Forensic Science

Forensic Science

Edited by
James Clifton

Larsen & Keller
www.larsen-keller.com

Forensic Science
Edited by James Clifton
ISBN: 978-1-63549-715-1 (Hardback)

Larsen & Keller
Published by Larsen and Keller Education,
5 Penn Plaza,
19th Floor,
New York, NY 10001, USA

Cataloging-in-Publication Data

Forensic science / edited by James Clifton.
p. cm.
Includes bibliographical references and index.
ISBN 978-1-63549-715-1
1. Forensic sciences. 2. Criminal investigation. I. Clifton, James.
HV8073 .F67 2018
363.25--dc23

Table of Contents

Preface

Forensic science refers to the field of science which is used in criminal investigations to analyze, preserve and collect evidence from the investigation scene. Some of the procedures used in solving crimes using forensic science are toxicology, fingerprint reports, DNA identification, anthropometry, etc. There are many sub-branches of forensic science such as digital forensics, computational forensics, forensic anthropology, forensic botany, forensic chemistry, forensic limnology, etc. Different approaches, evaluations and methodologies and advanced studies on forensic science have been included in this book. It provides deep information about the various concepts and theories related to this field. It is an essential guide for both academicians and those who wish to pursue this discipline further.

A detailed account of the significant topics covered in this book is provided below:

Chapter 1- Forensic science is the application of science to matters related to criminal and legal procedures. The evidence gathered during the investigation is analyzed and preserved. Some of the devices used in forensic science are drones, laser scanners and photogrammetry. This chapter elucidates the crucial theories and principles of forensic science.

Chapter 2- Forensic science can be divided into different categories. Digital forensics, forensic linguistics, forensic psychology, nuclear forensics and forensic pathology are some of the types of forensic science mentioned in this section. Forensic science is best understood in confluence with the major topics listed in the following chapter.

Chapter 3- Forensic economics applies theories of economics to the laws of a country. Forensic accounting, computational criminology, forensic anthropology, forensic facial reconstruction, forensic arts are some of the topics concerned with the subject matter. This chapter will provide an integrated understanding of forensic methodologies.

Chapter 4- Forensic engineering is the study of the objects that cause injury to any person or property due of a technical error in the product. This subject can be applied to both criminal and civil legal cases. Unexpected structural failures are a key event to which forensic engineering is applied. The chapter strategically encompasses and incorporates the major components and key concepts of forensic engineering, providing a complete understanding.

Chapter 5- Fingerprints are detailed and are almost unique. Fingerprint analysis is used to identify people, making it easier to solve crimes. The other methods of evidence collection are blood residue, forensic footwear evidence, DNA profiling, skid mark, MABMAT and trace evidence. The topics discussed in the chapter are of great importance to broaden the existing knowledge on the methods used in evidence collection.

Chapter 6- The tools and techniques used in forensic science are fingerprint powder, facial recognition system, bloodstain pattern analysis, autopsy, gait analysis, etc. The powder used by investigators in brushing for fingerprints is known as fingerprint powder whereas the application used in identifying a person's face is known as facial recognition system. The aspects elucidated in this chapter are of vital importance, and provide a better understanding of forensic science.

I would like to make a special mention of my publisher who considered me worthy of this opportunity and also supported me throughout the process. I would also like to thank the editing team at the back-end who extended their help whenever required.

Editor

1

Principles of Forensic Science

Forensic science is the application of science to matters related to criminal and legal procedures. The evidence gathered during the investigation is analyzed and preserved. Some of the devices used in forensic science are drones, laser scanners and photogrammetry. This chapter elucidates the crucial theories and principles of forensic science.

Forensic Science

Forensic science is the application of science to criminal and civil laws, mainly—on the criminal side—during criminal investigation, as governed by the legal standards of admissible evidence and criminal procedure.

Forensic scientists collect, preserve, and analyze scientific evidence during the course of an investigation. While some forensic scientists travel to the scene of the crime to collect the evidence themselves, others occupy a laboratory role, performing analysis on objects brought to them by other individuals.

In addition to their laboratory role, forensic scientists testify as expert witnesses in both criminal and civil cases and can work for either the prosecution or the defense. While any field could technically be *forensic*, certain sections have developed over time to encompass the majority of forensically related cases.

Etymology

The word *forensic* comes from the Latin term *forensis*, meaning "of or before the forum." The history of the term originates from Roman times, during which a criminal charge meant presenting the case before a group of public individuals in the forum. Both the person accused of the crime and the accuser would give speeches based on their sides of the story. The case would be decided in favor of the individual with the best argument and delivery. This origin is the source of the two modern usages of the word *forensic* – as a form of legal evidence and as a category of public presentation. In modern use, the term *forensics* in the place of *forensic science* can be considered correct, as the term *forensic* is effectively a synonym for *legal* or *related to courts*. However, the term is now so closely associated with the scientific field that many dictionaries include the meaning that equates the word *forensics* with *forensic science*.

History

Early Methods

The ancient world lacked standardized forensic practices, which aided criminals in escaping punishment. Criminal investigations and trials heavily relied on forced confessions and witness testimony. However, ancient sources do contain several accounts of techniques that foreshadow concepts in forensic science that were developed centuries later.

The first written account of using medicine and entomology to solve criminal cases is attributed to the book of *Xi Yuan Lu* (translated as *Washing Away of Wrongs*), written in China by Song Ci (1186–1249) in 1248, during the Song Dynasty. In one of the accounts, the case of a person murdered with a sickle was solved by an investigator who instructed everyone to bring his sickle to one location. (He realized it was a sickle by testing various blades on an animal carcass and comparing the wound.) Flies, attracted by the smell of blood, eventually gathered on a single sickle. In light of this, the murderer confessed. The book also offered advice on how to distinguish between a drowning (water in the lungs) and strangulation (broken neck cartilage), along with other evidence from examining corpses on determining if a death was caused by murder, suicide or an accident.

Methods from around the world involved saliva and examination of the mouth and tongue to determine innocence or guilt, as a precursor to the Polygraph test. In ancient India, some suspects were made to fill their mouths with dried rice and spit it back out. Similarly, in Ancient China, those accused of a crime would have rice powder placed in their mouths. In ancient middle-eastern cultures, the accused were made to lick hot metal rods briefly. It is thought that these tests had some validity since a guilty person would produce less saliva and thus have a drier mouth; the accused would be considered guilty if rice was sticking to their mouths in abundance or if their tongues were severely burned due to lack of shielding from saliva.

Origins of Forensic Science

Ambroise Paré's surgical work laid the groundwork for the development of forensic techniques in the following centuries.

In 16th-century Europe, medical practitioners in army and university settings began to gather information on the cause and manner of death. Ambroise Paré, a French army surgeon, systematically studied the effects of violent death on internal organs. Two Italian surgeons, Fortunato Fidelis and Paolo Zacchia, laid the foundation of modern pathology by studying changes that occurred in the structure of the body as the result of disease. In the late 18th century, writings on these topics began to appear. These included *A Treatise on Forensic Medicine and Public Health* by the French physician Francois Immanuele Fodéré and *The Complete System of Police Medicine* by the German medical expert Johann Peter Frank.

As the rational values of the Enlightenment era increasingly permeated society in the 18th century, criminal investigation became a more evidence-based, rational procedure – the use of torture to force confessions was curtailed, and belief in witchcraft and other powers of the occult largely ceased to influence the court's decisions. Two examples of English forensic science in individual legal proceedings demonstrate the increasing use of logic and procedure in criminal investigations at the time. In 1784, in Lancaster, John Toms was tried and convicted for murdering Edward Culshaw with a pistol. When the dead body of Culshaw was examined, a pistol wad (crushed paper used to secure powder and balls in the muzzle) found in his head wound matched perfectly with a torn newspaper found in Toms's pocket, leading to the conviction.

In Warwick 1816, a farm laborer was tried and convicted of the murder of a young maidservant. She had been drowned in a shallow pool and bore the marks of violent assault. The police found footprints and an impression from corduroy cloth with a sewn patch in the damp earth near the pool. There were also scattered grains of wheat and chaff. The breeches of a farm labourer who had been threshing wheat nearby were examined and corresponded exactly to the impression in the earth near the pool.

Toxicology and Ballistics

A method for detecting arsenious oxide, simple arsenic, in corpses was devised in 1773 by the Swedish chemist, Carl Wilhelm Scheele. His work was expanded, in 1806, by German chemist Valentin Ross, who learned to detect the poison in the walls of a victim's stomach.

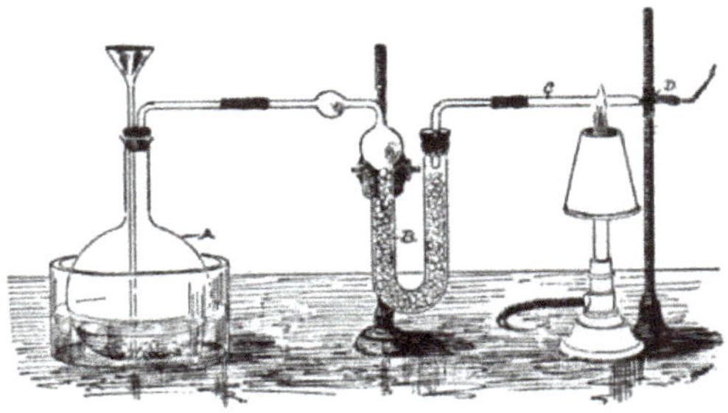

Apparatus for the arsenic test, devised by James Marsh.

James Marsh was the first to apply this new science to the art of forensics. He was called by the prosecution in a murder trial to give evidence as a chemist in 1832. The defendant, John Bodle, was accused of poisoning his grandfather with arsenic-laced coffee. Marsh performed the standard test by mixing a suspected sample with hydrogen sulfide and hydrochloric acid. While he was able to detect arsenic as yellow arsenic trisulfide, when it was shown to the jury it had deteriorated, allowing the suspect to be acquitted due to reasonable doubt.

Annoyed by that, Marsh developed a much better test. He combined a sample containing arsenic with sulfuric acid and arsenic-free zinc, resulting in arsine gas. The gas was ignited, and it decomposed to pure metallic arsenic, which, when passed to a cold surface, would appear as a silvery-black deposit. So sensitive was the test, known formally as the Marsh test, that it could detect as little as one-fiftieth of a milligram of arsenic. He first described this test in *The Edinburgh Philosophical Journal* in 1836.

Henry Goddard at Scotland Yard pioneered the use of bullet comparison in 1835. He noticed a flaw in the bullet that killed the victim and was able to trace this back to the mold that was used in the manufacturing process.

Anthropometry

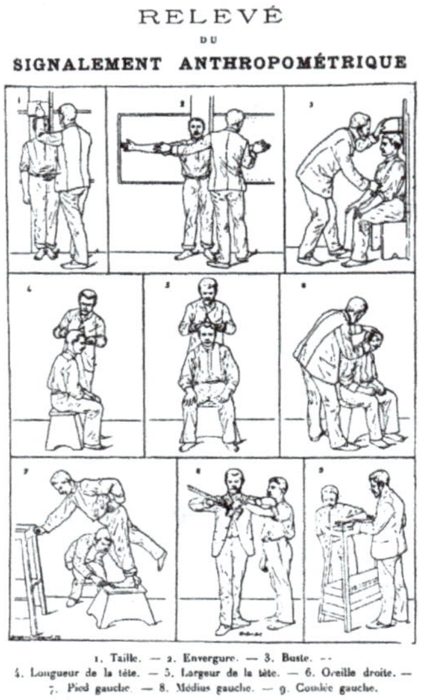

Frontispiece from Bertillon's *Identification anthropométrique* (1893), demonstrating the measurements needed for his anthropometric identification system.

The French police officer Alphonse Bertillon was the first to apply the anthropological technique of anthropometry to law enforcement, thereby creating an identification system based on physical measurements. Before that time, criminals could only be identified by name or photograph. Dissatisfied with the *ad hoc* methods used to identify captured criminals in France in the 1870s, he began his work on developing a reliable system of anthropometrics for human classification.

Bertillon created many other forensics techniques, including forensic document examination, the use of galvanoplastic compounds to preserve footprints, ballistics, and the dynamometer, used to determine the degree of force used in breaking and entering. Although his central methods were soon to be supplanted by fingerprinting, "his other contributions like the mug shot and the systematization of crime-scene photography remain in place to this day."

Fingerprints

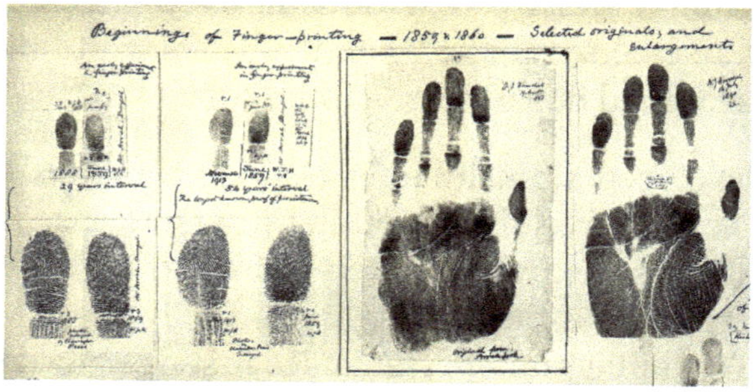

Fingerprints taken by William Herschel 1859/60.

Sir William Herschel was one of the first to advocate the use of fingerprinting in the identification of criminal suspects. While working for the Indian Civil Service, he began to use thumbprints on documents as a security measure to prevent the then-rampant repudiation of signatures in 1858.

In 1877 at Hooghly (near Calcutta), Herschel instituted the use of fingerprints on contracts and deeds, and he registered government pensioners' fingerprints to prevent the collection of money by relatives after a pensioner's death.

In 1880, Dr. Henry Faulds, a Scottish surgeon in a Tokyo hospital, published his first paper on the subject in the scientific journal *Nature*, discussing the usefulness of fingerprints for identification and proposing a method to record them with printing ink. He established their first classification and was also the first to identify fingerprints left on a vial. Returning to the UK in 1886, he offered the concept to the Metropolitan Police in London, but it was dismissed at that time.

Faulds wrote to Charles Darwin with a description of his method, but, too old and ill to work on it, Darwin gave the information to his cousin, Francis Galton, who was interested in anthropology. Having been thus inspired to study fingerprints for ten years, Galton published a detailed statistical model of fingerprint analysis and identification and encouraged its use in forensic science in his book *Finger Prints*. He had calculated that the chance of a "false positive" (two different individuals having the same fingerprints) was about 1 in 64 billion.

Women clerical employees of the LA Police Department getting fingerprinted and photographed in 1928.

Juan Vucetich, an Argentine chief police officer, created the first method of recording the fingerprints of individuals on file. In 1892, after studying Galton's pattern types, Vucetich set up the world's first fingerprint bureau. In that same year, Francisca Rojas of Necochea was found in a house with neck injuries whilst her two sons were found dead with their throats cut. Rojas accused a neighbour, but despite brutal interrogation, this neighbour would not confess to the crimes. Inspector Alvarez, a colleague of Vucetich, went to the scene and found a bloody thumb mark on a door. When it was compared with Rojas' prints, it was found to be identical with her right thumb. She then confessed to the murder of her sons.

A Fingerprint Bureau was established in Calcutta (Kolkata), India, in 1897, after the Council of the Governor General approved a committee report that fingerprints should be used for the classification of criminal records. Working in the Calcutta Anthropometric Bureau, before it became the Fingerprint Bureau, were Azizul Haque and Hem Chandra Bose. Haque and Bose were Indian fingerprint experts who have been credited with the primary development of a fingerprint classification system eventually named after their supervisor, Sir Edward Richard Henry. The Henry Classification System, co-devised by Haque and Bose, was accepted in England and Wales when the first United Kingdom Fingerprint Bureau was founded in Scotland Yard, the Metropolitan Police headquarters, London, in 1901. Sir Edward Richard Henry subsequently achieved improvements in dactyloscopy.

In the United States, Dr. Henry P. DeForrest used fingerprinting in the New York Civil Service in 1902, and by December 1905, New York City Police Department Deputy Commissioner Joseph A. Faurot, an expert in the Bertillon system and a fingerprint advocate at Police Headquarters, introduced the fingerprinting of criminals to the United States.

Uhlenhuth Test

The Uhlenhuth test, or the antigen–antibody precipitin test for species, was invented by Paul Uhlenhuth in 1901 and could distinguish human blood from animal blood, based on the discovery that the blood of different species had one or more characteristic proteins. The test represented a major breakthrough and came to have tremendous importance in forensic science. The test was further refined for forensic use by the Swiss chemist Maurice Müller in the 1960s.

DNA

Forensic DNA analysis was first used in 1984. It was developed by Sir Alec Jefferys, who realized that variation in the genetic code could be used to identify individuals and to tell individuals apart from one another. The first application of DNA profiles was used by Jefferys in a double murder mystery in a small England town called Narborough, Leicestershire in 1985. A 15-year-old school girl by the name of Lynda Mann was raped and murdered in Carlton Hayes psychiatric hospital. The police did not find a suspect but were able to obtain a semen sample.

In 1986, Dawn Ashworth, 15 years old, was also raped and strangled in a nearby village of Enderby. Forensic evidence showed that both killers had the same blood type. Richard Buckland became the suspect because he worked at Carlton Hayes psychiatric hospital, had been spotted near Dawn Ashworth's murder scene and knew unreleased details about the body. He later confessed to Dawn's murder but not Lynda's. Jefferys was brought into the case to analyze the semen samples. He concluded that there was no match between the samples and Buckland, who became the first person to be exonerated using DNA. Jefferys confirmed that the DNA profiles were identical for the two murder semen samples. To find the perpetrator, DNA samples from the entire male population, more than 4,000 aged from 17 to 34, of the town were collected. They all were compared to semen samples from the crime. A friend of Colin Pitchfork was heard saying that he had given his sample to the police claiming to be Colin. Colin Pitchfork was arrested in 1987 and it was found that his DNA profile matched the semen samples from the murder.

Because of this case, DNA databases were developed. There is the national (FBI) and international databases as well as the European countries (ENFSI : European Network of Forensic Science Institutes). These searchable databases are used to match crime scene DNA profiles to those already in a database.

Maturation

Police brought to bear the latest techniques of forensic science in their attempts to identify and capture the serial killer Jack the Ripper.

By the turn of the 20th century, the science of forensics had become largely established in the sphere of criminal investigation. Scientific and surgical investigation was widely employed by the Metropolitan Police during their pursuit of the mysterious Jack the Ripper, who had killed a number of prostitutes in the 1880s. This case is a watershed in the application of forensic science. Large teams of policemen conducted house-to-house inquiries throughout Whitechapel. Forensic material was collected and examined. Suspects were identified, traced and either examined more closely or eliminated from the inquiry. Police work follows the same pattern today. Over 2000 people were interviewed, "upwards of 300" people were investigated, and 80 people were detained.

The investigation was initially conducted by the Criminal Investigation Department (CID), headed by Detective Inspector Edmund Reid. Later, Detective Inspectors Frederick Abberline, Henry Moore, and Walter Andrews were sent from Central Office at Scotland Yard to assist. Initially, butchers, surgeons and physicians were suspected because of the manner of the mutilations. The alibis of local butchers and slaughterers were investigated, with the result that they were eliminated from the inquiry. Some contemporary figures thought the pattern of the murders indicated that the culprit was a butcher or cattle drover on one of the cattle boats that plied between London and mainland Europe. Whitechapel was close to the London Docks, and usually such boats docked on Thursday or Friday and departed on Saturday or Sunday. The cattle boats were examined, but the dates of the murders did not coincide with a single boat's movements, and the transfer of a crewman between boats was also ruled out.

At the end of October, Robert Anderson asked police surgeon Thomas Bond to give his opinion on the extent of the murderer's surgical skill and knowledge. The opinion offered by Bond on the character of the "Whitechapel murderer" is the earliest surviving offender profile. Bond's assessment was based on his own examination of the most extensively mutilated victim and the post mortem notes from the four previous canonical murders. In his opinion the killer must have been a man of solitary habits, subject to "periodical attacks of homicidal and erotic mania", with the character of the mutilations possibly indicating "satyriasis". Bond also stated that "the homicidal impulse may have developed from a revengeful or brooding condition of the mind, or that religious mania may have been the original disease but I do not think either hypothesis is likely".

The popular fictional character Sherlock Holmes was in many ways ahead of his time in his use of forensic analysis.

Handbook for Coroners, police officials, military policemen was written by the Austrian criminal jurist Hans Gross in 1893, and is generally acknowledged as the birth of the field of criminalistics. The work combined in one system fields of knowledge that had not been previously integrated, such as psychology and physical science, and which could be successfully used against crime. Gross adapted some fields to the needs of criminal investigation, such as crime scene photography. He went on to found the Institute of Criminalistics in 1912, as part of the University of Graz' Law School. This Institute was followed by many similar institutes all over the world.

In 1909, Archibald Reiss founded the *Institut de police scientifique* of the University of Lausanne (UNIL), the first school of forensic science in the world. Dr. Edmond Locard, became known as the "Sherlock Holmes of France". He formulated the basic principle of forensic science: "Every contact leaves a trace", which became known as Locard's exchange principle. In 1910, he founded what may have been the first criminal laboratory in the world, after persuading the Police Department of Lyon (France) to give him two attic rooms and two assistants.

Symbolic of the new found prestige of forensics and the use of reasoning in detective work was the popularity of the fictional character Sherlock Holmes, written by Arthur Conan Doyle in the late 19th century. He remains a great inspiration for forensic science, especially for the way his acute study of a crime scene yielded small clues as to the precise sequence of events. He made great use of trace evidence such as shoe and tire impressions, as well as fingerprints, ballistics and handwriting analysis, now known as questioned document examination. Such evidence is used to test theories conceived by the police, for example, or by the investigator himself. All of the techniques advocated by Holmes later became reality, but were generally in their infancy at the time Conan

Doyle was writing. In many of his reported cases, Holmes frequently complains of the way the crime scene has been contaminated by others, especially by the police, emphasising the critical importance of maintaining its integrity, a now well-known feature of crime scene examination. He used analytical chemistry for blood residue analysis as well as toxicology examination and determination for poisons. He used ballistics by measuring bullet calibres and matching them with a suspected murder weapon.

Late 19th–early 20th Centuries Figures

Hans Gross applied scientific methods to crime scenes and was responsible for the birth of criminalistics.

Edmond Locard expanded on Gross' work with Locard's Exchange Principle which stated "whenever two objects come into contact with one another, materials are exchanged between them". This means that every contact by a criminal leaves a trace. Locard was also known as the "Sherlock Holmes of France".

Alexander Lacassagne, who taught Locard, produced autopsy standards on actual forensic cases.

Alphonse Bertillon was a French criminologist and founder of Anthropometry (scientific study of measurements and proportions of the human body). He used anthropometry for identification, saying each individual is unique and by measuring aspect of physical difference, there could be a personal identification system. He created the Bertillon System around 1879, which was a way to identify criminals and citizens by measuring 20 parts of the body. In 1884, there was over 240 repeat offenders caught through the Bertillon system. Fingerprinting became more reliable than the Bertillon system.

20th Century

Alec Jeffreys invented the DNA profiling technique in 1984

Later in the 20th century several British pathologists, Mikey Rochman, Francis Camps, Sydney Smith and Keith Simpson pioneered new forensic science methods. Alec Jeffreys pioneered the use of DNA profiling in forensic science in 1984. He realized the scope of DNA fingerprinting, which uses variations in the genetic code to identify individuals. The method has since become important in forensic science to assist police detective work, and it has also proved useful in resolving paternity and immigration disputes. DNA fingerprinting was first used as a police forensic test to identify the rapist and killer of two teenagers, Lynda Mann and Dawn Ashworth, who were both murdered in Narborough, Leicestershire, in 1983 and 1986 respectively. Colin Pitchfork was identified and convicted of murder after samples taken from him matched semen samples taken from the two dead girls.

Forensic science has been fostered by a number of national forensic science learned bodies including the Chartered Society of Forensic Sciences, (founded in 1959), then known as the Forensic Science Society, publisher of *Science & Justice*;. American Academy of Forensic Sciences (founded 1948), publishers of the *Journal of Forensic Sciences*; the Canadian Society of Forensic Science (founded 1953), publishers of the *Journal of the Canadian Society of Forensic Science*; the British Academy of Forensic Sciences (founded 1960), publishers of *Medicine, science and the law*, and the Australian Academy of Forensic Sciences (founded 1967), publishers of the *Australian Journal of Forensic Sciences*.

21st century

In the past decade, documenting forensics scenes has become more efficient. People started using laser scanners, drones and photogrammetry to obtain 3D point clouds of accidents or crime scenes. Reconstruction of an accident scene on a highway using drones involves data acquisition time of only 10–20 minutes and can be performed without shutting down traffic.The results are not just accurate, in centimeters, for measurement to be presented in court but also easy to digitally preserve in the long term.

Subdivisions

Agents of the United States Army Criminal Investigation Division investigate a crime scene

Police forensic investigation in Ashton-under-Lyne, England, using a tent to protect the crime scene

- Art forensics concerns the art authentication cases to help research the work's authenticity. Art authentication methods are used to detect and identify forgery, faking and copying of art works, e.g. paintings.
- Computational forensics concerns the development of algorithms and software to assist forensic examination.
- Criminalistics is the application of various sciences to answer questions relating to examination and comparison of biological evidence, trace evidence, impression evidence (such as fingerprints, footwear impressions, and tire tracks), controlled substances, ballistics, firearm and toolmark examination, and other evidence in criminal investigations. In typical circumstances evidence is processed in a crime lab.
- Digital forensics is the application of proven scientific methods and techniques in order to recover data from electronic / digital media. Digital Forensic specialists work in the field as well as in the lab.
- Ear print analysis is used as a means of forensic identification intended as an identification tool similar to fingerprinting. An earprint is a two-dimensional reproduction of the parts of the outer ear that have touched a specific surface (most commonly the helix, antihelix, tragus and antitragus).
- Forensic accounting is the study and interpretation of accounting evidence.
- Forensic aerial photography is the study and interpretation of aerial photographic evidence.
- Forensic anthropology is the application of physical anthropology in a legal setting, usually for the recovery and identification of skeletonized human remains.
- Forensic archaeology is the application of a combination of archaeological techniques and forensic science, typically in law enforcement.
- Forensic astronomy uses methods from astronomy to determine past celestial constellations for forensic purposes.
- Forensic botany is the study of plant life in order to gain information regarding possible crimes.
- Forensic chemistry is the study of detection and identification of illicit drugs, accelerants used in arson cases, explosive and gunshot residue.
- Forensic dactyloscopy is the study of fingerprints.
- Forensic document examination or questioned document examination answers questions about a disputed document using a variety of scientific processes and methods. Many examinations involve a comparison of the questioned document, or components of the document, with a set of known standards. The most common type of examination involves handwriting, whereby the examiner tries to address concerns about potential authorship.
- Forensic DNA analysis takes advantage of the uniqueness of an individual's DNA to answer forensic questions such as paternity/maternity testing and placing a suspect at a crime scene, e.g. in a rape investigation.

- Forensic engineering is the scientific examination and analysis of structures and products relating to their failure or cause of damage.
- Forensic entomology deals with the examination of insects in, on and around human remains to assist in determination of time or location of death. It is also possible to determine if the body was moved after death using entomology.
- Forensic geology deals with trace evidence in the form of soils, minerals and petroleum.
- Forensic geomorphology is the study of the ground surface to look for potential location(s) of buried object(s).
- Forensic geophysics is the application of geophysical techniques such as radar for detecting objects hidden underground or underwater.
- Forensic intelligence process starts with the collection of data and ends with the integration of results within into the analysis of crimes under investigation.
- Forensic Interviews are conducted using the science of professionally using expertise to conduct a variety of investigative interviews with victims, witnesses, suspects or other sources to determine the facts regarding suspicions, allegations or specific incidents in either public or private sector settings.
- Forensic limnology is the analysis of evidence collected from crime scenes in or around fresh-water sources. Examination of biological organisms, in particular diatoms, can be useful in connecting suspects with victims.
- Forensic linguistics deals with issues in the legal system that requires linguistic expertise.
- Forensic meteorology is a site-specific analysis of past weather conditions for a point of loss.
- Forensic odontology is the study of the uniqueness of dentition, better known as the study of teeth.
- Forensic optometry is the study of glasses and other eyewear relating to crime scenes and criminal investigations.
- Forensic pathology is a field in which the principles of medicine and pathology are applied to determine a cause of death or injury in the context of a legal inquiry.
- Forensic podiatry is an application of the study of feet footprint or footwear and their traces to analyze scene of crime and to establish personal identity in forensic examinations.
- Forensic psychiatry is a specialized branch of psychiatry as applied to and based on scientific criminology.
- Forensic psychology is the study of the mind of an individual, using forensic methods. Usually it determines the circumstances behind a criminal's behavior.
- Forensic seismology is the study of techniques to distinguish the seismic signals generated by underground nuclear explosions from those generated by earthquakes.

- Forensic serology is the study of the body fluids.
- Forensic social work is the specialist study of social work theories and their applications to a clinical, criminal justice or psychiatric setting. Practitioners of forensic social work connected with the criminal justice system are often termed Social Supervisors, whilst the remaining use the interchangeable titles forensic social worker, approved mental health professional or forensic practitioner and they conduct specialist assessments of risk, care planning and act as an officer of the court.
- Forensic toxicology is the study of the effect of drugs and poisons on/in the human body.
- Forensic video analysis is the scientific examination, comparison and evaluation of video in legal matters.
- Mobile device forensics is the scientific examination and evaluation of evidence found in mobile phones, e.g. Call History and Deleted SMS, and includes SIM Card Forensics.
- Trace evidence analysis is the analysis and comparison of trace evidence including glass, paint, fibres and hair (e.g., using micro-spectrophotometry).
- Wildlife forensic science applies a range of scientific disciplines to legal cases involving non-human biological evidence, to solve crimes such as poaching, animal abuse, and trade in endangered species.
- Bloodstain pattern analysis is the scientific examination of blood spatter patterns found at a crime scene to reconstruct the events of the crime.

Questionable Techniques

Some forensic techniques, believed to be scientifically sound at the time they were used, have turned out later to have much less scientific merit or none. Some such techniques include:

- Comparative bullet-lead analysis was used by the FBI for over four decades, starting with the John F. Kennedy assassination in 1963. The theory was that each batch of ammunition possessed a chemical makeup so distinct that a bullet could be traced back to a particular batch or even a specific box. Internal studies and an outside study by the National Academy of Sciences found that the technique was unreliable due to improper interpretation, and the FBI abandoned the test in 2005.
- Forensic dentistry has come under fire: in at least two cases bite-mark evidence has been used to convict people of murder who were later freed by DNA evidence. A 1999 study by a member of the American Board of Forensic Odontology found a 63 percent rate of false identifications and is commonly referenced within online news stories and conspiracy websites. The study was based on an informal workshop during an ABFO meeting, which many members did not consider a valid scientific setting.
- By the late 2000s, scientists were able to show that it is possible to fabricate DNA evidence, thus "undermining the credibility of what has been considered the gold standard of proof in criminal cases."

Litigation Science

Litigation science describes analysis or data developed or produced *expressly* for use in a trial versus those produced in the course of independent research. This distinction was made by the U.S. 9th Circuit Court of Appeals when evaluating the admissibility of experts.

This uses demonstrative evidence, which is evidence created in preparation of trial by attorneys or paralegals.

International Demographics

In the United States there are over 14,500 forensic science technicians, as of 2014.

Examples in Popular Culture

Early-Mid 20th Century

Joseph Bell

The Argentinean writer Jorge Luis Borges claims that the police novel genre is inaugurated with Edgar Allan Poe's short story, "The Murders in the Rue Morgue". But it was Sherlock Holmes, the fictional character created by Sir Arthur Conan Doyle in works produced from 1887 to 1915, who first used forensic science as one of his investigating methods. Conan Doyle credited the inspiration for Holmes on his teacher at the medical school of the University of Edinburgh, the gifted surgeon and forensic detective Joseph Bell.

Agatha Christie's Hercule Poirot and Miss Marple, in books, films, and television series, use similar methods.

The comic strip *Dick Tracy* also featured a detective using a considerable number of forensic methods, although sometimes the methods were more fanciful than actually possible.

In comic books published by DC Comics, Barry Allen (alter ego of The Flash) is a forensic scientist for the Central City police department.

Defense attorney Perry Mason occasionally used forensic techniques, both in the novels and television series.

Late 20th Century - Early 21st Century

One of the earliest television series to focus on the scientific analysis of evidence was *Quincy, M.E.* (1976–83, and based loosely on an even earlier Canadian series titled *Wojeck*), with the title character, a medical examiner working in Los Angeles solving crimes through careful study. The opening theme of each episode featured a clip of the title character, played by Jack Klugman, beginning a lecture to a group of police officers with "Gentlemen, you are about to enter the most fascinating sphere of police work, the world of forensic medicine." Later series with similar premises include *Dexter*, *The Mentalist*, *CSI*, *Hawaii Five-0*, *Cold Case*, *Bones*, *Law & Order*, *Body of Proof*, *NCIS*, *Criminal Minds*, *Silent Witness*, *Detective Conan*, *Midsomer Murders* and *Waking the Dead*, depict glamorized versions of the activities of 21st-century forensic scientists.

Non-fiction TV shows such as *Forensic Files*, *The New Detectives*, *American Justice*, and Dayle Hinman's *Body of Evidence* have also popularized forensic science.

The Ace Attorney series features forensic science, mainly in *Apollo Justice: Ace Attorney* and the DS-only case in *Phoenix Wright: Ace Attorney*.

Realism Controversy

However, real-life crime scene investigators and forensic scientists warn that popular television shows like these (often naming some of these specific shows) do not give a realistic picture of the work -- wildlly distorting the nature of the work, and exaggerating the ease, speed, effectiveness, drama, glamour, influence and comfort level of their jobs -- which they describe as far more mundane, tedious and boring.

Some claim these modern TV shows have changed individuals' expectations of forensic science, sometimes unrealistically -- an influence termed the "CSI effect".

Further, research has suggested that public misperceptions about criminal forensics can create, in the mind of a juror, unrealistic expectations of forensic evidence -- which they expect to see before convicting -- implicitly biasing the juror towards the defendant. Citing the "CSI Effect," at least one researcher has suggested screening jurors for their level of influence from such TV programs

Controversies

Questions about certain areas of forensic science, such as fingerprint evidence and the assumptions behind these disciplines have been brought to light in some publications including the *New York Post*. The article stated that "No one has proved even the basic assumption: That everyone's fingerprint is unique." The article also stated that "Now such assumptions are being questioned – and with it may come a radical change in how forensic science is used by police departments and prosecutors." Law professor Jessica Gabel said on NOVA that forensic science "lacks the rigors, the standards, the quality controls and procedures that we find, usually, in science."

In America, on 25 June 2009, the Supreme Court issued a 5-to-4 decision in *Melendez-Diaz v. Massachusetts* stating that crime laboratory reports may not be used against criminal defendants at trial unless the analysts responsible for creating them give testimony and subject themselves to cross-examination. The Supreme Court cited the National Academies report *Strengthening Forensic Science in the United States* in their decision. Writing for the majority, Justice Antonin Scalia referred to the National Research Council report in his assertion that "Forensic evidence is not uniquely immune from the risk of manipulation."

In 2009, scientists indicated that it is possible to fabricate DNA evidence, therefore suggesting it is possible to falsely accuse or acquit a person or persons using forged evidence.

In America, another area of forensic science that has come under question in recent years is the lack of laws requiring the accreditation of forensic labs. Some states require accreditation, but some states do not. Because of this, many labs have been caught performing very poor work resulting in false convictions or acquittals. For example, it was discovered after an audit of the Houston Police Department in 2002 that the lab had fabricated evidence which led George Rodriguez being convicted of raping a fourteen-year-old girl. The former director of the lab, when asked, said that the total number of cases that could have been contaminated by improper work could be in the range of 5,000 to 10,000. This could have been avoided if the lab had been accredited by organizations such as ASCLD/Lab, which require crime labs to undergo rigorous assessments to show that they are able to perform multiple tests accurately. Once they become accredited, they are periodically re-evaluated to ensure that the lab is still functioning at its best. Periodic evaluations of a lab's performance by an independent organization will help to prevent scandals from occurring in forensic science laboratories.

Although forensic science has greatly enhanced the investigator's ability to solve crimes, it has limitations and must be scrutinized in and out of the courtroom to avoid the occurrence of wrongful convictions.

Forensic Science and Humanitarian Work

The International Committee of the Red Cross (ICRC) uses forensic science for humanitarian purposes to clarify the fate of missing persons after armed conflict, disasters or migration, and is one of the services related to Restoring Family Links and Missing Persons. Knowing what has happened to a missing relative can often make it easier to proceed with the grieving process and move on with life for families of missing persons.

Forensic science is used by various other organizations to clarify the fate and whereabouts of persons who have gone missing. Examples include the NGO Argentine Forensic Anthropology Team, working to clarify the fate of people who disappeared during the period of the 1976–1983 military dictatorship. The International Commission on Missing Persons (ICMP) uses forensic science to find missing persons, for example after the conflicts in the Balkans.

Crime Scene

A crime scene is any location that may be associated with a committed crime. Crime scenes contain physical evidence that is pertinent to a criminal investigation.This evidence is collected by crime scene investigators (CSIs) and Law enforcement.The location of a crime scene can be the place where the crime took place, or can be any area that contains evidence from the crime itself. Scenes are not only limited to a location, but can be any person, place, or object associated with the criminal behaviors that occurred.

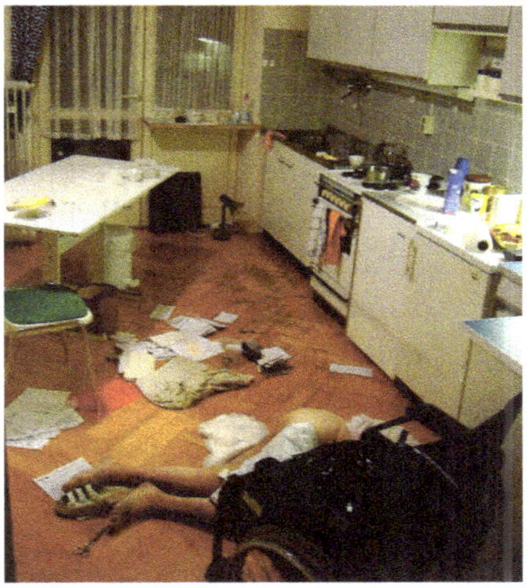

A crime scene

After a crime scene has been discovered, it is important that measures are taken to secure and protect the scene from contamination. In order to maintain the integrity of the scene, law enforcement must take action to block off the surrounding area as well as keep track of who comes in and goes out. By taking these precautions, officers can ensure that evidence that is collected can be used in court. Evidence that has become contaminated, tampered with, or mistreated can pollute the scene and cause a case to be thrown out of court.

It is important that everything that occurs during the analysis of a crime scene is documented. It is the job of the initial responding officer to make sure that the scene has an extremely coherent and summarized documentation. The documentation should include the officers observations and actions while at the scene. The initial responder is in charge of documenting the appearance and condition of the scene upon arrival. The initial responder will also gather statements and comments from witnesses, victims, and possible suspects. Several other documents are also generated so that a crime scene's integrity is kept intact. These documents include a list of who has been in contact with evidence (chain of custody), as well as a log of what evidence has been collected.

Preservation and Contamination

A crime scene is often preserved by setting up a blockade to control the movement in and out of a scene as well as maintaining the scene's integrity. A perimeter is taped off with barricade tape in order to keep only those necessary on site. This is done to prevent contaminated evidence. Investigators try to avoid contamination at all costs. While it is difficult to completely avoid contamination, many steps are taken to ensure the integrity of the crime scene remains intact. Officers take care to not eat, drink, smoke, or take their breaks near the crime scene. Anything leftover by the officers on scene could be mistaken for potential evidence and tamper with the success of the investigation.

Sequence of Events

The Initial Responding Officer receives a dispatch call and arrives at the location of the crime. This officer plays a crucial part in maintaining the integrity of the scene. Initial responders are in charge of securing the scene by setting up physical barriers to control the traffic in and around the area. The officer also documents his/her initial observations as well as the condition of the scene upon arrival. Once the crime scene investigation unit arrives on scene, being sure not to touch anything,an initial walkthrough is performed. This walkthrough helps the investigators get an understanding of what kind of crime has occurred. The unit notes on the presence of potential evidence and devises a plan for processing the scene. A second walkthrough is performed for the purpose of documentation. The unit will take pictures and draw sketches of the scene. Sometimes videos are taken to ensure every detail of the crime is documented. After a thorough documentation has been conducted, the CSI unit carefully collects all items that could be considered evidence. These items are tagged, logged, and packaged to ensure nothing is damaged or lost. All evidence from the scene is sent to the forensic laboratory for analysis. The forensic laboratory processes all pieces of evidence from the scene. Once the results are in they go the lead detective on the case.

Documentation

Photographs of all evidence are taken before anything is touched, moved, or otherwise further investigated. Evidence markers are placed next to each piece of evidence allowing for organization of the evidence. Sketching the scene is also a form of documentation at a crime scene. This allows for notes to be taken as well as to gauge distances and other information that may not be easily detected from only a photograph. The investigators will draw out locations of evidence and all other objects in the room. The sketch is usually drawn from an above point of view. Notes are taken by investigators to ensure memorization of their thoughts and suspicions about different pieces of evidence.

Evidence Collection

FBI agents collect evidence from a crime scene

Evidence comes in many different forms. It can be anything from a biological sample like blood, or everyday item like receipts or bank statements. Other types of evidence include: fibers, firearm residue, photographs or videos, and fingerprints. Forensic scientists analyze this evidence so they can come up with an explanation for why a crime occurred. Ensuring that evidence is collected in an accurate and timely manner helps officers to better understand what happened at the scene and aids in the investigation being completed successfully. Only the appropriate personnel with the proper knowledge and training should be collecting evidence. These individuals include, First Responders, Crime Scene Investigators, and other specialized personnel. Different types of evidence will sometimes need different methods of collection or specific containers. For instance, paper containers, such as bags,envelopes, or boxes, may be optimal for biological samples. Paper containers allow evidence that is not completely dry to continue drying. This type of collection protects those samples from deteriorating. When the evidence is collected properly there is less of a chance that the items collected will be damaged or contaminated.

Forensics uses a variety of different tools and techniques. Fingerprint collection through the use of grey or black magnetic powder. DNA and other bodily fluids are collected and, whether it is hair or fluid, for further examination in a lab. Shoe and tire prints can be collected using dental stone. Electronics are taken for examination by a technical expert to search for further evidence. Documents from the area are also taken for further examination. Ammunition and weapons are taken for matching to wounds and ballistics. Photographs of tool marks are taken because they can be matched to a weapon at a later time. Any other trace evidence is also collected. Trace evidence is anything left behind by a perpetrator or could have been transferred to the perpetrator. Interviews of both witnesses and victims of the crime are taken by law enforcement officials in order to gain knowledge and creating a timeline of events.

Chain of Custody

After evidence has been collected from the scene of the crime, it is placed in its appropriate container and then is labeled or tagged. The tag identifies the specific scene the evidence came from and establishes the "chain of custody". The chain of custody refers to the order in which evidence is handled by individuals who are involved in the case's investigation. The chain of custody is pertinent to the investigation and guarantees the physical security of all evidence that is part of the case. The following types of identifiers are needed to establish the chain:

- Initials or names of the person collecting the evidence, and all the subsequent people who have and will come in contact with the evidence.
- The date of collection and transfer
- The name of the agency, case number, and type of crime
- Voucher or property clerk number
- The name of the victim or the suspect
- Where the item is being stored
- A summary of what the item is

Types of Crime Scenes

Different types of crime scenes include outdoors, indoor, and conveyance. Outdoor crime scenes are the most difficult to investigate. The exposure to elements such as rain, wind, or heat, as well as animal activity, contaminates the crime scene and leads to the destruction of evidence. Indoor crime scenes have a significantly lower chance of contamination because of the lack of exposure.

The contamination here usually comes from the people factor. Conveyance crime scenes are crimes committed by means of transportation, such as robbery or auto theft. Each type of crime scene, along with the nature of the crime committed (robbery, homicide, rape, etc.) have different procedures.

Reconstruction

Crime scene *reconstruction* is the use of scientific methods, physical evidence, deductive reasoning, and their interrelationships to gain explicit knowledge of the series of events that surround the commission of a crime.

Crime Reconstruction

Crime reconstruction or crime scene reconstruction is the forensic science discipline in which one gains "explicit knowledge of the series of events that surround the commission of a crime using deductive and inductive reasoning, physical evidence, scientific methods, and their interrelationships." Gardner and Bevel explain that crime scene reconstruction "involves evaluating the context of a scene and the physical evidence found there in an effort to identify what occurred and in what order it occurred." Chisum and Turvey explain that "[h]olistic crime reconstruction is the development of actions and circumstances based on the system of evidence discovered and examined in relation to a particular crime. In this philosophy, all elements of evidence that come to light in a given case are treated as interdependent; the significance of each piece, each action, and each event falls and rises on the backs of the others."

Methods

Crime scene reconstruction has been described as putting together a jigsaw puzzle but doing so without access to the box top; the analyst does not know what the picture is supposed to look like. Furthermore, not all of the pieces are likely to be present, so there will be holes in the picture. However, if enough pieces of a puzzle are assembled in the correct order, the picture may become clear enough that the viewer is able to recognize the image and answer critical questions about it.

In forensic science, there are three areas of importance in finding the answers and determining the components of a crime scene: (1) specific incident reconstruction, (2) event reconstruction, and (3) physical evidence reconstruction. Specific incident reconstruction deals with road traffic accidents, bombings, homicides, and accidents of any severity. Event reconstruction looks at connections between evidence, sequence of events, and identity of those involved. Physical evidence reconstruction focuses on such items as firearms, blood traces, glass fragments, and any other objects that can be stripped for DNA analysis.

Expertise

To be competent as a crime scene reconstructionist, one must possess the requisite technical knowledge and have a thorough understanding of forensic investigations. There are no set educational requirements; however, many practicing crime scene reconstructionists possess undergraduate or graduate degrees in forensic science, chemistry, biology, physics, engineering, or criminal justice. In addition, a crime scene reconstructionist must have considerable experience in the investigation and analysis of crime scenes and physical evidence. Most crime scene reconstructionists have gained such experience either as a crime scene investigator, homicide investigator, or medicolegal death investigator.

Arguably, a crime scene reconstructionist is a forensic scientist who specializes in interpreting and assembling evidence in a coherent manner. Chisum and Turvey explain that to perform crime reconstruction one need not "be an expert in all forensic disciplines" but "must become an expert in only one: *the interpretation of the evidence in context.*" The crime scene reconstructionist may not be the person who carries out laboratory analysis of evidence such as developing DNA profiles or performing firearms and toolmark analysis; however, the competent crime scene reconstructionist must understand the meaning of each various piece of evidence and how it fits within the overall context of the scene. In this way, the crime scene reconstructionist is able to assemble the necessary puzzle pieces to make the picture visible.

Professional Associations

The Association for Crime Scene Reconstruction was formed in 1991 by a group of crime scene professionals who "saw a need for an organization that would encompass an understanding of the whole crime scene and the necessity of reconstructing that scene in order to better understand the elements of the crime and to recognize and preserve evidence." The association publishes a peer-reviewed journal and holds an annual conference in which members gain information about the latest techniques and technologies used in crime scene reconstruction and share case examples. Many crime scene reconstructionists are also members of the International Association of Bloodstain Pattern Analysts, the American Academy of Forensic Sciences, and the International Association for Identification or one of its state chapters.

Certification

The International Association for Identification (IAI) offers the only nationally-recognized Certified Crime Scene Reconstructionist program in the United States. To be eligible for certification, applicants must have a minimum of five years experience in the crime scene reconstruction field; must have completed a minimum of 120 hours of related professional training including coursework in bloodstain pattern analysis, shooting incident reconstruction, and other related areas; and, must meet other qualifications such as being published in a professional journal, presenting to a professional association, or being an active instructor in the field. Once approved by the board, applicants must pass a 300-question multiple choice examination and a series of practical questions involving actual analysis of crime scene evidence as presented in photographs. Certification is valid for five years. The IAI maintains a roster of certified crime scene reconstructionists on the organization's website.

Forensic Identification

Forensic identification is the application of forensic science, or "forensics", and technology to identify specific objects from the trace evidence they leave, often at a crime scene or the scene of an accident. Forensic means "for the courts".

Human Identification

People can be identified by their fingerprints. This assertion is supported by the philosophy of friction ridge identification, which states that friction ridge identification is established through the agreement of friction ridge formations, in sequence, having sufficient uniqueness to individualize.

Friction ridge identification is also governed by four premises or statements of facts:

1. Friction ridges develop on the fetus in their definitive form prior to birth.
2. Friction ridges are persistent throughout life except for permanent scarring, disease, or decomposition after death.
3. Friction ridge paths and the details in small areas of friction ridges are unique and never repeated.
4. Overall, friction ridge patterns vary within limits which allow for classification.

People can also be identified from traces of their DNA from blood, skin, hair, saliva, and semen by DNA fingerprinting, from their ear print, from their teeth or bite by forensic odontology, from a photograph or a video recording by facial recognition systems, from the video recording of their walk by gait analysis, from an audio recording by voice analysis, from their handwriting by handwriting analysis, from the content of their writings by their writing style (e.g. typical phrases, factual bias, and/or misspellings of words), or from other traces using other biometric techniques.

Droplets of human blood. In addition to analyzing for DNA, the droplets are round and show no spattering, indicating they impacted at a relatively slow velocity, in this case from a height of two feet.

Since forensic identification has been first introduced to the courts in 1980, the first exoneration due to DNA evidence was in 1989 and there have been 336 additional exonerations since then. Those who specialize in forensic identification continue to make headway with new discoveries and technological advances to make convictions more accurate.

Body identification is a subfield of forensics concerned with identifying someone from their remains.

Foot Creases

Feet also have friction ridges like fingerprints do. Friction ridges have been widely accepted as a form of identification with fingerprints but not entirely with feet. Feet have creases which remain over time due to the depth it reaches in the dermal layer of the skin, making them permanent. These creases are valuable when individualizing the owner. The concept of no two fingerprints are alike is also applied to foot creases. Foot creases can grow as early as 13 weeks after conception when the volar pads begin to grow and when the pads regress, the creases remain. When foot crease identification is used in a criminal case, it should be used in conjunction with morphology and friction ridges to ensure precise identification. There is record of foot crease identification used in a criminal case to solve a murder. Sometimes with marks left by the foot with ink, blood, mud, or other substances, the appearance of creases or ridges become muddled or extra creases may appear due to cracked skin, folded skin, or fissures. In order to truly compare morphological feature, the prints of feet must be clear enough to distinguish between individuals.

Downfalls

The two basic conceptual foundations of forensic identification is that everyone is individualized and unique. This individualization belief was invented by a police records clerk, Alphonse Bertillon, based on the idea that "nature never repeats," originating from the father of social statistics, Lambert Adolphe Jacques Quetelet. The belief was passed down through generations being generally accepted, but it was never scientifically proven. There was a study done intending to show that no two fingerprints were the same, but the results were inconclusive. Many modern forensic and evidentiary scholars collectively agree that individualization to one object, such as a fingerprint, bite mark, handwriting, or ear mark is not possible. In court cases, forensic scientists can fall victim to observer bias when not sufficiently blinded to the case or results of other pertinent tests. This has happened in cases like *United States v. Green* and *State v. Langill*. Also, the proficiency tests that forensic analysts must do are often not as demanding to be considered admissible in court.

Animal Identification

Wildlife Forensics

There are many different applications for wildlife forensics and below are only some of the procedures and processes used to distinguish species.

Species Identification: The important of species identification is most prominent in animal population that are illegally hunted, harvested, and traded, such as rhinoceroses, lions, and African elephants. In order to distinguish which species is which, mtDNA, or mitochondrial DNA, is the most used genetic marker because it's easier to type from highly decomposed and processed tissue compared to nuclear DNA. Additionally, the mitochondrial DNA has multiple copies per cell, which is another reason it's frequently used. When nuclear DNA is used, certain segments of the strands are amplified in order to compare those to segments of mitochondrial DNA. This comparison is used to figure out related genes and species proximity since distant relatives of animals are closer in proximity in the gene tree. That being said, the comparison process demands precision because mistakes can easily be made due to genes evolving and mutating in the evolution of species.

Determination of geographic origin: Determining the origin of a certain species aids research in population numbers and lineage data. Phylogenetic studies are most often used to find the broad geographic area of which a species reside. For example, in California seahorses were being sold for traditional medicinal purposes and the phylogenetic data of those seahorses led researchers to find their origin and from which population they came from and what species they were. In addition to phylogenetic data, assignment tests are used to find the probability of a species belonging to or originating from a specific population and genetic markers of a specimen are utilized. These types of tests are most accurate when all potential population's data have been gathered. Statistical analyses are used in assignment tests based on an individual's microsatellites or Amplified Fragment Length Polymorphisms (AFLPs). Using microsatellites in these studies is more favorable than AFLPs because the AFLPs required non-degraded tissue samples and higher errors have been reported when using AFLPs.

Domestic Animal Forensics

Domestic animals such as dogs and cats can be utilized to help solve criminal cases. These can include homicides, sexual assaults, or robberies. DNA evidence from dogs alone have helped over 20 criminal cases in Great Britain and the U.S. since 1996. There are only a few laboratories though that are able to process and analyze evidence or data from domestic animals. Forensics can be used in animal attacks as well. In cases like dog attacks, the hair blood, and saliva surrounding the wounds a victim has can be analyzed to find a match for the attacker. In the competitive realm, DNA analysis is used in many cases to find illegal substances in racehorses by urine samples and comparisons of STRs.

Product Identification

- Color copiers and maybe some color computer printers steganographically embed their identification number to some printouts as a countermeasure against currency forgeries.
- Copiers and computer printers can be potentially identified by the minor variants of the way they feed the paper through the printing mechanism, leaving banding artifacts. Analysis of the toners is also used.
- Documents are characterized by the composition of their paper and ink.
- Firearms can be identified by the striations on the bullets they fired and imprints on the cartridge casings.
- Paper shredders can be potentially identified in a similar way, by spacing and wear of their blades.
- Photo identification is used to detect and identify forged digital photos.
- Typewriters can be identified by minor variations of positioning and wear of their letters.
- Illegal drugs can be identified by which color it turns when a reagent is added during a color test. Gas Chromatography, Infrared Spectrometry or Mass Spectrometry is used in combination with the color test to identify the type of drug.

Networks

- Cars can be automatically found on CCTV records by automatic number plate recognition.
- Computers connected to the Internet can often be identified by their IP address or MAC address.
- Radio transceivers can be potentially identified by minute variations of their output signal.
- Social networks can be discovered by network analysis of banking, telecommunication and postal records.

Applications

Sometimes, manufacturers and film distributors may intentionally leave subtle forensic markings on their products to identify them in case of piracy or involvement in a crime. (*Cf.* watermark, digital watermark, steganography. DNA marking.)

Organizations

- Association of Firearm and Tool Mark Examiners
- Canadian Identification Society
- International Association for Identification

Forensic Profiling

Forensic profiling is the study of trace evidence in order to develop information which can be used by police authorities . This information can be used to identify suspects and convict them in a court of law.

The term "forensic" in this context refers to "information that is used in court as evidence" (Geradts & Sommer 2006, p. 10). The traces originate from criminal or litigious activities themselves. However traces are information that is not strictly dedicated to the court. They may increase knowledge in broader domains linked to security that deal with investigation, intelligence, surveillance, or risk analysis (Geradts & Sommer 2008, p. 26).

Forensic profiling is different than offender profiling, which only refers to the identification of an offender to the psychological profile of a criminal.

In particular, forensic profiling should refer to profiling in the information sciences sense, i.e., to "The process of 'discovering' correlations between data in data bases that can be used to identify and represent a human or nonhuman subject (individual or group), and/or the application of profiles (sets of correlated data) to individuate and represent a subject or to identify a subject as a member of a group or category" (Geradts & Sommer 2006, p. 41).

Profiling Techniques

Forensic profiling is generally conducted using datamining technology, as a means by which relevant patterns are discovered, and profiles are generated from large quantities of data.

A distinction of forms of profiles that are used in a given context is necessary before evaluating applications of data mining techniques for forensic profiling.

Data Available

The data available to law enforcement agencies are divided into two categories (Geradts & Sommer 2008, p. 15):

- Nominal data directly designates persons or objects (recidivists, intelligence files and suspect files, stolen vehicles or objects, etc.) and their relations. Nominal data may also be obtained in the framework of specific investigations, for instance a list of calls made with a mobile phone (card and/or phone) that cover a certain period of time, a list of people corresponding to a certain profile, or data obtained through surveillances;
- Crime data consist of traces that result from criminal activities: physical traces, other information collected at the scene, from witness or victims or some electronic traces, as well as reconstructed descriptions of cases (modus operandi, time intervals, duration and place) and their relations (links between cases, series).

Types

- DNA profiling Used for the identification of individuals on the basis of their respective DNA profiles.
- Digital Image Forensics. This covers: *image source identification* (which is based on specific characteristics of the image acquisition device or technology) and *malicious post-processing or tampering* (which aim is for instance to verify the integrity of particular features) (Popescu & Farid 2005).
- Illicit drug profiling, which refers to the systematic extraction and storage of chemical attributes of drugs seized in order to obtain indications on the manufacture and distribution processes, the size and the evolution of the market). (Terrettaz-Zufferey et al. Khanevski)
- Forensic Information Technology (forensic IT), which refers to the analysis of the digital traces that people leave when using information technology.
- [ffender profiling, i.e. psychological profiling of the criminal.

Issues

The use of profiling techniques represents threats to the privacy of the individual and to the protection of fundamental freedoms. Indeed, criminal data, i.e., data which are collected and processed for suppressing criminal offences, often consists of personal data. One of the issues is the re-use of personal data collected within one criminal investigation for another purpose than the one for which it was collected.

Several methods-including technical, legal, and behavioral-are available to address some of the issues associated with forensic profiling. For instance, in Europe the European Convention on Human Rights provides a number of instruments for the Protection of Individuals with regard to Automatic Processing of Personal Data.

References

- Donald E. Sheldon, Young S. Kim and Gregg Barak A Study of Juror Expectations and Demands Concerning Scientific Evidence: Does the 'CSI Effect' Exist? Vanderbilt Journal of Entertainment & Technology Law
- Kruse, Corinna (March 2010). "Producing Absolute Truth: CSI Science as Wishful Thinking". American Anthropologist. 112 (1): 79–91. doi:10.1111/j.1548-1433.2009.01198
- Chesen, Jeff (July 2008). "The 'CSI Effect'—There's No Such Thing as Questions, Just Hidden Answers". It's Evident. NCSTL. Retrieved 21 December 2010
- Isani, Shaeda (29 September 2010). "Quand la science enquête : imaginaires & représentations de la FASP criminalistique". Revue de l'Institut des Langues et des Cultures d'Europe et d'Amérique (in French). ILCEA. 2010 (12). ISBN 978-2-84310-180-9. Retrieved 7 January 2011
- Holmgren, Janne A.; Fordham, Judith (January 2011). "The CSI Effect and the Canadian and the Australian Jury". Journal of Forensic Sciences. 56 (S1): S63–S71. doi:10.1111/j.1556-4029.2010.01621
- Durnal, Evan W. (12 March 2010). "Crime scene investigation (as seen on TV)". Forensic Science International. 199 (1–3): 1–5 [4]. PMID 20227206. doi:10.1016/j.forsciint.2010.02.015
- Roane, Kit R (17 April 2005). "The CSI Effect". US News & World Report. Archived from the original on 3 February 2011. Retrieved 28 December 2010
- Shelton, Donald E (17 March 2008). "The 'CSI Effect': Does It Really Exist?". National Institute of Justice Journal. 259. Retrieved 21 December 2010
- Cole, S.A. (2009). "Forensics without uniqueness, conclusions without individualization: the new epistemology of forensic identification.". Law, Probability, and Risk (3 ed.). 8: 233–255. doi:10.1093/lpr/mgp016
- Mandal, Ananya (28 March 2010). "DNA evidence often overwhelms jurors to convict wrongly says research". Medical News. Retrieved 27 December 2010
- Massey, S. L. (2004). "Persistence of creases of the foot and their value for forensic identification purposes". Journal of Forensic Identification. 54 (3): 296
- Maddison, W. P. (1997). "Gene trees in species trees.". Systematic Biology. 46: 523–536. doi:10.1093/sysbio/46.3.523
- Stevens, Dennis J. (2008). An Introduction to American Policing. Jones & Bartlett Learning. p. 406. ISBN 978-0-7637-4893-7. Retrieved 21 December 2010
- Blake, J. W. (1959). "Identification of the New Born by Flexure Creases". Journal of Language, Identity, & Education. 9 (9): 3–5
- Manel, S.; Gaggiotti, O.E.; Waples, R.S. (March 2005). "Assignment methods: matching biological questions with appropriate techniques.". Trends in Ecology and Evolution (3 ed.). 20: 136–142. doi:10.1016/j.tree.2004.12.004
- Greenwood, Jill King (25 November 2006). "Criminals get tips from forensic television shows". Pittsburgh Tribune-Review. Retrieved 10 December 2010

2

Various Types of Forensic Science

Forensic science can be divided into different categories. Digital forensics, forensic linguistics, forensic psychology, nuclear forensics and forensic pathology are some of the types of forensic science mentioned in this section. Forensic science is best understood in confluence with the major topics listed in the following chapter.

Digital Forensics

Aerial photo of FLETC, where US digital forensics standards were developed in the 1980s and '90s

Digital forensics (sometimes known as digital forensic science) is a branch of forensic science encompassing the recovery and investigation of material found in digital devices, often in relation to computer crime. The term digital forensics was originally used as a synonym for computer forensics but has expanded to cover investigation of all devices capable of storing digital data. With roots in the personal computing revolution of the late 1970s and early 1980s, the discipline evolved in a haphazard manner during the 1990s, and it was not until the early 21st century that national policies emerged.

Digital forensics investigations have a variety of applications. The most common is to support or refute a hypothesis before criminal or civil (as part of the electronic discovery process) courts. Forensics may also feature in the private sector; such as during internal corporate investigations or intrusion investigation (a specialist probe into the nature and extent of an unauthorized network intrusion).

The technical aspect of an investigation is divided into several sub-branches, relating to the type of digital devices involved; computer forensics, network forensics, forensic data analysis and mobile device forensics. The typical forensic process encompasses the seizure, forensic imaging (acquisition) and analysis of digital media and the production of a report into collected evidence.

As well as identifying direct evidence of a crime, digital forensics can be used to attribute evidence to specific suspects, confirm alibis or statements, determine intent, identify sources (for example, in copyright cases), or authenticate documents. Investigations are much broader in scope than other areas of forensic analysis (where the usual aim is to provide answers to a series of simpler questions) often involving complex time-lines or hypotheses.

History

Prior to the 1980s crimes involving computers were dealt with using existing laws. The first computer crimes were recognized in the 1978 Florida Computer Crimes Act, which included legislation against the unauthorized modification or deletion of data on a computer system. Over the next few years the range of computer crimes being committed increased, and laws were passed to deal with issues of copyright, privacy/harassment (e.g., cyber bullying, cyber stalking, and online predators) and child pornography. It was not until the 1980s that federal laws began to incorporate computer offences. Canada was the first country to pass legislation in 1983. This was followed by the US Federal *Computer Fraud and Abuse Act* in 1986, Australian amendments to their crimes acts in 1989 and the British *Computer Misuse Act* in 1990.

1980s–1990s: Growth of the Field

The growth in computer crime during the 1980s and 1990s caused law enforcement agencies to begin establishing specialized groups, usually at the national level, to handle the technical aspects of investigations. For example, in 1984 the FBI launched a *Computer Analysis and Response Team* and the following year a computer crime department was set up within the British Metropolitan Police fraud squad. As well as being law enforcement professionals, many of the early members of these groups were also computer hobbyists and became responsible for the field's initial research and direction.

One of the first practical (or at least publicized) examples of digital forensics was Cliff Stoll's pursuit of hacker Markus Hess in 1986. Stoll, whose investigation made use of computer and network forensic techniques, was not a specialized examiner. Many of the earliest forensic examinations followed the same profile.

Throughout the 1990s there was high demand for these new, and basic, investigative resources. The strain on central units lead to the creation of regional, and even local, level groups to help handle the load. For example, the British National Hi-Tech Crime Unit was set up in 2001 to provide a national infrastructure for computer crime; with personnel located both centrally in London and with the various regional police forces (the unit was folded into the Serious Organised Crime Agency (SOCA) in 2006).

During this period the science of digital forensics grew from the ad-hoc tools and techniques developed by these hobbyist practitioners. This is in contrast to other forensics disciplines which developed from work by the scientific community. It was not until 1992 that the term "computer forensics" was used in academic literature (although prior to this it had been in informal use); a paper by Collier and Spaul attempted to justify this new discipline to the forensic science world. This swift development resulted in a lack of standardization and training. In his 1995 book, "*High-Technology Crime: Investigating Cases Involving Computers*", K. Rosenblatt wrote:

Seizing, preserving, and analyzing evidence stored on a computer is the greatest forensic challenge facing law enforcement in the 1990s. Although most forensic tests, such as fingerprinting and DNA testing, are performed by specially trained experts the task of collecting and analyzing computer evidence is often assigned to patrol officers and detectives.

2000s: Developing Standards

Since 2000, in response to the need for standardization, various bodies and agencies have published guidelines for digital forensics. The Scientific Working Group on Digital Evidence (SWGDE) produced a 2002 paper, "*Best practices for Computer Forensics*", this was followed, in 2005, by the publication of an ISO standard (ISO 17025, *General requirements for the competence of testing and calibration laboratories*). A European lead international treaty, the Convention on Cybercrime, came into force in 2004 with the aim of reconciling national computer crime laws, investigative techniques and international co-operation. The treaty has been signed by 43 nations (including the US, Canada, Japan, South Africa, UK and other European nations) and ratified by 16.

The issue of training also received attention. Commercial companies (often forensic software developers) began to offer certification programs and digital forensic analysis was included as a topic at the UK specialist investigator training facility, Centrex.

Since the late 1990s mobile devices have become more widely available, advancing beyond simple communication devices, and have been found to be rich forms of information, even for crime not traditionally associated with digital forensics. Despite this, digital analysis of phones has lagged behind traditional computer media, largely due to problems over the proprietary nature of devices.

Focus has also shifted onto internet crime, particularly the risk of cyber warfare and cyberterrorism. A February 2010 report by the United States Joint Forces Command concluded:

Through cyberspace, enemies will target industry, academia, government, as well as the military in the air, land, maritime, and space domains. In much the same way that airpower transformed the battlefield of World War II, cyberspace has fractured the physical barriers that shield a nation from attacks on its commerce and communication.

The field of digital forensics still faces unresolved issues. A 2009 paper, "Digital Forensic Research: The Good, the Bad and the Unaddressed", by Peterson and Shenoi identified a bias towards Windows operating systems in digital forensics research. In 2010 Simson Garfinkel identified issues facing digital investigations in the future, including the increasing size of digital media, the wide availability of encryption to consumers, a growing variety of operating systems and file formats, an increasing number of individuals owning multiple devices, and legal limitations on investigators. The paper also identified continued training issues, as well as the prohibitively high cost of entering the field.

Development of Forensic Tools

During the 1980s very few specialized digital forensic tools existed, and consequently investigators often performed live analysis on media, examining computers from within the operating system using existing sysadmin tools to extract evidence. This practice carried the risk of modifying data on the disk, either inadvertently or otherwise, which led to claims of evidence tampering. A number of tools were created during the early 1990s to address the problem.

The need for such software was first recognized in 1989 at the Federal Law Enforcement Training Center, resulting in the creation of IMDUMP (by Michael White) and in 1990, SafeBack (developed by Sydex). Similar software was developed in other countries; DIBS (a hardware and software solution) was released commercially in the UK in 1991, and Rob McKemmish released *Fixed Disk Image* free to Australian law enforcement. These tools allowed examiners to create an exact copy of a piece of digital media to work on, leaving the original disk intact for verification. By the end of the 1990s, as demand for digital evidence grew more advanced commercial tools such as EnCase and FTK were developed, allowing analysts to examine copies of media without using any live forensics. More recently, a trend towards "live memory forensics" has grown resulting in the availability of tools such as WindowsSCOPE.

More recently, the same progression of tool development has occurred for mobile devices; initially investigators accessed data directly on the device, but soon specialist tools such as XRY or Radio Tactics Aceso appeared.

Forensic Process

A portable Tableau write-blocker attached to a hard drive

A digital forensic investigation commonly consists of 3 stages: acquisition or imaging of exhibits, analysis, and reporting. Ideally acquisition involves capturing an image of the computer's volatile memory (RAM) and creating an exact sector level duplicate (or "forensic duplicate") of the media, often using a write blocking device to prevent modification of the original. However, the growth in size of storage media and developments such as cloud computing have led to more use of 'live' acquisitions whereby a 'logical' copy of the data is acquired rather than a complete image of the physical storage device. Both acquired image (or logical copy) and original media/data are hashed (using an algorithm such as SHA-1 or MD5) and the values compared to verify the copy is accurate.

During the analysis phase an investigator recovers evidence material using a number of different methodologies and tools. In 2002, an article in the *International Journal of Digital Evidence* referred to this step as "an in-depth systematic search of evidence related to the suspected crime." In 2006, forensics researcher Brian Carrier described an "intuitive procedure" in which obvious evidence is first identified and then "exhaustive searches are conducted to start filling in the holes."

The actual process of analysis can vary between investigations, but common methodologies include conducting keyword searches across the digital media (within files as well as unallocated and slack space), recovering deleted files and extraction of registry information (for example to list user accounts, or attached USB devices).

The evidence recovered is analysed to reconstruct events or actions and to reach conclusions, work that can often be performed by less specialised staff. When an investigation is complete the data is presented, usually in the form of a written report, in lay persons' terms.

Application

Camera manufacturer	Canon
Camera model	Canon EOS 400D DIGITAL
Exposure time	1/60 sec (0.016666666666667)
F-number	f/4.5
ISO speed rating	400
Date and time of data generation	11:06, August 27, 2010
Lens focal length	31 mm
Show extended details	

An example of an image's Exif metadata that might be used to prove its origin

Digital forensics is commonly used in both criminal law and private investigation. Traditionally it has been associated with criminal law, where evidence is collected to support or oppose a hypothesis before the courts. As with other areas of forensics this is often as part of a wider investigation spanning a number of disciplines. In some cases the collected evidence is used as a form of intelligence gathering, used for other purposes than court proceedings (for example to locate, identify or halt other crimes). As a result, intelligence gathering is sometimes held to a less strict forensic standard.

In civil litigation or corporate matters digital forensics forms part of the electronic discovery (or eDiscovery) process. Forensic procedures are similar to those used in criminal investigations, often with different legal requirements and limitations. Outside of the courts digital forensics can form a part of internal corporate investigations.

A common example might be following unauthorized network intrusion. A specialist forensic examination into the nature and extent of the attack is performed as a damage limitation exercise. Both to establish the extent of any intrusion and in an attempt to identify the attacker. Such attacks were commonly conducted over phone lines during the 1980s, but in the modern era are usually propagated over the Internet.

The main focus of digital forensics investigations is to recover objective evidence of a criminal activity (termed actus reus in legal parlance). However, the diverse range of data held in digital devices can help with other areas of inquiry.

Attribution

> Meta data and other logs can be used to attribute actions to an individual. For example, personal documents on a computer drive might identify its owner.

Alibis and statements

> Information provided by those involved can be cross checked with digital evidence. For example, during the investigation into the Soham murders the offender's alibi was disproved

when mobile phone records of the person he claimed to be with showed she was out of town at the time.

Intent

As well as finding objective evidence of a crime being committed, investigations can also be used to prove the intent (known by the legal term mens rea). For example, the Internet history of convicted killer Neil Entwistle included references to a site discussing *How to kill people.*

Evaluation of source

File artifacts and meta-data can be used to identify the origin of a particular piece of data; for example, older versions of Microsoft Word embedded a Global Unique Identifer into files which identified the computer it had been created on. Proving whether a file was produced on the digital device being examined or obtained from elsewhere (e.g., the Internet) can be very important.

Document authentication

Related to "Evaluation of source," meta data associated with digital documents can be easily modified (for example, by changing the computer clock you can affect the creation date of a file). Document authentication relates to detecting and identifying falsification of such details.

Limitations

One major limitation to a forensic investigation is the use of encryption; this disrupts initial examination where pertinent evidence might be located using keywords. Laws to compel individuals to disclose encryption keys are still relatively new and controversial.

Legal Considerations

The examination of digital media is covered by national and international legislation. For civil investigations, in particular, laws may restrict the abilities of analysts to undertake examinations. Restrictions against network monitoring, or reading of personal communications often exist. During criminal investigation, national laws restrict how much information can be seized. For example, in the United Kingdom seizure of evidence by law enforcement is governed by the PACE act. During its existence early in the field, the "International Organization on Computer Evidence" (IOCE) was one agency that worked to establish compatible international standards for the seizure of evidence.

In the UK the same laws covering computer crime can also affect forensic investigators. The 1990 computer misuse act legislates against unauthorised access to computer material; this is a particular concern for civil investigators who have more limitations than law enforcement.

An individuals right to privacy is one area of digital forensics which is still largely undecided by courts. The US Electronic Communications Privacy Act places limitations on the ability of law enforcement or civil investigators to intercept and access evidence. The act makes a distinction between stored communication (e.g. email archives) and transmitted communication (such as

VOIP). The latter, being considered more of a privacy invasion, is harder to obtain a warrant for. The ECPA also affects the ability of companies to investigate the computers and communications of their employees, an aspect that is still under debate as to the extent to which a company can perform such monitoring.

Article 5 of the European Convention on Human Rights asserts similar privacy limitations to the ECPA and limits the processing and sharing of personal data both within the EU and with external countries. The ability of UK law enforcement to conduct digital forensics investigations is legislated by the Regulation of Investigatory Powers Act.

Digital Evidence

Digital evidence can come in a number of forms

When used in a court of law digital evidence falls under the same legal guidelines as other forms of evidence; courts do not usually require more stringent guidelines. In the United States the Federal Rules of Evidence are used to evaluate the admissibility of digital evidence, the United Kingdom PACE and Civil Evidence acts have similar guidelines and many other countries have their own laws. US federal laws restrict seizures to items with only obvious evidential value. This is acknowledged as not always being possible to establish with digital media prior to an examination.

Laws dealing with digital evidence are concerned with two issues: integrity and authenticity. Integrity is ensuring that the act of seizing and acquiring digital media does not modify the evidence (either the original or the copy). Authenticity refers to the ability to confirm the integrity of information; for example that the imaged media matches the original evidence. The ease with which digital media can be modified means that documenting the chain of custody from the crime scene, through analysis and, ultimately, to the court, (a form of audit trail) is important to establish the authenticity of evidence.

Attorneys have argued that because digital evidence can theoretically be altered it undermines the reliability of the evidence. US judges are beginning to reject this theory, in the case *US v. Bonallo* the court ruled that "the fact that it is possible to alter data contained in a computer is plainly insufficient to establish untrustworthiness." In the United Kingdom guidelines such as those issued by ACPO are followed to help document the authenticity and integrity of evidence.

Digital investigators, particularly in criminal investigations, have to ensure that conclusions are based upon factual evidence and their own expert knowledge. In the US, for example, Federal Rules of Evidence state that a qualified expert may testify "in the form of an opinion or otherwise" so long as:

(1) the testimony is based upon sufficient facts or data, (2) the testimony is the product of reliable principles and methods, and (3) the witness has applied the principles and methods reliably to the facts of the case.

The sub-branches of digital forensics may each have their own specific guidelines for the conduct of investigations and the handling of evidence. For example, mobile phones may be required to be placed in a Faraday shield during seizure or acquisition to prevent further radio traffic to the device. In the UK forensic examination of computers in criminal matters is subject to ACPO guidelines. There are also international approaches to providing guidance on how to handle electronic evidence. The "Electronic Evidence Guide" by the Council of Europe offers a framework for law enforcement and judicial authorities in countries who seek to set up or enhance their own guidelines for the identification and handling of electronic evidence.

Investigative Tools

The admissibility of digital evidence relies on the tools used to extract it. In the US, forensic tools are subjected to the Daubert standard, where the judge is responsible for ensuring that the processes and software used were acceptable. In a 2003 paper Brian Carrier argued that the Daubert guidelines required the code of forensic tools to be published and peer reviewed. He concluded that "open source tools may more clearly and comprehensively meet the guideline requirements than would closed source tools." In a 2011 article Josh Brunty stated that the scientific validation of the technology and software associated with performing a digital forensic examination is critical to any laboratory process. He argued that "the science of digital forensics is founded on the principles of repeatable processes and quality evidence therefore knowing how to design and properly maintain a good validation process is a key requirement for any digital forensic examiner to defend their methods in court."

Branches

Digital forensics investigation is not restricted to retrieve data merely from the computer, as laws are breached by the criminals and small digital devices (e.g. PDAs, smart phones, flash sticks) are now extensively used. Some of these devices got volatile memory while some got non-volatile memory. Sufficient methodologies are available to retrieve data from volatile memory, however there is lack of detailed methodology or a framework for data retrieval from non-volatile memory sources. Depending on the type of devices, media or artifacts, digital forensics investigation is branched into various types.

Computer Forensics

The goal of computer forensics is to explain the current state of a digital artifact; such as a computer system, storage medium or electronic document. The discipline usually covers computers, embedded systems (digital devices with rudimentary computing power and onboard memory) and static memory (such as USB pen drives).

Computer forensics can deal with a broad range of information; from logs (such as internet history) through to the actual files on the drive. In 2007 prosecutors used a spreadsheet recovered from the computer of Joseph E. Duncan III to show premeditation and secure the death penalty. Sharon Lopatka's killer was identified in 2006 after email messages from him detailing torture and death fantasies were found on her computer.

Mobile phones in a UK Evidence bag

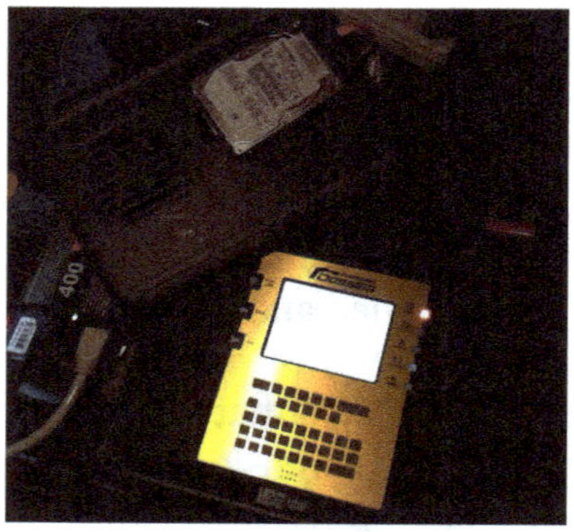

Private Investigator & Certified Digital Forensics Examiner Imaging a hard drive in the field for forensic examination.

Mobile Device Forensics

Mobile device forensics is a sub-branch of digital forensics relating to recovery of digital evidence or data from a mobile device. It differs from Computer forensics in that a mobile device will have an inbuilt communication system (e.g. GSM) and, usually, proprietary storage mechanisms. Investigations usually focus on simple data such as call data and communications (SMS/Email) rather than in-depth recovery of deleted data. SMS data from a mobile device investigation helped to exonerate Patrick Lumumba in the murder of Meredith Kercher.

Mobile devices are also useful for providing location information; either from inbuilt gps/location tracking or via cell site logs, which track the devices within their range. Such information was used to track down the kidnappers of Thomas Onofri in 2006.

Network Forensics

Network forensics is concerned with the monitoring and analysis of computer network traffic, both local and WAN/internet, for the purposes of information gathering, evidence collection, or intrusion detection. Traffic is usually intercepted at the packet level, and either stored for later analysis or filtered in real-time. Unlike other areas of digital forensics network data is often volatile and rarely logged, making the discipline often reactionary.

In 2000 the FBI lured computer hackers Aleksey Ivanov and Gorshkov to the United States for a fake job interview. By monitoring network traffic from the pair's computers, the FBI identified passwords allowing them to collect evidence directly from Russian-based computers.

Forensic Data Analysis

Forensic Data Analysis is a branch of digital forensics. It examines structured data with the aim to discover and analyse patterns of fraudulent activities resulting from financial crime.

Database Forensics

Database forensics is a branch of digital forensics relating to the forensic study of databases and their metadata. Investigations use database contents, log files and in-RAM data to build a timeline or recover relevant information.

Education and Research

Academic centre of education and research in forensic sciences:

North America: Penn State University offers Security and Risk Analysis Major, Master of Professional Studies in Information Sciences, Master of Professional Studies in Homeland Security, and Ph.D. in Information Sciences and Technology in the digital forensics area.

Forensic Pathology

The heart of a murder victim

Forensic pathology is pathology that focuses on determining the cause of death by examining a corpse. A post mortem is performed by a medical examiner, usually during the investigation of criminal law cases and civil law cases in some jurisdictions. Coroners and medical examiners are also frequently asked to confirm the identity of a corpse.

Scope of Forensic Pathology

Forensic pathology is an application of medical jurisprudence. The *forensic pathologist*:

- Is a medical doctor who has completed training in anatomical pathology and who has subsequently specialized in forensic pathology. The requirements for becoming a "fully qualified" forensic pathologist vary from country to country. Some of the different requirements are discussed below.
- Performs autopsies/postmortem examinations to determine the cause of death. The autopsy report contains an opinion about :
    - The pathologic process, injury, or disease that directly results in or initiates a series of events that lead to a person's death (also called mechanism of death), such as a bullet wound to the head, exsanguination caused by a stab wound, manual or ligature strangulation, myocardial infarction resulting from coronary artery disease, etc.), and
    - The "manner of death", the circumstances surrounding the cause of death, which in most jurisdictions include:
        - Homicide
        - Accidental
        - Natural
        - Undetermined
- The autopsy also provides an opportunity for other issues raised by the death to be addressed, such as the collection of trace evidence or determining the identity of the deceased.
- Examines and documents wounds and injuries, both at autopsy and occasionally in a clinical setting.
- Collects and examines tissue specimens under the microscope (histology) in order to identify the presence or absence of natural disease and other microscopic findings such as asbestos bodies in the lungs or gunpowder particles around a gunshot wound.
- Collects and interprets toxicological analyses on body tissues and fluids to determine the chemical cause of accidental overdoses or deliberate poisonings.
- Forensic pathologists also work closely with the medico-legal authority for the area concerned with the investigation of sudden and unexpected deaths i.e. the coroner (England and Wales), procurator fiscal (Scotland) or coroner or medical examiner (United States).
- Serves as an expert witness in courts of law testifying in civil or criminal law cases.

In an autopsy, he/she is often assisted by an autopsy/mortuary technician (sometimes called a diener in the USA).

Forensic physicians, sometimes referred to as 'forensic medical examiners' or 'police surgeons' (in the UK until recently), are medical doctors trained in the examination of, and provision of medical treatment to, living victims of assault (including sexual assault) and those individuals who find themselves in police custody. Many forensic physicians in the UK practise clinical forensic medicine part-time, whilst they also practice family medicine, or another medical specialty.

In the United Kingdom, Membership of the Royal College of Pathologists is not a prerequisite of appointment as a Coroner's *Medical Expert*, i.e. doctors in the UK that are not forensic pathologists or pathologists are allowed to perform medicolegal autopsies, simply because of the vague wording of 'The Coroners Act', which merely stipulates a 'suitably qualified medical practitioner', i.e. anyone on the GMC Register.

Investigation of Death

Deaths where there is a known cause and those considered unnatural are investigated. In most jurisdictions this is done by a *"forensic pathologist", coroner, medical examiner*, or hybrid *medical examiner-coroner* offices.

Terminology is not Consistent Across Jurisdictions

In some jurisdictions, the title of "Medical Examiner" is used by a non-physician, elected official involved in medicolegal death investigation. In others, the law requires the medical examiner to be a physician, pathologist, or forensic pathologist.

Similarly, the title "coroner" is applied to both physicians and non-physicians. Historically, coroners were not all physicians (most often serving primarily as the town mortician). However, in some jurisdictions the title of "Coroner" is exclusively used by physicians.

Canadian Coroners

In Canada, there is a mix of coroner and medical examiner systems, depending on the province or territory. In Ontario, coroners are licensed physicians, usually but not exclusively family physicians. In Quebec, there is a mix of medical and non-medical coroners, whereas in British Columbia, there is predominantly a non-physician coroner system. Alberta and Nova Scotia are examples of ME systems

Coroners and Medical Examiners in the United States

In the United States, a coroner is typically an elected public official in a particular geographic jurisdiction who investigates and certifies deaths. The vast majority of coroners lack a Doctor of Medicine degree and the amount of medical training that they have received is highly variable, depending on their profession (e.g. law enforcement, judges, funeral directors, emergency medical technicians, nurses).

In contrast, a medical examiner is typically a physician who holds the degree of Doctor of Medicine or Doctor of Osteopathic Medicine. Ideally, a medical examiner has completed both a pathology residency and a fellowship in forensic pathology. In some jurisdictions, a medical examiner must be both a doctor and a lawyer, with additional training in forensic pathology.

History

In German-speaking Europe, lectures on forensic pathology were regularly held in Freiburg in the mid 18th century and Vienna in 1804. Scientists like Auguste Ambroise Tardieu, Johann Ludwig Casper and Carl Liman made great effort to develop forensic pathology into a science based on empirics.

Forensic pathology was first recognized in the United States by the American Board of Pathology in 1959.

In Canada, it was formally recognized in 2003, and a formal training program (a fellowship) is currently being established under the auspices of the Royal College of Physicians and Surgeons of Canada.

Education

In most English speaking countries, forensic pathology is a subspecialty of anatomical pathology. Training requirements differ from country to country.

Australia

There are currently three paths to qualify as a forensic pathologist in Australia. The first is to train solely in forensic pathology (although a significant amount of anatomical pathology knowledge is still required) and pass two examinations for forensic pathology only. The second is to commence training in anatomical pathology, and complete an initial anatomical pathology examination, which takes a minimum of three years; then go on to train solely in forensic pathology and complete a forensic pathology examination, which takes a minimum of two years. The third is to complete a minimum 5 years' training in anatomical pathology to qualify as a fellow in anatomical pathology, then complete a post-fellowship year in forensic pathology (a minimum twelve months further training plus successful completion of an examination).

Canada

In Canada, anatomical pathology is a five-year residency. Residents who wish to become forensic pathologists must then complete a one-year fellowship in forensic pathology. Forensic pathology is a sub-specialty by the Royal College of Physicians and Surgeons. Two schools that have training programs are the University of Toronto and Mcmaster University.

India

In India, the speciality is commonly referred to as Forensic Medicine and Toxicology or Legal Medicine. After completion of medical graduation (MBBS), one has to complete three years of study and training including thesis research, which leads to award of degree of MD (Forensic Medicine). One can also alternately pass the board examination conducted by National Board of Examinations, leading to awarding of Diplomate of National Board (DNB).

The majority of the specialists are attached to the Department of Forensic Medicine and Toxicology in various medical colleges. The classification of posts includes Assistant Professor (Lecturer), Associate Professor (Reader) and Professor. The work profile of the specialists includes conducting autopsies and clinical forensic examinations; apart from teaching the medical students. They have to regularly appear in the courts as expert witnesses. A typical department in a government institution conducts 100 to 5000 autopsies a year depending upon the jurisdiction. Apart from this the clinical forensic examinations constitute a major part of the work and number of cases can run up to 10000 a year in an average institution.

The largest association of the specialty is Indian Academy of Forensic Medicine (IAFM), which also publishes its quarterly Journal of Indian Academy of Forensic Medicine regularly. This association has a specialist member strength of more than 1000.

Indonesia

In Indonesia, forensic medicine, also known as legal medicine (*"kedokteran kehakiman"*), is a 3-year specialty program that can be taken directly after completing medical school. It is separate from anatomical pathology and clinical pathology. Upon completion of the program, a forensic medicine specialist will obtain the title *Spesialis Forensik*, or *Sp.F.* He or she may be addressed in public as *Dokter Forensik* ("forensic doctor"). Note that there is no pre-medicine program, making the total duration of formal education for one to become a forensic specialist 8 years.

Forensic medicine is also a mandatory round during medical school clerkship. Medical students assist the doctors on autopsies, and they may also be allowed to perform an autopsy under supervision, and to witness in the court.

United Kingdom

In the UK, anatomical pathology is a five-year residency. Successful candidates are eligible for inclusion on the specialist register of the General Medical Council (GMC) having obtained Membership of the Royal College of Pathologists (United Kingdom).

A specialist training (ST) post is applied for after the foundation year to enter a training program in Histopathology. Imminent changes as a result of the Tooke report may require two years or more to be fulfilled on general rotational placements before the option of histopathology arises. However, the Royal College have not yet issued their response to this matter. It is then necessary to obtain the MRCPath Part I examination in Histopathology, after which it is then possible to apply to one of few training posts in Forensic Pathology in the UK. Current approved centres include Belfast, Liverpool, Leicester, Cardiff, London, Sheffield, Glasgow and Dundee. Not all the posts are currently actively training. Following 3 years training in Forensic Pathology and completion of the FRCPath Part II slanted to Forensic Pathology you may then obtain CCT (certificate of completion of training) and work as a Consultant Forensic Pathologist. Another option is to obtain the full FRCPath in general histopathology, followed by another 18–24 months of training in forensic pathology, which will qualify the candidates with either the Diploma of the Royal College of Pathologists in Forensic Pathology (DipRCPath (forensic)), or the Diploma in Medical Jurisprudence (DMJ). In England & Wales you will also need to be Home Office Accredited, which will require checks of your training portfolio and completion of a security check and the Expert Witness Training Course run by the Forensic Science Service.

Foreign graduates and specialists need to apply to the GMC and the RCPath directly to practise Forensic Pathology in the United Kingdom.

United States

In the United States, forensic pathologists typically complete at least one year of additional training (a fellowship) after completing an anatomical pathology residency and having passed the "board" examination administered by The American Board of Pathology or The American Osteopathic Board of Pathology ("board-certified"). Becoming an anatomic pathologist in the United States requires completing a residency in anatomic pathology, which is on-the-job training one must perform upon completing medical school before one may practice unsupervised. *Anatomic pathology* (as it is called) by itself is a three-year residency. Most U.S. pathologists complete a combined residency in both anatomic and *clinical pathology*, which requires a total of four years.

In the United States, all told, the education after high school is typically 13–15 years in duration (4 years undergraduate training + 4 years medical school + 4–5 years residency [anatomic and clinical pathology combined] + 1-2 year forensic pathology fellowship). Generally, the biggest hurdle is gaining admission to medical school, although the pass rate for anatomic and forensic pathology board examinations (in the U.S.) is approximately 80-90 and 90-100 percent, respectively. The courts do not require American Board of Pathology certification in order for a witness to be qualified as an expert in the field of forensic pathology, and there are several "diploma mills" that give online certificates in the field.

Forensic Linguistics

Forensic linguistics, legal linguistics, or language and the law, is the application of linguistic knowledge, methods and insights to the forensic context of law, language, crime investigation, trial, and judicial procedure. It is a branch of applied linguistics.

There are principally three areas of application for linguists working in forensic contexts:

- understanding language of the written law,
- understanding language use in forensic and judicial processes, and
- the provision of linguistic evidence.

The discipline of forensic linguistics is not homogenous; it involves a range of experts and researchers in different areas of the field.

History

The phrase *forensic linguistics* first appeared in 1968 when Jan Svartvik, a professor of linguistics, used it in an analysis of statements by Timothy John Evans.

During the early days of forensic linguistics in the United Kingdom, the legal defense for many criminal cases questioned the authenticity of police statements. At the time, customary police procedure for taking suspects' statements dictated that it be in a specific format, rather than in the suspect's own words. Statements by witnesses are very seldom made in a coherent or orderly

fashion, with speculation and backtracking done out loud. The delivery is often too fast-paced, causing important details to be left out.

Early work of forensic linguistics in the United States concerned the rights of individuals with regard to understanding their Miranda rights during the interrogation process. An early application of forensic linguistics in the United States was related to the status of trademarks as words or phrases in the language. One of the bigger cases involved fastfood giant McDonald's claiming that it had originated the process of attaching unprotected words to the 'Mc' prefix (referred to as McWords) and was unhappy with Quality Inns International's intention of opening a chain of economy hotels to be called 'McSleep.'

In the 1980s, Australian linguists discussed the application of linguistics and sociolinguistics to legal issues. They discovered that a phrase such as ' *the same language* ' is open to interpretation. Aboriginal people have their own understanding and use of 'English', something that is not always appreciated by speakers of the dominant version of English, i.e., 'white English'. The Aboriginal people also bring their own culturally based, interactional styles to the interview.

The 2000s saw a considerable shift in the field of forensic linguistics, which has been described as a coming-of-age of the discipline. Not only does the field have professional associations such as the International Association of Forensic Linguistics (IAFL) founded in 1993, and the Austrian Association for Legal Linguistics (AALL) founded in 2017, it can now provide the scientific community with a range of textbooks such as Coulthard and Johnson (2007), Gibbons (2003) and Olsson (2008).

Areas of Study

The range of topics within forensic linguistics is diverse, but research occurs in the following areas:

The Language of Legal Texts

The study of the language of legal texts encompasses a wide range of forensic texts. That includes the study of text types and forms of analysis. Any text or item of spoken language can potentially be a forensic text when it is used in a legal or criminal context. This includes analysing the linguistics of documents as diverse as Acts of Parliament (or other law-making body), private wills, court judgements and summonses and the statutes of other bodies, such as States and government departments. One important area is that of the transformative effect of Norman French and Ecclesiastic Latin on the development of the English common law, and the evolution of the legal specifics associated with it. It can also refer to the ongoing attempts at making legal language more comprehensible to laypeople.

A popular forensic linguistics understanding of the relationship between language and law has been voiced by Leisser who states that:

- "It is indeed hard to deny that the rule of law is in fact the rule of language. It seems that there cannot be law without language. Kelsen (1945: 161) wrote that 'just as everything King Midas touched turned into gold, everything to which the law refers becomes law, i.e. something legally existing'. The concept of law is conveyed and mediated entirely through the structures of human language and it is thus plausible to assume that everything the law touches is therefore also touched by language. This is particularly evident in the fact that all processes of legal meaning-making and meaning-seeking are inextricably tied to the language system. [...] Law is defined as a set of linguistic signs which is ascribed the societal power to control human conduct."

The Language of Legal Processes

Among other things, this area examines language as it is used in cross-examination, evidence presentation, judge's direction, police cautions, police testimonies in court, summing up to a jury, interview techniques, the questioning process in court and in other areas such as police interviews.

Forensic Text Types

Emergency Call

In an emergency call, the recipient or emergency operator's ability to extract primarily linguistic information in threatening situations and to come up with the required response in a timely manner is crucial to the successful completion of the call. Intonational emphasis, voice pitch and the extent to which there is cooperation between the caller and the recipient at any one time are also very important in analysing an emergency call. Full cooperation includes frank and timely responses.

Urgency plays a role in emergency calls, so hesitations, signs of evasiveness, and incomplete or overly short answers indicate that the caller might be making a false or hoax call. A genuine call has distinctive interlocking and slight overlap of turns. The recipient trusts the caller to provide accurate information and the caller trusts the recipient to ask only pertinent questions. If the caller uses a rising pitch at the end of every turn, it might represent a lack of commitment; the recipient's use of a rising pitch indicates doubt or desire for clarification. The call ideally moves from nil knowledge on the part of the recipient to a maximum amount of knowledge in a minimum possible period of time. This makes the emergency call unlike any other kind of service encounter.

Ransom Demands or other Threat Communication

Threat is a counterpart of a promise and is an important feature in a ransom demand. Ransom demands are also examined to identify between genuine and false threats. An example of a ransom note analysis can be seen in the case of the Lindbergh kidnapping, where the first ransom note (sometimes referred to as the Nursery Note) stated: *"We warn you for making anyding public or for notify the Polise the child is in gut care."* From the sentence, the kidnapper makes the claim that the child is in good hands but to make such a claim, the note would have to be written before the perpetrator enters the premises. Therefore, the claim is false (at the time of writing) since the kidnapper had not even encountered the child when he wrote the note.

Kidnappers may write statements that later end up being true, such as "your child is being held in a private location" being written ahead of time.

Suicide Letters

A suicide note is typically brief, concise and highly propositional with a degree of evasiveness. A credible suicide letter must be making a definite unequivocal proposition in a situational context.

The proposition of genuine suicide is thematic, directed to the addressee (or addressees) and relevant to the relationship between them. Suicide notes generally have sentences alluding to the act of killing oneself, or the method of suicide that was undertaken. The contents of a suicide note could be intended to make the addressee suffer or feel guilt. Genuine suicide letters are short, typically less than 300 words in length. Extraneous or irrelevant material is often excluded from the text.

Death Row Statements

Death row statements either admit the crime, leaving the witness with an impression of honesty and forthrightness; or deny the crime, leaving the witness with an impression of innocence. They may also denounce witnesses as dishonest, critique law enforcement as corrupt in an attempt to portray innocence or seek an element of revenge in their last moments (Olsson 2004). Death row statements are within the heavily institutionalized setting of death row prisons. The Forensic Linguistics Institute holds a corpus of these documents and is conducting research on them.

Social Media

Social media statements are often context specific, and their interpretation can be highly subjective. Forensic application of a selection of stylistic and stylometric techniques in a simulated authorship attribution case involving texts has been done in relation to Facebook. Analysis of social media postings can reveal whether they are illegal (e.g. sexist) or unethical (e.g. intended to harm) or whether they are not (e.g. simply provocative or free speech).

Use of Linguistic Evidence in Legal Proceedings

These areas of application have varying degrees of acceptability or reliability within the field. Linguists have provided evidence in:

- Trademark and other intellectual property disputes
- Disputes of meaning and use
- Author identification (determining who wrote an anonymous text by making comparisons to known writing samples of a suspect; such as threat letters, mobile phone texts or emails)
- Forensic stylistics (identifying cases of plagiarism)
- Voice identification, also known as forensic phonetics, used to determine, through acoustic qualities, if the voice on a tape recorder is that of the defendant)
- Discourse analysis (the analysis of the structure of written or spoken utterance to determine who is introducing topics or whether a suspect is agreeing to engage in criminal conspiracy)
- Language analysis (forensic dialectology) tracing the linguistic history of asylum seekers (Language Analysis for the Determination of Origin)
- Reconstruction of mobile phone text conversations
- Forensic phonetics

Specialist databases of samples of spoken and written natural language (called corpora) are now frequently used by forensic linguists. These include corpora of suicide notes, mobile phone texts, police statements, police interview records and witness statements. They are used to analyse language, understand how it is used, and to reduce the effort needed to identify words that tend to occur near each other (collocations or collocates).

Author Identification

The identification of whether a given individual said or wrote something relies on analysis of their idiolect, or particular patterns of language use (vocabulary, collocations, pronunciation, spelling, grammar, etc). The idiolect is a theoretical construct based on the idea that there is linguistic variation at the group level and hence there may also be linguistic variation at the individual level. William Labov has stated that nobody has found a "homogenous data" in idiolects, and there are many reasons why it is difficult to provide such evidence.

Firstly, language is not an inherited property, but one which is socially acquired. Because acquisition is continuous and life-long, an individual's use of language is always susceptible to variation from a variety of sources, including other speakers, the media and macro-social changes. Education can have a profoundly homogenizing effect on language use. Research into authorship identification is ongoing. The term authorship attribution is now felt to be too deterministic.

The paucity of documents (ransom notes, threatening letters, etc) in most criminal cases in a forensic setting means there is often too little text upon which to base a reliable identification. However, the information provided may be adequate to eliminate a suspect as an author or narrow down an author from a small group of suspects.

Authorship measures that analysts use include word length average, average number of syllables per word, article frequency, type-token ratio, punctuation (both in terms of overall density and syntactic boundaries) and the measurements of hapax legomena (unique words in a text). Statistical approaches include factor analysis, Bayesian statistics, Poisson distribution, multivariate analysis, and discriminant function analysis of function words.

The Cusum (Cumulative Sum) method for text analysis has also been developed. Cusum analysis works even on short texts and relies on the assumption that each speaker has a unique set of habits, thus rendering no significant difference between their speech and writing. Speakers tend to utilize two to three letter words in a sentence and their utterances tend to include vowel-initial words.

In order to carry out the Cusum test on habits of utilizing two to three letter words and vowel-initial words in a sentential clause, the occurrences of each type of word in the text must be identified and the distribution plotted in each sentence. The Cusum distribution for these two habits will be compared with the average sentence length of the text. The two sets of values should track each other. Any altered section of the text would show a distinct discrepancy between the values of the two reference points. The tampered section will exhibit a different pattern from the rest of the text.

Forensic Stylistics

This discipline subjects written or spoken materials (or both), to scientific analysis for determination and measurement of content, meaning, speaker identification, or determination of authorship, in identifying plagiarism.

One of the earliest cases where forensic stylistics was used to detect plagiarism was the case of Helen Keller's short story "The Frost King". The blind American author was accused of plagiarism in 1892 with regard to the short story. Upon investigation, The Frost King was found to have been plagiarised from Margaret Canby's book *Frost Fairies* which had been read to her some time ago. Keller was discovered to have made only minute changes to common words and phrases and used less common words to put the same point across, suggesting mere alterations to original ideas.

Keller used 'vast wealth' instead of 'treasure' (approximately 230 times less common in the language) 'bethought' instead of 'concluded' (approximately 450 times less common), 'bade them' instead of 'told them' (approximately 30 times less common). Keller used the phrase 'ever since that time' whilst Canby chose 'from that time' (the latter 50 times more common than the former). Keller also used ' I cannot imagine' whereas Canby used ' I do not know'. 'Know' is approximately ten times more common than 'imagine'.

Keller relied on a lexis that is less common when compared to Canby's. The Flesch and Flesch-Kincaid readability test showed that Canby's text showing more originality compared to Keller's. Canby's text obtained a higher grade on the reading ease scale compared to Keller's. The distinctions between Keller and Canby's text are at the lexical and phrasal level.

Other examples of plagiarism include the cases between Richard Condon, author of The Manchurian Candidate and English novelist Robert Graves; and between Martin Luther King Jr and Archibald Carey.

Judging by the text in *The Manchurian Candidate*, Condon's work is seen to be rich in clichés such as *"in his superstitious heart of hearts."* While Helen Keller took pride in using rare phrases and avoids common source words, Condon was fond of expanding existing words into phrases and existing phrases into more extensive ones. Condon was also found to have borrowed from a wide range of Graves' work.

In the plagiarism case of Martin Luther King Jr, almost half of his doctoral dissertation was discovered to have been copied from another theology student. King simply changed the names of the mountains and used much more alliteration and assonance.

Carey's and Graves' texts (source texts) were noticeably shorter, pithier and simpler in structure while Condon's and King's texts relied on 'purple' devices, extending the existing text and flourish their language significantly.

Discourse Analysis

Discourse analysis deals with analyzing written, oral, or sign language use, or any significant semiotic event. According to the method, the close analysis of a covert recording can produce useful deductions. The use of 'I' instead of 'We' in a recording highlights non-complicity in a conspiracy. The utterance of 'yeah' and 'uh-huh' as responses indicate that the suspect understands the suggestion, while feedback markers such as 'yeah' and 'uh-huh' do not denote the suspect's agreement to the suggestion. Discourse analysts are not always allowed to testify but during preparation for a case they are often useful to lawyers.

Linguistic Dialectology

This refers to the study of dialects in a methodological manner based on anthropological information. It is becoming more important to conduct systematic studies of dialects, especially within the English language, because they are no longer as distinct as they once were due to the onslaught of mass media and population mobility. Political and social issues have also caused languages to straddle geographical borders resulting in certain language varieties spoken in multiple countries, leading to complications when determining an individual's origin by means of his/her language or dialect.

Dialectology was used during the investigations into the Yorkshire Ripper tape hoax.

Forensic Phonetics

The forensic phonetician is concerned with the production of accurate transcriptions of what was being said. Transcriptions can reveal information about a speaker's social and regional background. Forensic phonetics can determine similarities between the speakers of two or more separate recordings. Voice recording as a supplement to the transcription can be useful as it allows victims and witnesses to indicate whether the voice of a suspect is that of the accused, i.e., alleged criminal.

A man accused of manufacturing the drug Ecstasy was mis-heard by the police transcriber as 'hallucinogenic' The police transcriber heard *"but if it's as you say it's hallucinogenic, it's in the Sigma catalogue."* However, the actual utterance was *"but if it's as you say it's German, it's in the Sigma catalogue."*

Another disputed utterance was between a police officer and a suspect. One of the topics of conversation was a third man known as 'Ernie'. The poor signal of the recording made 'Ernie' sound like 'Ronnie'. The surveillance tape presented acoustic problems- an intrusive electronic-sounding cackle, the sound of the car engine, the playing of the car radio, the movement of the target vehicle, and the intrusive noise coincided with the first syllable of the disputed name.

Forensic speechreading is the complement of forensic voice identification. Transcripts of surveilled video records can sometimes allow expert speechreaders to identify speech content or style where the identity of the talker is apparent from the video record.

Examples

Evidence from forensic linguistics has more power to eliminate someone as a suspect than to prove him or her guilty. Linguistic expertise has been employed in criminal cases to defend an individual suspected of a crime, and during government investigations. Forensic linguists have given expert evidence in a wide variety of cases, including abuse of process, where police statements were found to be too similar to have been independently produced by police officers; the authorship of hate mail; the authorship of letters to an Internet child pornography service; the contemporaneity of an arsonist's diary; the comparison between a set of mobile phone texts and a suspect's police interview, and the reconstruction of a mobile phone text conversation. Some well-known examples include an appeal against the conviction of Derek Bentley and the identification of Theodore Kaczynski as the so-called "Unabomber".

The criminal laboratories *Bundeskriminalamt* (in Germany) and the *Nederlands Forensisch Instituut* (in the Netherlands) both employ forensic linguists.

Forensic linguistics contributed to the overturning of Derek Bentley's conviction for murder in 1998 although there were other non-linguistic issues. Nineteen-year-old Bentley, who was functionally illiterate, had been hanged in 1953 for his part in the murder of PC Sidney Miles; he had been convicted partly on the basis of his statement to police, allegedly transcribed verbatim from a spoken monologue. When the case was reopened, a forensic linguist found that the frequency and usage of the word "then" in police transcripts suggested the transcripts were not verbatim statements but had been partially authored by police interviewers; this and other evidence led to Bentley's posthumous pardon.

In the case of Theodore Kaczynski, who was eventually convicted of being the "Unabomber", family members recognized his writing style from the published 35,000-word *Industrial Society and Its Future* (commonly called the "Unabomber Manifesto"), and notified the authorities. FBI agents searching Kaczynski's hut found hundreds of documents written by Kaczynski but not published anywhere. An analysis produced by FBI Supervisory Special Agent James R. Fitzgerald identified numerous lexical items and phrases common to the two documents. Some were more distinctive than others, but the prosecution argued that even the more common words and phrases being used by Kaczynski became distinctive when used in combination with each other.

Forensic linguistic evidence also played a role in the investigation of the 2005 disappearance of Julie Turner, a 40-year-old woman living in Yorkshire. After she was reported missing, her partner received several text messages from Julie's mobile phone, such as "Stopping at jills, back later need to sort my head out", and "Tell kids not to worry. sorting my life out. (sic) be in touch to get some things". Investigators found that letters written by Turner's friend Howard Simmerson shared several unusual orthographic and punctuation features with the text messages, suggesting that Simmerson had been aware of the contents of the messages. Simmerson was eventually found guilty of Turner's murder.

Forensic linguist John Olsson gave evidence in a murder trial on the meaning of 'jooking' in connection with a stabbing.

During the appeal against the conviction of the Bridgewater Four, the forensic linguist examined the written confession of Patrick Molloy, one of the defendants – a confession which he had retracted immediately – and a written record of an interview which the police claimed took place immediately before the confession was dictated. Molloy denied that the interview had ever taken place, and the analysis indicated that the answers in the interview were not consistent with the questions being asked. The linguist came to the conclusion that the interview had been fabricated by police. The conviction against the Bridgewater Four was quashed before the linguist in the case, Malcolm Coulthard, could produce his evidence.

In an Australian case reported by Eagleson, a "farewell letter" had apparently been written by a woman prior to her disappearance. The letter was compared with a sample of her previous writing and that of her husband. Eagleson came to the conclusion that the letter had been written by the husband of the missing woman, who subsequently confessed to having written it and to having killed his wife. The features analysed included sentence breaks, marked themes, and deletion of prepositions.

Additional Concepts

Linguistic Fingerprinting

A linguistic fingerprint is a concept put forward by some scholars that each human being uses language differently, and that this difference between people involves a collection of markers which stamps a speaker/writer as unique; similar to a fingerprint. Under this view, it is assumed that every individual uses languages differently and this difference can be observed as a fingerprint. It is formed as a result of merged language style. A person's linguistic fingerprint can be reconstructed from the individual's daily interactions and relate to a variety of self-reported personality characteristics, situational variables and physiological markers (e.g. blood pressure, cortisol, testosterone). In the process of an investigation, the emphasis should be on the relative rather than absolute difference between the authors and how investigators can classify their texts. John Olsson, however, argues that although the concept of linguistic fingerprinting is attractive to law enforcement agencies, there is so far little hard evidence to support the notion.

Variation

Intra-author variations are the ways in which one author's texts differ from each other. Inter-author variations are the ways in which different authors' writing varies. Two texts by one author do not necessarily vary less than texts by two different authors.

- Genre: When texts are being measured in different genres, considerable variation is observed even though they are by the same author.
- Text Type: Personal letters contain more inter-relationship bonding strategies than academic articles or term papers.
- Fiction vs. Non-Fiction: Some fiction writers are journalists. Due to the different demands of each medium, they can be completely different from one another and this results in intra-author variation.
- Private vs Public: A politician writing a political speech, which is a public text, will differ greatly from a private text to a friend or family member.
- Time lapse: The greater the time lapse between two works, the greater the likely variation. Language changes more than we realize in a relatively short span of time, influencing our susceptibility to language changes around us.
- Disguise: A writer can publish pseudonymously or anonymously, disguising output to prevent recognition.

Forensic Transcription

The two main types of transcriptions are written documents and video and audio records. Accurate, reliable text transcription is important because the text is the data which becomes the available evidence. If a transcription is wrong, the evidence is altered. If there is failure to transcribe the full text, evidence is once again altered unwittingly. There must be emphasis on the text being the evidence. A transcription of an audio file should never be assumed to be completely accurate. Each type of transcription contains its own problems. A handwritten document might contain unusual spellings which may result in ambiguous meanings, illegible handwriting and illustrations that are difficult to comprehend. A scanned document is tricky, as it may alter the original document. Audio and video documents can include repetitions, hesitation, nonsensical talk, jargon which can be hard to understand and speakers mumbling incoherently and inaudibly. Non-linguistic sounds such as crying and laughing may also be included in the audio and video text which cannot be transcribed easily. Because of this, civil libertarians argued that interrogations in major criminal cases should be recorded and the recordings kept, as well as transcribed.

Forensic Psychology

Forensic psychology is the intersection between psychology and the justice system. It involves understanding fundamental legal principles, particularly with regard to expert witness testimony and the specific content area of concern (e.g., competence to stand trial, child custody and visitation, or workplace discrimination), as well as relevant jurisdictional considerations (e.g., in the United States, the definition of insanity in criminal trials differs from state to state) in order to be able to interact appropriately with judges, attorneys, and other legal professionals. An important aspect of forensic psychology is the ability to testify in court as an expert witness, reformulating psychological findings into the legal language of the courtroom, providing information to legal personnel in a way that can be understood. Further, in order to be a credible witness, the forensic psychologist must understand the philosophy, rules, and standards of the judicial system. Primarily, they must understand the adversarial system. There are also rules about hearsay evidence and most importantly, the exclusionary rule. Lack of a firm grasp of these procedures will result in the forensic psychologist losing credibility in the courtroom. A forensic psychologist can be trained in clinical, social, organizational, or any other branch of psychology.

Generally, a forensic psychologist is designated as an expert in a specific field of study. The number of areas of expertise in which a forensic psychologist qualifies as an expert increases with experience and reputation. Forensic neuropsychologists are generally asked to appear as expert witnesses in court to discuss cases that involve issues with the brain or brain damage. They may also deal with issues of whether a person is legally competent to stand trial.

Questions asked by the court of a forensic psychologist are generally not questions regarding psychology but are legal questions and the response must be in language the court understands. For example, a forensic psychologist is frequently appointed by the court to assess a defendant's competence to stand trial. The court also frequently appoints a forensic psychologist to assess the state of mind of the defendant at the time of the offense. This is referred to as an evaluation of the defendant's sanity or insanity (which relates to criminal responsibility) at the time of the offense. These are not primarily psychological questions but rather legal ones. Thus, a forensic psychologist must be able to translate psychological information into a legal framework.

Forensic psychologists may be called on to provide sentencing recommendations, treatment recommendations, or any other information the judge requests, such as information regarding mitigating factors, assessment of future risk, and evaluation of witness credibility. Forensic psychology also involves training and evaluating police or other law enforcement personnel, providing law enforcement with criminal profiles, and in other ways working with police departments. Forensic psychologists may work with any party and in criminal or family law. In the United States, they may also help with jury selection.

Training and Education

Forensic psychologists may hold a Ph.D. or Psy.D. in clinical psychology, social psychology, organizational psychology, or experimental psychology. In order for a psychologist to practice as a forensic psychologist in the United States, it is preferable but not necessary that the individual be a state licensed psychologist and receive certification as a Diplomate in Forensic Psychology by the American Board of Forensic Psychology (although the latter is less important to judges). Ideally, the psychologist would have some years of postdoctoral experience in forensic psychology and have training and supervision in forensic psychology. However, practices vary from state to state and from jurisdiction to jurisdiction. In the United States legal system, the ultimate authority is the judge and the judge may select whomever he or she sees fit to qualify as an expert.

In other countries, training and practitioner requirements vary. In the United Kingdom, for example, a person must obtain the Graduate Basis for Registration with the British Psychological Society—normally through an undergraduate degree. This would be followed by Stages 1 (academic) and 2 (supervised practice) of the Diploma in Forensic Psychology (which would normally take 3 years full-time and 4 years part-time). Assessment occurs via examination, research, supervised practice, and the submission of a portfolio showing expertise across a range of criminological and legal applications of psychology. Once qualified as a "Chartered" psychologist (with a specialism in forensic psychology), a practitioner must engage in Continued Professional Development and demonstrate how much, of what kind, each year, in order to renew his/her practising certificate.

Professional Opportunities in Forensic Psychology

There are numerous professional positions and employment possibilities for forensic psychologists. They can be practiced at several different employment settings.

Academic Researcher

Academic forensic psychologists engage in teaching, researching, training, and supervision of students, and other education-related activities. These professionals usually have an advanced degree in Psychology (most likely a PhD). While their main focus is research, it is not unusual for them to take on any of the other positions of forensic psychologists. These professionals may be employed at various settings, which include colleges and universities, research institutes, government or private agencies, and mental health agencies. Forensic psychology research pertains to psychology and the law, whether it be criminal or civil. Researchers test hypotheses empirically and apply the research on issues related to psychology and the law. They may also conduct research on mental health law and policy evaluation. Some famous psychologists in the field include Saul Kassin, very widely known for studying false confessions, and Elizabeth Loftus, known for her research on eyewitness memory. She has provided expert witness testimony for many cases.

Consultant to Law Enforcement

Forensic psychologists also assist with law enforcement. They work in collaboration with the police force or other law enforcement agencies. Law enforcement psychologists are responsible for assisting law enforcement personnel. They are frequently trained to help with crisis intervention, including post-trauma and suicide. Other duties of law enforcement psychologists include development of police training programs, stress management, personnel management, and referral of departmental personnel as well as their families for specialized treatment and counseling. Of course, ethical issues may arise, such as the question of who the client is (the police officer referred or the department, in regards to confidentiality).

Correctional Psychologist

Correctional psychologists work with inmates and offenders in correctional settings. They serve both the role of an evaluator and a treatment provider to those who have been imprisoned or on parole or probation. Correctional psychologists may also take on the role of researcher or expert witness and frequently perform a wide range of psychological testing.

Evaluator

These forensic psychologists take on the role of evaluating parties in criminal or civil cases on mental health issues related to their case. For criminal cases, they may be called on to evaluate issues including, but not limited to, defendants' competence to stand trial, their mental state at the time of the offense (insanity), and their risk for future violent acts. For civil cases, they may be called on to evaluate issues including, but not limited to, an individual's psychological state after an accident or the families of custody cases. Any assessment made by an evaluator is not considered a counseling session, and therefore whatever is said or done is not confidential. It is the obligation of the evaluator to inform the parties that everything in the session will be open to scrutiny in a forensic report or expert testimony. Evaluators work closely with expert witnesses (discussed below) as many are called into court to testify with what they have come to conclude from their evaluations. They have a variety of employment settings, such as forensic and state psychiatric hospitals, mental health centers, and private practice. Evaluators usually have had training as clinical psychologists.

Expert Witness

Unlike fact witnesses, who are limited to testifying about what they know or have observed, expert witnesses have the ability to express opinion because, as their name suggests, they are presumed to be "experts" in a certain topic. They possess specialized knowledge about the topic. Expert witnesses are called upon to testify on matters of mental health (clinical expertise) or other areas of expertise such as social, experimental, cognitive, or developmental. The role of being an expert witness is not primary and it is usually performed in conjunction with another role such as that of researcher, academic, evaluator, or clinical psychologist. Clinical forensic psychologists evaluate a defendant and are then called upon as expert witnesses to testify on the mental state of the defendant.

In the past, expert witnesses primarily served the court rather than the litigants. Nowadays, that very rarely happens and most expert witness recruitment is done by trial attorneys. But regardless of who calls in the expert, it is the judge who determines the acceptability of the expert witness.

All ethical expert witnesses must be able to resolve the issue of relating to the case and being an advocate. They must decide between loyalty to their field of expertise or to the outcome of the case.

Treatment Provider

Treatment providers are forensic psychologists who administer psychological intervention or treatment to individuals in both criminal and civil cases who require or request these services. In criminal proceedings, treatment providers may be asked to provide psychological interventions to individuals who require treatment for the restoration of competency, after having been determined by the courts as incompetent to stand trial. They may be asked to provide treatment for the mental illness of those deemed insane at the crime. They may also be called to administer treatment to minimize the likelihood of future acts of violence for individuals who are at a high risk of committing a violent offense. As for civil proceedings, treatment providers may have to treat families going through divorce and/or custody cases. They may also provide treatment to individuals who have suffered psychological injuries due to some kind of trauma. Treatment providers and evaluators work in the same types of settings: forensic and state psychiatric hospitals, mental health centers, and private practice. Not surprisingly, their work may greatly overlap. And although not ethically encouraged, the same forensic psychologist may take on both the role of treatment provider and evaluator for the same client.

Trial Consultant

Forensic psychologists often are involved in trial consulting and are part of legal psychology. A trial consultant, a jury consultant, or a litigation consultant, are social scientists who work with legal professionals such as trial attorneys to aid in case preparation, which includes selection of jury, development of case strategy, and witness preparation. They rely heavily on research. Trial consultants may also attend seminars directed at the improvement of jury selection and trial presentation skills. Becoming a trial consultant does not necessarily require a doctoral degree or even a bachelor's degree. All that is really needed is some level of training.

Trial consultants are faced with many ethical issues. They are not only social scientists; they may be entrepreneurs as well, marketing their business and keeping fixed costs. This is a challenge to their ethical responsibilities as applied researchers who need to be following guidelines of ethical research. Trial consultants are hired by attorneys and conflicts may arise when each party has a different viewpoint on a certain issue, such as which prospective jurors should be excused, whether the jurors' preferences are appropriate for the case or not, etc. They must always keep in mind that they are employees of the attorneys and are not able to make the ultimate decisions regarding the case.

Distinction between Forensic and Therapeutic Evaluation

A forensic psychologist's interactions with and ethical responsibilities to the client differ widely from those of a psychologist dealing with a client in a clinical setting.

- Scope. Rather than the broad set of issues a psychologist addresses in a clinical setting, a forensic psychologist addresses a narrowly defined set of events or interactions of a non-clinical nature.

- Importance of client's perspective. A clinician places primary importance on understanding the client's unique point of view, while the forensic psychologist is interested in accuracy, and the client's viewpoint is secondary.
- Voluntariness. Usually in a clinical setting a psychologist is dealing with a voluntary client. A forensic psychologist evaluates clients by order of a judge or at the behest of an attorney.
- Autonomy. Voluntary clients have more latitude and autonomy regarding the assessment's objectives. Any assessment usually takes their concerns into account. The objectives of a forensic examination are confined by the applicable statutes or common law elements that pertain to the legal issue in question.
- Threats to validity. While the client and therapist are working toward a common goal, although unconscious distortion may occur, in the forensic context there is a substantially greater likelihood of intentional and conscious distortion.
- Relationship and dynamics. Therapeutic interactions work toward developing a trusting, empathic therapeutic alliance, a forensic psychologist may not ethically nurture the client or act in a "helping" role, as the forensic evaluator has divided loyalties and there are substantial limits on confidentiality he can guarantee the client. A forensic evaluator must always be aware of manipulation in the adversary context of a legal setting. These concerns mandate an emotional distance that is unlike a therapeutic interaction.
- Pace and setting. Unlike therapeutic interactions which may be guided by many factors, the forensic setting with its court schedules, limited resources, and other external factors, place great time constraints on the evaluation without opportunities for reevaluation. The forensic examiner focuses on the importance of accuracy and the finality of legal dispositions.

Forensic Psychology Practice

The forensic psychologist views the client or defendant from a different point of view than does a traditional clinical psychologist. Seeing the situation from the client's point of view or "empathizing" is not the forensic psychologist's task. Traditional psychological tests and interview procedure are not sufficient when applied to the forensic situation. In forensic evaluations, it is important to assess the consistency of factual information across multiple sources. Forensic evaluators must be able to provide the source on which any information is based. Treating psychologists do not routinely assess response bias or performance validity, whereas forensic psychologist usually do. Forensic media psychology is a sub-specialty in forensic psychology that analyzes behavior related to social media, intellectual property, entertainment, including film, television, etc., medical education and other areas where media is used in behavioral psychology.

Forensic psychologists perform a wide range of tasks within the criminal justice system.

Malingering

An important and pressing question in any type of forensic assessment is the issue of malingering and deception. In some criminal cases, the court views malingering or feigning illness as obstruction of justice and sentences the defendant accordingly.

Competency Evaluations

If there is a question of the accused's competency to stand trial, a forensic psychologist is appointed by the court to examine and assess the individual. The individual may be in custody or may have been released on bail. Based on the forensic assessment, a recommendation is made to the court whether or not the defendant is competent to proceed to trial. If the defendant is considered incompetent to proceed, the report or testimony will include recommendations for the interim period during which an attempt at restoring the individual's competency to understand the court and legal proceedings, as well as participate appropriately in their defense will be made. Often, this is an issue of committed, on the advice of a forensic psychologist, to a psychiatric treatment facility until such time as the individual is deemed competent.

As a result of *Ford v. Wainwright*, a case by a Florida inmate on death row that was brought before the Supreme Court of the United States, forensic psychologists are appointed to assess the competency of an inmate to be executed in death penalty cases.

Sanity Evaluations

The forensic psychologist may also be appointed by the court to evaluate the defendant's state of mind at the time of the offense. These are defendants who the judge, prosecutor, or public defender believe, through personal interaction with the defendant or through reading the police report, may have been significantly impaired at the time of the offense.

Other Evaluations

Forensic psychologists are frequently asked to make an assessment of an individual's dangerousness or risk of re-offending. They may provide information and recommendations necessary for sentencing purposes, grants of probation, and the formulation of conditions of parole, which often involves an assessment of the offender's ability to be rehabilitated. They are also asked questions of witness credibility and malingering. Occasionally, they may also provide criminal profiles to law enforcement.

Due to the Supreme Court decision upholding involuntary commitment laws for predatory sex offenders in *Kansas v. Hendricks*, it is likely that forensic psychologists will become involved in making recommendations in individual cases of end-of-sentence civil commitment decisions.

Ethical Implications

A forensic psychologist generally practices within the confines of the courtroom, incarceration facilities, and other legal setting. It is important to remember that the forensic psychologist is equally likely to be testifying for the prosecution as for the defense attorney. A forensic psychologist does not take a side, as do the psychologists described below. The ethical standards for a forensic psychologist differ from those of a clinical psychologist or other practicing psychologist because the forensic psychologist is not an advocate for the client and nothing the client says is guaranteed to be kept confidential. This makes evaluation of the client difficult, as the forensic psychologist needs and wants to obtain all information while it is often not in the client's best interest to provide it. The client has no control over how that information is used. Despite the signing of a waiver of confidentiality, most clients do not realize the nature of the evaluative situation. Furthermore, the interview techniques differ from those typical of a clinical psychologist and require an understanding of the criminal mind and criminal and violent behavior. For example, even indicating to a defendant being interviewed that an effort will be made to get the defendant professional help may be grounds for excluding the expert's testimony.

In addition, the forensic psychologist deals with a range of clients unlike those of the average practicing psychologist. Because the client base is by and large criminal, the forensic psychologist is immersed in an abnormal world. As such, the population evaluated by the forensic psychologist is heavily weighted with specific personality disorders.

The typical grounds for malpractice suits also apply to the forensic psychologist, such as wrongful commitment, inadequate informed consent, duty and breach of duty, and standards of care issues. Some situations are more clear cut for the forensic psychologist. The duty to warn, which is mandated by many states, is generally not a problem because the client or defendant has already signed a release of information, unless the victim is not clearly identified and the issue of the identifiability of the victim arises. However, in general the forensic psychologist is less likely to encounter malpractice suits than a clinical psychologist. The forensic psychologist does have some additional professional liability issues. As mentioned above, confidentiality in a forensic setting is more complicated that in a clinical setting as the client or defendant is apt to misinterpret the limits of confidentiality despite being warned and signing a release.

Forensic Photography

Footwear impressions left at a crime scene.

Forensic photography, also referred to as crime scene photography, is an activity that records the initial appearance of the crime scene and physical evidence, in order to provide a permanent record for the courts. Crime scene photography differs from other variations of photography because crime scene photographers usually have a very specific purpose for capturing each image.

Crime scenes can be major sources of physical evidence that is used to associate or link suspects to scenes, victims to scenes, and suspects to victims. This is Locard's exchange principle. It is the basic tenet of why crime scenes should be investigated. Anything found at a crime scene can be physical evidence. In scientific crime scene investigation, the first activities at the crime scene are essential for the successful preservation of the physical evidence. The first responder and ultimately the crime scene investigator have the obligation to make the scene secure and ensure that any further activities at the scene do not change the evidence. The use of a multilevel security method would accomplish this task. The preliminary scene survey is the first on-scene activity. Precautions are taken for transient and conditional evidence during the survey.

All forensic photography must consider three elements at a crime scene: the subject, the scale, and a reference object. Also, the overall forensic photographs must be shown a neutral and accurate representation.

Features of Crime Scene Photography

Common photography related to creative and artistic photography often shows their results in a different way. Creative and artistic photographs are perfectly fine. However, the forensic photography is different. They should serve several purposes.

For people who were at the original crime scene, forensic photos will help refresh their memory as time goes by. People who could not be present at the original crime scene, it provides them with the opportunity to see the crime scene and the evidence within the crime scene.

Furthermore, the forensic photos can be utilized by law enforcement professionals who will become involved with crime and will be utilized later when the crime case goes to trial. Judge, jury, attorney and witnesses can reuse and utilize forensic photos for lawful evidence or references. Sometimes, forensic photos can be the only way to collect lawful evidences; therefore, the following points should be considered :

1. Document the crime scene and the evidence within the crime scene.
2. Collect the evidence. These images can then be later used as examination-quality photographs by experts/analysts from the forensic laboratory.

Crime Scene Evidence

Crime scenes are the source of the physical evidence that is used to associate or link suspects to scenes, victims to scenes, and suspects to victims. Any item found at a crime scene can be physical evidence; it can be labeled as the debris of criminal activity. There is considerable overlap among identifications, but evidence can be categorized into the following broad groups based on its origin, composition, or method of creation:

1. Biological evidence — any evidence derived from a living item. Includes physiological fluids, plants, and some biological pathogens.
2. Chemical evidence — any evidence with identifiable chemicals present.
3. Patterned evidence — any evidence with a pattern or predictable pattern of appearance.

4. Trace evidence — any evidence of such a small size so as to be overlooked, not easily seen or not easily recognized.

In addition to identifying the type of physical evidence found at a crime scene, it is necessary to obtain valuable investigative information from the analysis of the items of physical evidence.

1. Determination of corpus delicti — the evidence is used to determine if a crime has taken place.
2. Modus operandi identification — criminals repeat behavior. Repeated methods of entry, for example, by kicking in a back door with the same shoe leaving the same footwear impressions throughout the crime scene.
3. Association or linkage — the Locard Exchange Principle — transfer of evidence by contact.
4. Disproving/supporting victim/suspect/witness statements — the evidence may or may not support what these groups say.
5. Identification of suspects/victims/crime scene location — fingerprints and even DNA can be used to identify who was present at a crime scene.
6. Provide for investigative leads for detectives — the use of the physical evidence to give information to detectives that will assist them in locating victims and suspects.

Essential 3 Steps on Crime Scene

The first activities at the crime scene are essential for the successful preservation of the physical evidence.

First Responders

The crime scene investigator is rarely the first person at a crime scene. Most first responders work on reflex or instinct at the scene. Their tasks are to save lives or apprehend suspects. Unfortunately, that may mean that physical evidence may be inadvertently altered, changed, or lost due to the actions of a first responder. The crime scene investigator needs to communicate with the first responders to determine if any changes or alterations have occurred at the scene before the scene investigator arrived.

Crime Scene Security

Locard's exchange principle is the basis for the use of physical evidence in a criminal investigation, it is extremely important for the crime scene to be made secure and restrict the access to the crime scene by nonessential people. Many agencies allow easy access to crime scenes by anyone in the agency. Most media persons are kept out but changes to the scene and evidence can change in attempts to protect victims.

Preliminary scene survey

The preliminary scene survey or walk-through is the crime scene investigator's first opportunity to view the target area crime scene. A simple visual search for obvious physical evidence can be accomplished at this time. It is during this first viewing of the crime scene that the scene investigator should note any transient or temporary items of evidence and protect them immediately. Melting snow footwear impression are examples of this transient evidence.

Methods

All photographs must contain three elements: the subject, a scale, and a reference object. Crime scene photographs should always be in focus, with the subject of the photograph as the main object of the scene. There should always be a scale or ruler present. This will allow the investigators the ability to resize the image to accurately reconstruct the scene. The overall photographs must be a fair and accurate representation of what is seen. Any change in color may misidentify an object for investigators and possibly jurors.

In this photograph, the white balance, or color of lighting, is incorrect. The overall composition of the photograph has a yellow tone. This photograph is not an accurate representation of the scene.

Although it is a closer depiction of the scene than the photograph directly above, this image is also incorrect. The color balance of this photograph depicts the overall scene as having a blue hue.

This photograph shows the door in the correct composition and depicts the colors correctly. The tones of the walls and the "Notice" sign are white, as seen at the scene.

Comparison of image color balance. Andrew R. Reitnauer 34 –
Crime Scene Response and Evidence Collection Security Supervision and Management
(Fourth Edition), 2015, 443–459 doi:10.1016/B978-0-12-800113-4.00034-1

Preliminary overall photographs should attempt to capture the locations of evidence and identifying features of the scene, such as addresses, vehicle identification numbers and serial numbers, footwear/tire mark impressions, and the conditions of the scene. While the purpose of the overall photograph is to document the conditions of the scene and the relationship of objects, the medium range photograph serves to document the appearance of an object.

In all photographs, a scale must be included, as well as a marker to indicate the identity of the object in question. Again, objects of medium-range photographs must be a fair and accurate representation of what is seen. Adjusting the photographic principles or lighting may allow the photographer to achieve this goal.

Photogrpah 1

Photogrpah 2

In figure, Photograph 2 is a correct representation.

Photograph 1 has too much light. It means that the photographer failed to catch proper light to describe object. By adjusting the flash, photographer should adjust camera flash to capture the object.

In general, the basic components of macro or evidentiary photography are as follows: If any evidentiary photographs are to be taken for use in a critical comparison examination at a later time, guidelines must be followed in accordance with the best practices of digital evidence.

1. The digital image must be captured in a lossless compression format. The two widely accepted lossless compression formats are tagged image file format (TIFF) and RAW. TIFF is a universal file type, whereas RAW files are proprietary based upon the manufacturer of the camera. Specialized software may be required to open and enhance a RAW image.

2. The camera must be on a grounded platform, such as a copy stand or tripod. In general, the human body cannot stop natural vibrations with a camera shutter speed slower than 1/60 of a second. Using a grounded platform will allow the subject matter to be in complete focus.

3. The camera shutter must be controlled by a remote cord or by using the timer mode. The simple action of depressing the shutter control will cause the camera to vibrate, losing focus of the subject matter.

Documentation

The responding officer must also maintain a photo log if any photographic documentation is taken. The log should contain the date and time of the photograph, the subject matter, and any additional notes. These logs must be maintained within a case file or incident report, as they are a part of the examination record and discoverable material at trial.

Photograph Log

Date:______________________________

Location:____________________________

Incident number:______________________

Supervisor:__________________________

Date	Time	Initials	Subject	Comments

Digital Photography

Photographers must understand principles of photography first. When the photographers take the photographs itself, they must consider three components. The three components are ISO, Shutter speed and aperture.

The International Organization for Standardization (ISO) is an international standard-setting body composed of representatives from various national standards organizations. The actual meaning in photography is a camera's sensitivity to light.

ISO

Photograph 1
Shutter Speed : 0.4 Focus : 6.3
ISO 100

Photograph 2
Shutter Speed : 0.4 Focus : 6.3
ISO 1600

By adjusting ISO, the photographs can be shown differently in same environment. In dark environment, ISO makes light sensor of camera more sensitive. It helps photographers to meet proper light in dark or harsh condition. Among above two photographs, the photograph 1 is a proper representation because it shows clear objects with proper brightness. However, ISO has high possibility to make camera noise which is visual distortion. Too much dependence on ISO can distort the image. For that reason, the photographers must understand ISO before using it.

Shutter Speed

Shutter speed is the length of time when the film or digital sensor inside the camera is exposed to light. Object and image can be shown differently by shutter speed. Below are the examples.

Photograph 1
Focus 2.8 ISO 800
Camera Shutter Speed : 1/25

Photogrpah 2
Focus 2.8 ISO 800
Camera Shutter Speed : 1/400

These two photographs are taken under same situation except for camera shutter speed. In above situation, slow shutter speed makes image more clear and bright because the low shutter speed takes more light than high shutter speed. However, the high shutter speed often is necessary for moving object.

Above two photographs are taken under same situation except for camera shutter speed. In case of moving object, the low shutter speed is not proper to capture the object. It needs faster shutter speed to capture it. Shutter speed has pros and cons. For capturing a moving object, photographers must use a high shutter speed. However, the image can be very dark. Low shutter speed must be used when capturing a clear image or object under the harsh condition, but it is hard to capture the moving objects.

Aperture(Focus)

Aperture means that the extent of a sharpness of an image that is shown through the lens. So, it is one of really important things to photographers. High aperture (High focus) means hard sharpness like photograph1. Every Low aperture (low focus) means soft sharpness.

Photograph 1
Focus 11 ISO 1600
Camera Shutter Speed : 1/30

Photogrpah 2
Focus 2.8 ISO 1600
Camera Shutter Speed : 0.5

The photograph 1 shows all objects very clearly because of the high aperture. The photograph 2 image shows an object with right focus but rest of the objects are all blurred because of low aperture.

Use of Flash

External flash units are helpful tools when responding to a crime scene and for the proper documentation of evidence. The white balance of a photo flash unit is set to mimic daylight to ensure the proper color balance of the subject matter. The photographer must be mindful of the reflections that can occur due to the directionality of the flash and the position of the subject matter. To avoid flash reflections, as demonstrated below examples, the flash must either be removed from the camera body, creating an angle, or bounced off of the ceiling.

Photograph 1

Flash : Ceiling bound (Indirect flash)

Photogrpah 2

Flash : Direct flash

Equipment

The tools required to properly document the crime scene include:

- Notepad
- Clipboard and/or digital tablet device
- Graph paper
- Writing instruments (pens, pencils, markers)
- Still camera with external flash and extra batteries
- Video camera
- Tripod
- Measurement instruments (tape measures, rulers, electronic measuring devices, perspective grids, etc.)
- Evidence identification and position markers or placards
- Photographic log
- Compass

Fit for Court

The images must be clear and usually have scales. They serve to not only remind investigators of the scene, but also to provide a tangible image for the court to better enable them to understand what happened. The use of several views taken from different angles helps to minimise the problem of parallax. Overall images do not have scales and serve to show the general layout, such as the house where the murder is thought to have occurred. Context images show evidence in context, like how the knife was next to the sofa. Close up images show fine detail of an artifact, such as a bloody fingerprint on the knife.

Road traffic incident (RTI) photographs show the overall layout at the scene taken from many different angles, with close-ups of significant damage, or trace evidence such as tire marks at a traffic collision. As with crime scene photography, it is essential that the site is pristine and untouched as far as is possible. Some essential intervention, such as rescuing a trapped victim, must be recorded in the notes made at the time by the photographer, so that the authenticity of the photographs can be verified.

As with all evidence a chain of custody must be maintained for crime scene photographs. Sometimes a CSI (forensic photographer) will process his/her own film or there is a specific lab for it. Regardless of how it is done any person who handles the evidence must be recorded. Secure Digital Forensic Imaging methods may be applied to help ensure against tampering and improper disclosure. Accident scene pictures should also be identified and sourced, police photographs taken at the scene often being used in civil cases.

Analysis of Historic Photographs

Original Tay Bridge from the north

Photograph of 1880 showing fallen Tay Bridge

Crime or accident scene photographs can often be re-analysed in cold cases or when the images need to be enlarged to show critical details. Photographs made by film exposure usually contain much information which may be crucial long after the photograph was taken. They can readily be digitised by scanning, and then enlarged to show the detail needed for new analysis. For example, controversy has raged for a number of years over the cause of the Tay Bridge disaster of 1879 when a half-mile section of the new bridge collapsed in a storm, taking an express train down into the estuary of the river Tay. At least 75 passengers and crew were killed in the disaster.

The set of photographs taken a few days after the accident have been re-analysed in 1999–2000 by digitising them and enlarging the files to show critical details. The originals were of very high resolution since a large plate camera was used with a small aperture, plus a small grain film. The re-analysed pictures shed new light on why the bridge fell, suggesting that design flaws and defects in the cast iron columns which supported the centre section led directly to the catastrophic failure. Alternative explanations that the bridge was blown down by the wind during the storm that night, or that the train derailed and hit the girders are unlikely. The re-analysis supports the original court of inquiry conclusions, which stated that the bridge was "badly designed, badly built and badly maintained".

Forensic Biology

Forensic biology is the application of biology to law enforcement.

It includes the subdisciplines of forensic anthropology, forensic botany, forensic entomology, forensic odontology, forensic toxicology and various DNA or protein based techniques.

Applications

Forensic biology has been used to prove a suspect was at a crime scene, identify illegal products from endangered species, solve crimes by matching crime scene evidence to suspects, investigate airplane bird strikes, and investigate bird collisions with wind turbines.

Disciplines

Forensic Anthropology

Forensic anthropology is for identification and recovery of remains. In extreme cases where conventional techniques are unable to determine the identity of the remains, anthropologists are sometimes able to deduce certain characteristics based on the skeletal remains. Race, sex, age and stature can often be determined by both measuring the remains and looking for structural clues in the bones.

Forensic Botany

Forensic botanists look to plant life in order to gain information regarding possible crimes. Leaves, seeds and pollen found either on a body or at the scene of a crime can offer valuable information regarding the timescales of a crime and also if the body has been moved between two or more different locations. The forensic study of pollen is known as forensic palynology and can often produce specific findings of location of death, decomposition and time of year. The knowledge of systematics leads to identification of evidences at crime scene. The morphological and anatomical study revels in collection of samples from crime scene and its in vitro analysis. It leads to proper submission of evidences in court of law.

Forensic Ornithology

Bird remains can be identified, first and foremost from feathers (which are distinctive to a particular species at both macroscopic and microscopic levels).

Forensic Odontology

Odontologists or dentists can be used in order to aid in an identification of degraded remains. Remains that have been buried for a long period or which have undergone fire damage often contain few clues to the identity of the individual. Tooth enamel, as the hardest substance in the human body, often endures and as such odontologists can in some circumstances compare recovered remains to dental records.

Forensic Toxicology

Forensic toxicology is the use of toxicology and other disciplines such as analytical chemistry, pharmacology and clinical chemistry to aid medical or legal investigation of death, poisoning, and drug use. The primary concern for forensic toxicology is not the legal outcome of the toxicological investigation or the technology utilized, but rather the obtainment and interpretation of results.

DNA-based Techniques

DNA-based evidence has become a significant tool that many law enforcement investigators now have at their disposal. DNA evidence can definitively link a suspect to either a crime scene or victim. Nuclear DNA evidence has been recovered from blood, semen, saliva, skin cells and hair. Furthermore, Mitochondrial DNA can be recovered from both bone and teeth dating back thousands of years. Laboratory analysis of DNA evidence generally involves the sample being amplified and quantified by a form of the Polymerase chain reaction known as Quantitative PCR or qPCR. (PCR) amplification of any sample recovered followed by sequencing via Capillary electrophoresis in order to obtain a DNA profile which can be compared to suspect DNA.

DNA can also be extracted from animals and used to at least identify the species, for example bird or bat remains on an airplane or wind turbine.

Popular Culture

In popular culture, forensic biology is frequently portrayed in shows like *Law & Order*, *Bones*, *CSI*, *Dexter* and *Castle*.

Forensic Chemistry

Forensic chemistry is the application of chemistry and its subfield, forensic toxicology, in a legal setting. A forensic chemist can assist in the identification of unknown materials found at a crime scene. Specialists in this field have a wide array of methods and instruments to help identify unknown substances. These include high-performance liquid chromatography, gas chromatography-mass spectrometry, atomic absorption spectroscopy, Fourier transform infrared spectroscopy, and thin layer chromatography. The range of different methods is important due to the destructive nature of some instruments and the number of possible unknown substances that can be found at a scene. Forensic chemists prefer using nondestructive methods first, to preserve evidence and to determine which destructive methods will produce the best results.

Along with other forensic specialists, forensic chemists commonly testify in court as expert witnesses regarding their findings. Forensic chemists follow a set of standards that have been proposed by various agencies and governing bodies, including the Scientific Working Group on the Analysis of Seized Drugs. In addition to the standard operating procedures proposed by the group, specific agencies have their own standards regarding the quality assurance and quality control of their results and their instruments. To ensure the accuracy of what they are reporting, forensic chemists routinely check and verify that their instruments are working correctly and are still able to detect and measure various quantities of different substances.

Role in Investigations

Chemists were able to identify the explosive ANFO at the scene of the Oklahoma City bombing.

Forensic chemists' analysis can provide leads for investigators, and they can confirm or refute their suspicions. The identification of the various substances found at the scene can tell investigators what to look for during their search. During fire investigations, forensic chemists can determine if an accelerant such as gasoline or kerosene was used; if so, this suggests that the fire was intentionally set. Forensic chemists can also narrow down the suspect list to people who would have access to the substance used in a crime. For example, in explosive investigations, the identification of RDX or C-4 would indicate a military connection as those substances are military grade explosives. On the other hand, the identification of TNT would create a wider suspect list, since it is used by demolition companies as well as in the military. During poisoning investigations, the detection of specific poisons can give detectives an idea of what to look for when they are interviewing potential suspects. For example, an investigation that involves ricin would tell investigators to look for ricin's precursors, the seeds of the castor oil plant.

Forensic chemists also help to confirm or refute investigators' suspicions in drug or alcohol cases. The instruments used by forensic chemists can detect minute quantities, and accurate measurement can be important in crimes such as driving under the influence as there are specific blood alcohol content cutoffs where penalties begin or increase. In suspected overdose cases, the quantity of the drug found in the person's system can confirm or rule out overdose as the cause of death.

History

Early History

A bottle of strychnine extract was once easily obtainable in apothecaries.

Throughout history, a variety of poisons have been used to commit murder, including arsenic, nightshade, hemlock, strychnine, and curare. Until the early 19th century, there were no methods to accurately determine if a particular chemical was present, and poisoners were rarely punished for their crimes. In 1836, one of the first major contributions to forensic chemistry was introduced by British chemist James Marsh. He created the Marsh test for arsenic detection, which was subsequently used successfully in a murder trial. It was also during this time that forensic toxicology began to be recognized as a distinct field. Mathieu Orfila, the "father of toxicology", made great advancements to the field during the early 19th century. A pioneer in the development of forensic microscopy, Orfila contributed to the advancement of this method for the detection of blood and semen. Orfila was also the first chemist to successfully classify different chemicals into categories such as corrosives, narcotics, and astringents.

The next advancement in the detection of poisons came in 1850 when a valid method for detecting vegetable alkaloids in human tissue was created by chemist Jean Stas. Stas's method was quickly adopted and used successfully in court to convict Count Hippolyte Visart de Bocarmé of murdering his brother-in-law by nicotine poisoning. Stas was able to successfully isolate the alkaloid from the organs of the victim. Stas's protocol was subsequently altered to incorporate tests for caffeine, quinine, morphine, strychnine, atropine, and opium.

The wide range of instrumentation for forensic chemical analysis also began to be developed during this time period. The early 19th century saw the invention of the spectroscope by Joseph von Fraunhofer. In 1859, chemist Robert Bunsen and physicist Gustav Kirchhoff expanded on Fraunhofer's invention. Their experiments with spectroscopy showed that specific substances created a unique spectrum when exposed to specific wavelengths of light. Using spectroscopy, the two scientists were able to identify substances based on their spectrum, providing a method of identification for unknown materials. In 1906 botanist Mikhail Tsvet invented paper chromatography, an early predecessor to thin layer chromatography, and used it to separate and examine the plant proteins that make up chlorophyll. The ability to separate mixtures into their individual components allows forensic chemists to examine the parts of an unknown material against a database of known products. By matching the retention factors for the separated components with known values, materials can be identified.

Modernization

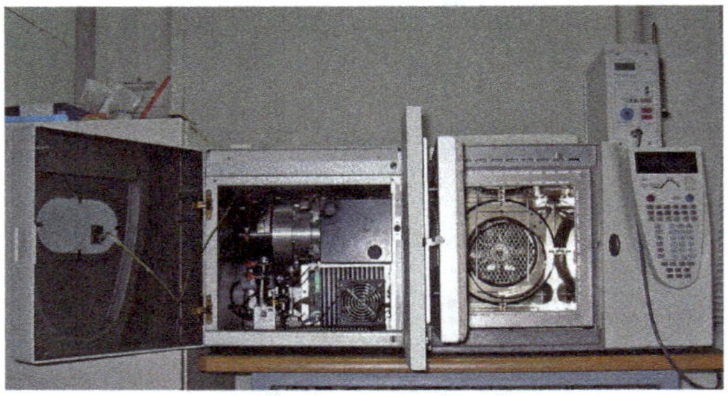

A GC-MS unit with doors open. The gas chromatograph is on the right and the mass spectrometer is on the left.

Modern forensic chemists rely on numerous instruments to identify unknown materials found at a crime scene. The 20th century saw many advancements in technology that allowed chemists to detect smaller amounts of material more accurately. The first major advancement in this century came during the 1930s with the invention of a spectrometer that could measure the signal produced with infrared (IR) light. Early IR spectrometers used a monochromator and could only measure light absorption in a very narrow wavelength band. It was not until the coupling of an interferometer with an IR spectrometer in 1949 by Peter Fellgett that the complete infrared spectrum could be measured at once. Fellgett also used the Fourier transform, a mathematical method that can break down a signal into its individual frequencies, to make sense of the enormous amount of data received from the complete infrared analysis of a material. Since then, Fourier transform infrared spectroscopy (FTIR) instruments have become critical in the forensic analysis of unknown material because they are nondestructive and extremely quick to use. Spectroscopy was further advanced in 1955 with the invention of the modern atomic absorption (AA) spectrophotometer by Alan Walsh. AA analysis can detect specific elements that make up a sample along with their concentrations, allowing for the easy detection of heavy metals such as arsenic and cadmium.

Advancements in the field of chromatography arrived in 1953 with the invention of the gas chromatograph by Anthony T. James and Archer John Porter Martin, allowing for the separation of volatile liquid mixtures with components which have similar boiling points. Nonvolatile liquid mixtures could be separated with liquid chromatography, but substances with similar retention times could not be resolved until the invention of high-performance liquid chromatography (HPLC) by Csaba Horváth in 1970. Modern HPLC instruments are capable of detecting and resolving substances whose concentrations are as low as parts per trillion.

One of the most important advancements in forensic chemistry came in 1955 with the invention of gas chromatography-mass spectrometry (GC-MS) by Fred McLafferty and Roland Gohlke. The coupling of a gas chromatograph with a mass spectrometer allowed for the identification of a wide range of substances. GC-MS analysis is widely considered the "gold standard" for forensic analysis due to its sensitivity and versatility along with its ability to quantify the amount of substance present. The increase in the sensitivity of instrumentation has advanced to the point that minute impurities within compounds can be detected potentially allowing investigators to trace chemicals to a specific batch and lot from a manufacturer.

Methods

Forensic chemists rely on a multitude of instruments to identify unknown substances found at a scene. Different methods can be used to determine the identity of the same substance, and it is up to the examiner to determine which method will produce the best results. Factors that forensic chemists might consider when performing an examination are the length of time a specific instrument will take to examine a substance and the destructive nature of that instrument. They prefer using nondestructive methods first, to preserve the evidence for further examination. Nondestructive techniques can also be used to narrow down the possibilities, making it more likely that the correct method will be used the first time when a destructive method is used.

Spectroscopy

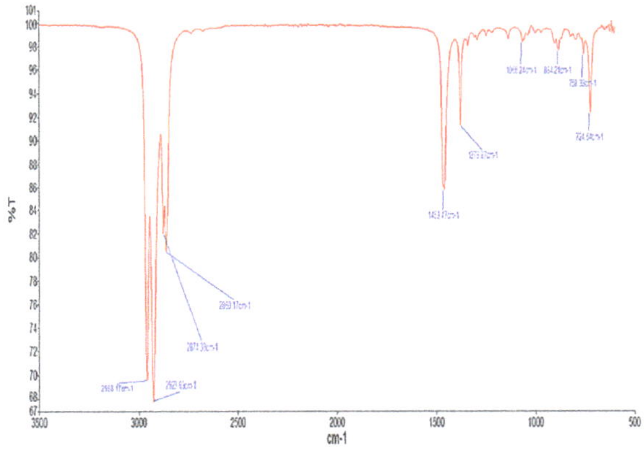

ATR FTIR spectrum for hexane showing percent transmittance (%T) versus wavenumber (cm^{-1}).

The two main standalone spectroscopy techniques for forensic chemistry are FTIR and AA spectroscopy. FTIR is a nondestructive process that uses infrared light to identify a substance. The attenuated total reflectance sampling technique eliminates the need for substances to be prepared before analysis. The combination of nondestructiveness and zero preparation makes ATR FTIR analysis a quick and easy first step in the analysis of unknown substances. To facilitate the positive identification of the substance, FTIR instruments are loaded with databases that can be searched for known spectra that match the unknown's spectra. FTIR analysis of mixtures, while not impossible, presents specific difficulties due to the cumulative nature of the response. When analyzing an unknown that contains more than one substance, the resulting spectra will be a combination of the individual spectra of each component. While common mixtures have known spectra on file, novel mixtures can be difficult to resolve, making FTIR an unacceptable means of identification. However, the instrument can be used to determine the general chemical structures present, allowing forensic chemists to determine the best method for analysis with other instruments. For example, a methoxy group will result in a peak between 3,030 and 2,950 wavenumbers (cm^{-1}).

Atomic absorption spectroscopy (AAS) is a destructive technique that is able to determine the elements that make up the analyzed sample. AAS performs this analysis by subjecting the sample to an extremely high heat source, breaking the atomic bonds of the substance, leaving free atoms.

Radiation in the form of light is then passed through the sample forcing the atoms to jump to a higher energy state. Forensic chemists can test for each element by using a corresponding wavelength of light that forces that element's atoms to a higher energy state during the analysis. For this reason, and due to the destructive nature of this method, AAS is generally used as a confirmatory technique after preliminary tests have indicated the presence of a specific element in the sample. The concentration of the element in the sample is proportional to the amount of light absorbed when compared to a blank sample. AAS is useful in cases of suspected heavy metal poisoning such as with arsenic, lead, mercury, and cadmium. The concentration of the substance in the sample can indicate whether heavy metals were the cause of death.

Chromatography

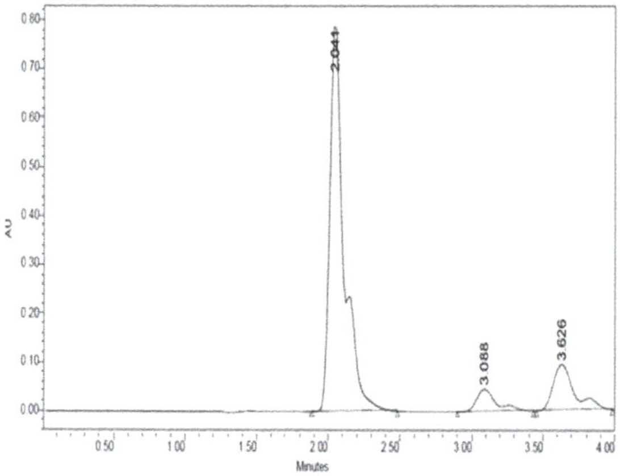

HPLC readout of an Excedrin tablet. Peaks from left to right are acetaminophen, aspirin, and caffeine.

Spectroscopy techniques are useful when the sample being tested is pure, or a very common mixture. When an unknown mixture is being analyzed it must be broken down into its individual parts. Chromatography techniques can be used to break apart mixtures into their components allowing for each part to be analyzed separately. Thin layer chromatography (TLC) is a quick alternative to more complex chromatography methods. TLC can be used to analyze inks and dyes by extracting the individual components. This can be used to investigate notes or fibers left at the scene since each company's product is slightly different and those differences can be seen with TLC. The only limiting factor with TLC analysis is the necessity for the components to be soluble in whatever solution is used to carry the components up the analysis plate. This solution is called the mobile phase. The forensic chemist can compare unknowns with known standards by looking at the distance each component traveled. This distance, when compared to the starting point, is known as the retention factor (R_f) for each extracted component. If each R_f value matches a known sample, that is an indication of the unknown's identity.

High-performance liquid chromatography can be used to extract individual components from a mixture dissolved in a solution. HPLC is used for nonvolatile mixtures that would not be suitable for gas chromatography. This is useful in drug analysis where the pharmaceutical is a combination drug since the components would separate, or elute, at different times allowing for the verification of each component. The eluates from the HPLC column are then fed into various detectors that produce a peak on a graph relative to its concentration as it elutes off the column. The most common type of detector is an ultraviolet-visible spectrometer as the most common item of interest tested with HPLC, pharmaceuticals, have UV absorbance.

Gas chromatography (GC) performs the same function as liquid chromatography, but it is used for volatile mixtures. In forensic chemistry, the most common GC instruments use mass spectrometry as their detector. GC-MS can be used in investigations of arson, poisoning, and explosions to determine exactly what was used. In theory, GC-MS instruments can detect substances whose concentrations are in the femtogram (10^{-15}) range. However, in practice, due to signal-to-noise ratios and other limiting factors, such as the age of the individual parts of the instrument, the practical detection limit for GC-MS is in the picogram (10^{-12}) range. GC-MS is also capable of quantifying the substances it detects; chemists can use this information to determine the effect the substance would have on an individual. GC-MS instruments need around 1,000 times more of the substance to quantify the amount than they need simply to detect it; the limit of quantification is typically in the nanogram (10^{-9}) range.

Forensic Toxicology

Forensic toxicology is the study of the pharmacodynamics, or what a substance does to the body, and pharmacokinetics, or what the body does to the substance. To accurately determine the effect a particular drug has on the human body, forensic toxicologists must be aware of various levels of tolerance that an individual can build up as well as the therapeutic index for various pharmaceuticals. Toxicologists are tasked with determining whether any toxin found in a body was the cause of or contributed to an incident, or whether it was at too low a level to have had an effect. While the determination of the specific toxin can be time-consuming due to the number of different substances that can cause injury or death, certain clues can narrow down the possibilities. For example, carbon monoxide poisoning would result in bright red blood while death from hydrogen sulfide would cause the brain to have a green hue.

Toxicologists are also aware of the different metabolites that a specific drug could break down into inside the body. For example, a toxicologist can confirm that a person took heroin by the presence in a sample of 6-monoacetylmorphine, which only comes from the breakdown of heroin. The constant creation of new drugs, both legal and illicit, forces toxicologists to keep themselves apprised of new research and methods to test for these novel substances. The stream of new formulations means that a negative test result does not necessarily rule out drugs. To avoid detection, illicit drug manufacturers frequently change the chemicals' structure slightly. These compounds are often not detected by routine toxicology tests and can be masked by the presence of a known compound in the same sample. As new compounds are discovered, known spectra are determined and entered into the databases that can be downloaded and used as reference standards. Laboratories also tend to keep in-house databases for the substances they find locally.

Standards

SWGDRUG analysis categories		
Category A	**Category B**	**Category C**
• Infrared spectroscopy	• Capillary electrophoresis	• Color tests
• Mass spectrometry	• Gas chromatography	• Fluorescence spectroscopy
• Nuclear magnetic resonance spectroscopy	• Ion-mobility spectrometry	• Immunoassay
	• Liquid chromatography	• Melting point analysis

SWGDRUG analysis categories		
Category A	**Category B**	**Category C**
• Raman spectroscopy • X-ray diffractometry	• Microcrystalline tests • Pharmaceutical identifiers • Thin-layer chromatography • *Cannabis only:* Macroscopic and microscopic examination	• Ultraviolet spectroscopy

Guidelines have been set up by various governing bodies regarding the standards that are followed by practicing forensic scientists. For forensic chemists, the international Scientific Working Group for the Analysis of Seized Drugs (SWGDRUG) presents recommendations for the quality assurance and quality control of tested materials. In the identification of unknown samples, protocols have been grouped into three categories based on the probability for false positives. Instruments and protocols in category A are considered the best for uniquely identifying an unknown material, followed by categories B and then C. To ensure the accuracy of identifications SWGDRUG recommends that multiple tests using different instruments be performed on each sample, and that one category A technique and at least one other technique be used. If a category A technique is not available, or the forensic chemist decides not to use one, SWGDRUG recommends that at least three techniques be used, two of which must be from category B. Combination instruments, such as GC-MS, are considered two separate tests as long as the results are compared to known values individually For example, the GC elution times would be compared to known values along with the MS spectra. If both of those match a known substance, no further tests are needed.

Standards and controls are necessary in the quality control of the various instruments used to test samples. Due to the nature of their work in the legal system, chemists must ensure that their instruments are working accurately. To do this, known controls are tested consecutively with unknown samples. By comparing the readouts of the controls with their known profiles the instrument can be confirmed to have been working properly at the time the unknowns were tested. Standards are also used to determine the instrument's limit of detection and limit of quantification for various common substances. Calculated quantities must be above the limit of detection to be confirmed as present and above the limit of quantification to be quantified. If the value is below the limit the value is not considered reliable.

Testimony

The standardized procedures for testimony by forensic chemists are provided by the various agencies that employ the scientists as well as SWGDRUG. Forensic chemists are ethically bound to present testimony in a neutral manner and to be open to reconsidering their statements if new information is found. Chemists should also limit their testimony to areas they have been qualified in regardless of questions during direct or cross-examination.

Individuals called to testify must be able to relay scientific information and processes in a manner that lay individuals can understand. By being qualified as an expert, chemists are allowed to give their opinions on the evidence as opposed to just stating the facts. This can lead to competing opinions from experts hired by the opposing side. Ethical guidelines for forensic chemists require that testimony be given in an objective manner, regardless of what side the expert is testifying for. Forensic experts that are called to testify are expected to work with the lawyer who issued the summons and to assist in their understanding of the material they will be asking questions about.

Education

Forensic chemistry positions require a bachelor's degree or similar in a natural or physical science as well as laboratory experience in general, organic, and analytical chemistry. Once in the position, individuals are trained in the protocols that are performed at that specific lab until they can prove they are competent to perform all experiments without supervision.. Practicing chemists already in the field are expected to have continuing education to maintain their proficiency.

Forensic Toxicology

Forensic toxicology is the use of toxicology and other disciplines such as analytical chemistry, pharmacology and clinical chemistry to aid medical or legal investigation of death, poisoning, and drug use. The primary concern for forensic toxicology is not the legal outcome of the toxicological investigation or the technology utilized, but rather the obtainment and interpretation of results. A toxicological analysis can be done to various kinds of samples. A forensic toxicologist must consider the context of an investigation, in particular any physical symptoms recorded, and any evidence collected at a crime scene that may narrow the search, such as pill bottles, powders, trace residue, and any available chemicals. Provided with this information and samples with which to work, the forensic toxicologist must determine which toxic substances are present, in what concentrations, and the probable effect of those chemicals on the person.

Determining the substance ingested is often complicated by the body's natural processes, as it is rare for a chemical to remain in its original form once in the body. For example: heroin is almost immediately metabolised into another substance and further to morphine, making detailed investigation into factors such as injection marks and chemical purity necessary to confirm diagnosis. The substance may also have been diluted by its dispersal through the body; while a pill or other regulated dose of a drug may have grams or milligrams of the active constituent, an individual sample under investigation may only contain micrograms or nanograms.

Examples

Urine

A urine sample is urine that has come from the bladder and can be provided or taken post-mortem. Urine is less likely to be infected with viruses such as HIV or Hepatitis B than blood samples. Many drugs have a higher concentration and can remain for much longer in urine than blood. Collection of urine samples can be taken in a noninvasive way which does not require professionals for collection. Urine is used for qualitative analysis as it cannot give any indication of impairment due to the fact that drug presence in urine only indicates prior exposure.

Blood

A blood sample of approximately 10 ml (0.35 imp fl oz; 0.34 US fl oz) is usually sufficient to screen and confirm most common toxic substances. A blood sample provides the toxicologist with a profile of the substance that the subject was influenced by at the time of collection; for this reason, it is the sample of choice for measuring blood alcohol content in drunk driving cases.

Hair Sample

Hair is capable of recording medium to long-term or high dosage substance abuse. Chemicals in the bloodstream may be transferred to the growing hair and stored in the follicle, providing a rough timeline of drug intake events. Head hair grows at rate of approximately 1 to 1.5 cm a month, and so cross sections from different sections of the follicle can give estimates as to when a substance was ingested. Testing for drugs in hair is not standard throughout the population. The darker and coarser the hair the more drug that will be found in the hair. If two people consumed the same amount of drugs, the person with the darker and coarser hair will have more drug in their hair than the lighter haired person when tested. This raises issues of possible racial bias in substance tests with hair samples.

Other

Other bodily fluids and organs may provide samples, particularly samples collected during an autopsy. A common autopsy sample is the gastric contents of the deceased, which can be useful for detecting undigested pills or liquids that were ingested prior to death. In highly decomposed bodies, traditional samples may no longer be available. The vitreous humour from the eye may be used, as the fibrous layer of the eyeball and the eye socket of the skull protects the sample from trauma and adulteration. Other common organs used for toxicology are the brain, liver, and spleen.

The inspection of the contents of the stomach must be part of every postmortem examination if possible because it may provide qualitative information concerning the nature of the last meal and the presence of abnormal constituents. Using it as a guide to the time of death, however, is theoretically unsound and presents many practical difficulties, although it may have limited applicability in some exceptional instances. Generally, using stomach contents as a guide to time of death involves an unacceptable degree of imprecision and is thus liable to mislead the investigator and the court. Characteristic cell types from food plants can be used to identify a victim's last meal; knowledge about which can be useful in determining the victim's whereabouts or actions prior to death (Bock and Norris, 1997). Some of these cell types include (Dickison, 2000):

- sclereids (pears)
- starch grains (potatoes and other tubers)
- raphide crystals (pineapple)
- druse crystals (citrus, beets, spinach)
- silica bodies (cereal grasses and bamboos)

In a case where a young woman had been stabbed to death, witnesses reported that she had eaten her last meal at a particular fast food restaurant. However, her stomach contents did not match the limited menu of the restaurant, leading investigators to conclude that she had eaten at some point after being seen in the restaurant. The investigation led to the apprehension of a man whom the victim knew, and with whom she had shared her actual final meal (Dickison, 2000). Time since death can be approximated by the state of digestion of the stomach contents. It normally takes at least a couple of hours for food to pass from the stomach to the small intestine; a meal still largely in the stomach implies death shortly after eating, while an empty or nearly-empty stomach suggests a longer time period between eating and death (Batten, 1995). However, there are numerous mitigating factors to take into account: the extent to which the food had been chewed, the amount of fat and protein present, physical activity undertaken by the victim prior to death, mood of the victim, physiological variation from person to person. All these factors affect the rate at which food passes through the digestive tract. Pathologists are generally hesitant to base a precise time of death on the evidence of stomach contents alone.

Other Organisms

Bacteria, maggots and other organisms that may have ingested some subject matter may have also ingested any toxic substance within it.

Detection and Classification

Detection of drugs and pharmaceuticals in biological samples is usually done by an initial screening and then a confirmation of the compound(s), which may include a quantitation of the compound(s). The screening and confirmation are usually, but not necessarily, done with different analytical methods. Every analytical method used in forensic toxicology should be carefully tested by performing a validation of the method to ensure correct and indisputable results at all times. A testing laboratory involved in forensic toxicology should adhere to a quality programme to ensure the best possible results and safety of any individual.

The choice of method for testing is highly dependent on what kind of substance one expects to find and the material on which the testing is performed. Biological samples are more complex to analyze because of factors such as the matrix effect and the metabolism and conjugation of the target compounds.

Gas Chromatography

Gas-liquid chromatography is of particular use in examining volatile organic compounds.

Detection of Metals

The compounds suspected of containing a metal are traditionally analyzed by the destruction of the organic matrix by chemical or thermal oxidation. This leaves the metal to be identified and quantified in the inorganic residue, and it can be detected using such methods as the Reinsch test, emission spectroscopy or X-ray diffraction. Unfortunately, while this identifies the metals present it removes the original compound, and so hinders efforts to determine what may have been ingested. The toxic effects of various metallic compounds can vary considerably.

Nonvolatile Organic Substances

Drugs, both prescribed and illicit, pesticides, natural products, pollutants and industrial compounds are some of the most common nonvolatile compounds encountered. Screening methods include thin-layer chromatography, gas-liquid chromatography and immunoassay. For complete legal identification, a second confirmatory test is usually also required. The trend today is to use liquid chromatography tandem mass spectrometry, preceded with sample workup as liquid-liquid extraction or solid phase extraction. Older methods include: spot test, typically the Marquis Reagent, Mecke Reagent, and Froehde's reagent for opiates, Marquis Reagent and Simon's reagent for amphetamine, methamphetamine and other analogs, like MDMA, the Scott's test for cocaine, and the modified Duquenois reagent for marijuana and other cannabinoids. For compounds that don't have a common spot test, like benzodiazepines, another test may be used, typically mass spectrometry, or spectrophotometry.

Nuclear Forensics

Nuclear forensics is the investigation of nuclear materials to find evidence for the source, the trafficking, and the enrichment of the material. The material can be recovered from various sources including dust from the vicinity of a nuclear facility, or from the radioactive debris following a nuclear explosion.

Results of nuclear forensic testing are used by different organisations to make decisions. The information is typically combined with other sources of information such as law enforcement and intelligence information.

History

The first seizures of nuclear or otherwise radioactive material were reported in Switzerland and Italy in 1991. Later, reports of incidents of nuclear material occurred in Germany, the Czech Republic, Hungary and other central European countries. Nuclear Forensics became a new branch of scientific research with the intent of not only determining the nature of the material, but also the intended use of the seized material as well as its origin and about the potential trafficking routes. Nuclear forensics relies on making these determinations through measurable parameters including, but not limited to chemical impurities, isotopic composition, microscopic appearance, and microstructure. By measuring these parameters, conclusions can be drawn as to the origin of the material. Identification of these parameters is an ongoing area of research, however, data interpretation also relies on the availability of reference information and on knowledge of the fuel cell operations.

The first investigative radiochemical measurements began in the early days of nuclear fission. In 1944, the US Air Force made the first attempts to detect fissiogenic ^{133}Xe in the atmosphere in order to indicate the production of plutonium through the irradiation of uranium and chemical reprocessing in an effort to gather intelligence on the status of the German nuclear program. However, no ^{133}Xe was detected. In the subsequent years it became increasingly valuable to gather information on the Soviet nuclear weapons program, which resulted in the development of technologies that could gather airborne particles in a WB-29 weather reconnaissance plane. On September 3, 1949, these particles were used to determine that the detonation time of the first Soviet atomic test, "Joe 1". Further analysis revealed that this bomb was a replicate of the "Fat Man", which was the bomb dropped on Nagasaki in 1945. This investigative methodology combined radiochemistry and other techniques to gather intelligence on nuclear activities.

The first seizures of nuclear materials from trafficking in the early 1990s allowed the nuclear forensic methodology to be adopted by a wider scientific community. When scientific laboratories outside the weapons and intelligence community took an interest in this methodology was when the term "Nuclear Forensics" was coined. Unlike standard forensics, nuclear forensics focuses mainly on the nuclear or radioactive material and aims to provide knowledge of the intended use of the materials.

In 1994 560 grams of plutonium and uranium oxide were intercepted at Munich airport in an airplane coming from Moscow. The precise composition was 363 grams plutonium (87% of which was Plutonium-239) and 122 grams of uranium.

Chronometry

Determining a nuclear material's age is critical to nuclear forensic investigations. Dating techniques can be utilized to identify a material's source as well as procedures performed on the material. This can aid in determining the information about the potential participant in the "age" of the material of interest. Nuclides, related through radioactive decay processes will have relative sample concentrations that can be predicted using parent-daughter in-growth equations and relevant half-lives. Because radioactive isotopes decay at a rate determined by the amount of the isotope in a sample and the half-life of the parent isotope, the relative amount of the decay products compared to the parent isotopes can be used to determine "age". Heavy element nuclides have a 4n+2 relationship, where the mass number divided by 4 leaves a remainder of two. The decay network begins with ^{238}Pu and proceeds through the in-growth of long-lived ^{234}U, ^{230}Th, and ^{226}Ra. If any member of the 4n+2 decay chain is purified it will immediately begin to produce descendant species. The time since a sample was last purified can be calculated from the ratio of any two concentrations among the decaying nuclides.

Essentially, if a nuclear material has been put through a refinement process to remove the daughter species, the time elapsed since purification can be "back-calculated" using radiochemical separation techniques in conjunction with analytical measurement of the existing parent-daughter ratios. For example, the α decay of ^{239}Pu to ^{235}U can be used as an example of this procedure. with the assumption of a perfect purification time T_0 then there will be a linear relationship between the in-growth of ^{235}U and time elapsed since purification. There are, however, various instances where the correlation is not as clear. This strategy may not apply when the parent-daughter pair achieve secular equilibrium very rapidly or when the half-life of the daughter nuclide is significantly shorter than the time that has elapsed since purification of the nuclear material, e.g. $^{237}Np/^{233}Pa$. Another possible complication is if in environmental samples, non-equivalent metal/ion transport for parents and daughter species may complicate or invalidate the use of chronometric measurements. Special age-dating relationships exist, including the commonly employed $^{234}U/^{230}Th$ and $^{241}Pu/^{241}Am$ chronometers. In special circumstances, parent-granddaughter relationships can be used to elucidate the age of nuclear materials when the material is intentionally made to look older through the addition of daughter nuclides.

Chronometry is based on the concept that the composition of the nuclear material changes as samples are prepared and analyzed. This barrier can be substantial for species that decay quickly or whose daughter products put forth spectral interferences. The decay of ^{233}U, for example, has a $t_{1/2}$~1.6x10^{5} years which is rapid in comparison to many species and yield ^{229}Th, which emits an α particle that is isoenergetic, having the same energy, as the parent. To avoid this, freshly prepared samples as well as complementary analysis methods are used for confident nuclear materials characterization. The decay of nuclear samples makes rapid analysis methods highly desirable.

Separations

Chemical separation techniques are frequently utilized in nuclear forensics as a method of reducing the interferences and to facilitate the measurement of low level radionuclides. Purification that occurs rapidly as progeny in-growth begins immediately following purification is ideal.

Anion Exchange

Anion exchange separation methods are widely used in the purification of actinides and actinide bearing materials through the use of resin columns. The anionic actinide complexes are retained by anion exchange sites that are on the resin and neutral species pass through the column unretained. Then the retained species can be eluted from the column by conversion to a neutral complex, typically by changing the mobile phase passed through the resin bed. Anion exchange-based separations of actinides, while valued for there simplicity and widely used, tend to be time consuming and are infrequently automated. Most are still dependent on gravity. Speeding up the flow of the mobile phase tends to introduce problems such as impurities and jeopardize future investigations. Hence, there is still a need for development of this technique to satisfy the nuclear forensic research priorities.

Co-Precipitation

Actinide isolation by co-precipitation is frequently used for samples of relatively large volumes to concentrate analytes and remove interferences. Actinide carriers include iron hydroxides, lanthanide fluorides/hydroxides, manganese dioxide, and a few other species.

Analysis

A wide range of instrumental techniques are employed in nuclear forensics. Radiometric counting techniques are useful when determining decay products of species with short half-lives. However, for longer half-lives, inorganic mass spec is a powerful means of carrying out elemental analysis and determining isotopic relationships. Microscopy approaches can also be useful in characterization of a nuclear material.

Counting Techniques

Counting techniques of α,β,γ or neutron can be used as approaches for the analysis of nuclear forensic materials that emit decay species. The most common of these are alpha and gamma spectroscopy. β counting is used infrequently because most short lived β-emitters also give off characteristic γ-rays and produce very broad counting peaks. Neutron counting are found more rarely in analytical labs due in part to shielding concerns should such neutron emitters be introduced into a counting facility.

Alpha-particle Spectroscopy

Alpha-particle spectroscopy is a method of measuring the radionuclides based on emission of α particles. They can be measured by a variety of detectors, including liquid scintillation counters, gas ionization detectors, and ion-implanted silicon semiconductor detectors. Typical alpha-particle spectrometers have low backgrounds and measure particles ranging from 3 to 10 MeV. Radionuclides that decay through α emission tend to eject α particles with discrete, characteristic energies between 4 and 6 MeV. These energies become attenuated as they pass through the layers of sample. Increasing the distance between the source and the detector can lead to improved resolution, but decreased particle detection.

The advantages of alpha-particle spectroscopy include relatively inexpensive equipment costs, low backgrounds, high selectivity, and good throughput capabilities with the use of multi-chamber systems. There are also disadvantages of alpha-particle spectroscopy. One disadvantage is that there must be significant sample preparation to obtain useful spectroscopy sources. Also, spectral interferences or artifacts from extensive preparation prior to counting, to minimize this high purity acids are needed. Another disadvantage is that measurements require a large quantity of material which can also lead to poor resolution. Also, undesired spectral overlap and long analysis times are disadvantages.

Gamma Spectroscopy

Gamma spectroscopy yields results that are conceptually equivalent to alpha-particle spectroscopy, however, can result in sharper peaks due to reduced attenuation of energy. Some radionuclides produce discrete γ-rays that produce energy between a few KeV to 10 MeV which can be measured with a gamma-ray spectrometer. This can be accomplished without destroying the sample. The most common gamma-ray detector is a semiconductor germanium detector which allow for a greater energy resolution than alpha-particle spectroscopy, however gamma spectroscopy only has an efficiency of a few percent. Gamma spectroscopy is a less sensitive method due to low detector efficiency and high background. However, gamma spectroscopy has the advantage of having less time consuming sample procedures and portable detectors for field use.

Mass Spectrometry

Mass spec techniques are essential in nuclear forensics analysis. Mass spec can provide elemental and isotopic information. Mass spec also requires less sample mass relative to counting techniques. For nuclear forensic purposes it is essential that the mass spectrometry offers excellent resolution in order to distinguish between similar analytes, e.g. ^{235}U and ^{236}U. Ideally, mass spec should offer excellent resolution/mass abundance, low backgrounds, and proper instrumental function.

Thermal Ionization MS

In thermal ionization mass spectrometry, small quantities of highly purified analyte are deposited onto a clean metal filament, rhenium or tungsten are typically used. The sample is heated in a vacuum of the ion source by applying a current to the filaments. A portion of the analyte will be ionized by the filament and then are directed down the flight tube and separated based on mass to charge ratios. Major disadvantages include time consuming sample preparation and inefficient analyte ionization.

Multi-collector Inductively Coupled Plasma-mass Spectrometry

This is a frequently used technique in nuclear forensics. In this technique a purified sample is nebulized in a spray chamber and then aspirated into a plasma. The high temperature of the plasma leads to sample dissociation and high efficiency of ionization of the analyte. The ions then enter the mass spectrometer where they are discriminated based on mass based on a double focusing system. Ions of various masses are detected simultaneously by a bank of detectors similar to those used in the thermal ionization mass spec. MC-ICP-MS has a more rapid analysis because i does not require lengthy filament preparation. For high quality, however, there is a requirement for extensive sample cleanup. Argon plasma is also less stable and requires relatively expensive equipment as well as skilled operators.

Secondary-Ion MS

SIMS is a micro-analytical technique valuable for three-dimensional analysis of a materials elemental composition and isotopic ratios. This method can be utilized in characterization of bulk materials with a detection limit in the low parts per billion (10^{-9} or ng/g) range. Particles as small as a few 100 nanometer can be detected. Ion production in this technique is dependent on the bombardment of solid samples with a focused beam of primary ions. The sputtered, secondary ions are directed onto the mass spectrometry system to be measured. The secondary ions are a result of kinetic energy transfer from the primary ions. These primary ions penetrate into the solid sample to some depth. This method can be used to detect any element, however the sputtering process is highly matrix dependent and ion yields vary.

This method is especially useful, because it can be fully automated to find uranium particles in a sample of many million particles in a matter of hours. Particles of interest can then be imaged and further analyzed with very high isotopic precision.

Additional Nuclear Forensic Methods

Numerous additional approaches may be employed in the interrogation of seized nuclear material. In contrast to previously mentioned analysis techniques, these approaches have received relatively low attention in recent years in terms of novel advancement, and, typically, require greater quantities of sample.

Scanning Electron Microscope

The scanning electron microscope can provide images of an object's surface at high magnification with a resolution on the order of nanometers. A focused beam of energetic electrons is scanned over the sample and electrons that a backscattered or emitted from the sample surface are detected. Images are constructed via measuring the fluctuations of electrons from the sample beam scanning position. This data is useful in determining what process may have been employed in the materials production and to distinguish between materials of differing origins. Measurement of backscattered electrons elucidate the average atomic number of the area being scanned. The emitted, or secondary electrons provide topological information. This is a relatively straight forward technique, however samples must be amenable to being under a vacuum and may require pre-treatment.

X-Ray Fluorescence

X-ray fluorescence offers rapid and non-destructive determination of the elemental composition of a nuclear material based on the detection of characteristic X-rays. Direct sample irradiation allows for minimal sample preparation and portable instrumentation for field deployment. The detection limit is 10 ppm. This is well above mass spectrometry. This technique tends to be hindered by matrix affects, which must be corrected for.

Neutron Activation Analysis

Neutron activation analysis is a powerful non-destructive method of analyzing elements of mid to high atomic number. This method combines excitation by nuclear reaction and the radiation counting techniques to detect various materials. The measurement of characteristic radiation, following the bombardment completion, is indicative of the elements of interest. The equation for the production product is given by: $A + n \rightarrow B^{*} + \gamma$ where A is the starting analyte, n is the incoming neutron, B^{*} is the excited product and γ is the detected radiation that results from the de-excitation of the product species.

The advantages of this technique include multi-element analysis, excellent sensitivity, and high selectivity, and no time-consuming separation procedures. One disadvantage is the requirement of a nuclear reactor for sample preparation.

References

- M Reith; C Carr; G Gunsch (2002). "An examination of digital forensic models". International Journal of Digital Evidence. Retrieved 2 August 2010
- Various (2009). Eoghan Casey, ed. Handbook of Digital Forensics and Investigation. Academic Press. p. 567. ISBN 0-12-374267-6. Retrieved 27 August 2010
- Maarten Van Horenbeeck (24 May 2006). "Technology Crime Investigation". Archived from the original on 17 May 2008. Retrieved 17 August 2010
- Sarah Mocas (February 2004). "Building theoretical underpinnings for digital forensics research". Digital Investigation. 1 (1): 61–68. ISSN 1742-2876. doi:10.1016/j.diin.2003.12.004
- Gohlke, Roland S.; McLafferty, Fred W. (May 1993). "Early Gas Chromatography/Mass Spectrometry". Journal of the American Society for Mass Spectrometry. 4 (5): 367–371. PMID 24234933. doi:10.1016/1044-0305(93)85001-e. Retrieved September 27, 2015
- Warren G. Kruse; Jay G. Heiser (2002). Computer forensics: incident response essentials. Addison-Wesley. p. 392. ISBN 0-201-70719-5
- Wells, Doris (March 26, 2012). "In Brief: Law 101: Legal Guide for the Forensic Expert". National Institute of Justice. Retrieved October 13, 2016
- Nikolin, B; Imamović, B; Medanhodzić-Vuk, S; Sober, M (May 2004). "High Performance Liquid Chromatography in Pharmaceutical Analyses". Bosnian Journal of Basic Medical Sciences. 4 (2): 5–9. PMID 15629016
- Miller, Marilyn T; Peter, Massey. Chapter 1 - Crime Scene Investigations. San Diego: Academic Press. pp. 3–15. ISBN 9780128012451
- Glaser, Alexander; Tom Bielefeld. "Nuclear Forensics - Revision 5 Capabilities, Limits, and the "CSI Effect"" (PDF). Retrieved 25 November 2013
- Wennig, Robert (April 2009). "Back to the Roots of Modern Analytical Toxicology: Jean Servais Stas and the Bocarmé Murder Case" (PDF). Drug Testing and Analysis. 1 (4): 153–155. PMID 20355192. doi:10.1002/dta.32

- GL Palmer; I Scientist; H View (2002). "Forensic analysis in the digital world". International Journal of Digital Evidence. Retrieved 2 August 2010
- Forbes, Patricia, ed. (2015). Monitoring of Air Pollutants: Sampling, Sample Preparation and Analytical Techniques. Comprehensive Analytical Chemistry. Vol. 70. Elsevier. p. 274. ISBN 9780444635532 – via Google Books
- "Scientific Working Group for the Analysis of Seized Drugs (SWGDRUG) Recommendations" (PDF). 7.1. June 9, 2016. Retrieved January 4, 2017
- Stanley, Floyd E.; Stalcup A.M.; Spitz, H.B (2013). "A Brief Introduction to Analytical Methods in Nuclear Forensics". J Radioanal Nucl Chem. 295: 1385–1393. doi:10.1007/s10967-012-1927-3

3

Forensic Methodologies: An Integrated Study

Forensic economics applies theories of economics to the laws of a country. Forensic accounting, computational criminology, forensic anthropology, forensic facial reconstruction, forensic arts are some of the topics concerned with the subject matter. This chapter will provide an integrated understanding of forensic methodologies.

Forensic Economics

Forensic Economics as defined by the National Association of Forensic Economics (nafe.net) is the scientific discipline that applies economic theories and methods to matters within a legal framework. Forensic economics covers, but is not limited to:

- The calculation of pecuniary damages in personal and commercial litigation.
- The analysis of liability, such as the statistical analysis of discrimination, the analysis of market power in antitrust disputes, and fraud detection.
- Other matters subject to legal review, such as public policy analysis, and business, property, and asset valuation.

In a 2012 paper by Eric Zitzewitz entitled "Forensic Economics," *Journal of Economic Literature* 2012, 50(3), 731-769, published by the American Economic Association, "Forensic Economics" was defined as the application of economics to the detection and quantification of harm from behavior that has become the subject of litigation.

The only difference between these two definitions is that one suggests the application of science is itself a scientific discipline. Notwithstanding this distinction, both definitions refer to the application of economics. While courts may dictate what economic issues are to be addressed, the economic science that is applied must be that which is taught and practiced in the world at large. Clearly, it is not a set of theories and methods that only exist for litigation purposes. This fact is an important one for those interested in entering the profession to recognize.

Examples of Applications of Economics in Litigation

- Economic Damages in Injury and Death
- Antitrust liability and economic damages
- Unfair Practices in International Trade

- Economic Damages in Copyright Violation and Patent Infringement
- Contract Violations
- Discrimination
- Economic Damages Related to Physical and Emotional Abuse

A graduate degree in the relevant sub-field of economics is the usual qualification for an economist offering to serve as an economic expert in litigation. The National Association of Forensic Economics is a good reference for trained economists interested in learning the idiosyncrasies of litigation.

Forensic Accounting

Forensic accounting, forensic accountancy or financial forensics is the specialty practice area of accounting that describes engagements that result from actual or anticipated disputes or litigation. "The work performed and reports issued will often provide answers to the how, where, what, why and who. However, ultimately the court decides." (David Malamed, Forensic Accountant, Toronto Ontario.) "Forensic" means "suitable for use in a court of law", and it is to that standard and potential outcome that forensic accountants generally have to work. Forensic accountants, also referred to as forensic auditors or investigative auditors, often have to give expert evidence at the eventual trial. All of the larger accounting firms, as well as many medium-sized and boutique firms and various police and government agencies have specialist forensic accounting departments. Within these groups, there may be further sub-specializations: some forensic accountants may, for example, just specialize in insurance claims, personal injury claims, fraud, anti-money-laundering, construction, or royalty audits.

Financial forensic engagements may fall into several categories. For example:

- Economic damages calculations, whether suffered through tort or breach of contract;
- Post-acquisition disputes such as earnouts or breaches of warranties;
- Bankruptcy, insolvency, and reorganization;
- Securities fraud;
- Tax fraud;
- Money laundering;
- Business valuation; and
- Computer forensics/e-discovery.

Forensic accountants often assist in professional negligence claims where they are assessing and commenting on the work of other professionals. Forensic accountants are also engaged in marital and family law of analyzing lifestyle for spousal support purposes, determining income available for child support and equitable distribution.

Engagements relating to criminal matters typically arise in the aftermath of fraud. They frequently involve the assessment of accounting systems and accounts presentation—in essence assessing if the numbers reflect reality.

Some forensic accountants specialize in forensic analytics which is the procurement and analysis of electronic data to reconstruct, detect, or otherwise support a claim of financial fraud. The main steps in forensic analytics are (a) data collection, (b) data preparation, (c) data analysis, and (d) reporting. For example, forensic analytics may be used to review an employee's purchasing card activity to assess whether any of the purchases were diverted or divertible for personal use.

Forensic Accountants

Forensic accountants, investigative accountants or expert accountants may be involved in recovering proceeds of crime and in relation to confiscation proceedings concerning actual or assumed proceeds of crime or money laundering. In the United Kingdom, relevant legislation is contained in the Proceeds of Crime Act 2002. Forensic accountants typically hold the following qualifications; Certified Forensic Accounting Professional [Certified Forensic Auditors] (CFA - England & Wales) granted by the Forensic Auditors Certification Board of England and Wales (FACB), Certified Fraud Examiners (CFE - US / International),Certificate Course on Forensic Accounting and Fraud Detection (FAFD) by Institute of Chartered Accountants of India (ICAI), Certified Public Accountants (CPA - US) with AICPA's [Certified in Financial Forensics est. 2008] (CFF) Credentials, Chartered Accountants (CA - Canada), Certified Management Accountants (CMA - Canada), Chartered Professional Accountants (CPA - Canada)), Chartered Certified Accountants (CCA - UK), or Certified Forensic Investigation Professionals (CFIP). In India there is a separate breed of forensic accountants called Certified Forensic Accounting Professionals.

The Certified Forensic Accountant (CRFAC) program from the American Board of Forensic Accounting assesses Certified Public Accountants (CPAs) knowledge and competence in professional forensic accounting services in a multitude of areas. Forensic accountants may be involved in both litigation support (providing assistance on a given case, primarily related to the calculation or estimation of economic damages and related issues) and investigative accounting (looking into illegal activities). The American Board of Forensic Accounting was established in 1993. The American Board of Forensic Accounting offers the "Forensic Accounting Review". The CRFAC is a valuable credential and covers the broad base of forensic accounting knowledge. The American Board of Forensic Accounting offers many programs.

In 2016, the Forensic Auditors Certification Board (FACB) of England and Wales was established by the major forensic auditing and accounting bodies from across the world with its registered address in London. FACB is a professional bodies membership body comprising the International Institute of Certified Forensic Accountants (IICFA) of USA, Institute of Forensic Auditors of Zimbabwe (IFA), Institute of Forensic Accountants of Pakistan (IFAP), Institute of Certified Forensic Accountants (ICFA) of USA and Canada and the Institute of Forensic Accountants of Nigeria (IFA). FACB plays several roles and one the roles is standardization of the examination and certification of forensic auditors globally. Forensic auditors and accountants sit for one examination that is set by FACB and upon passing and meeting all the professional requirements, are awarded the credential, Certified Forensic Auditor (CFA) or the Registered Forensic Auditor (RFA) for practitioners who intend to go into public practice. All certification is renewed on an annual basis. Apart from practitioners certification, FACB is an oversight body which accredits prospective member organization before admission as part of quality checks. Persons with the FACB credential can practice as forensic auditors on a global scale.

Large accounting firms often have a forensic accounting department.

Forensic accounting and fraud investigation methodologies are different than internal auditing. Thus forensic accounting services and practice should be handled by forensic accounting experts, not by internal auditing experts. Forensic accountants may appear on the crime scene a little later than fraud auditors, but their major contribution is in translating complex financial transactions and numerical data into terms that ordinary laypersons can understand. That is necessary because if the fraud comes to trial, the jury will be made up of ordinary laypersons. On the other hand, internal auditors move on checklists that may not surface the evidence that the jury or regulatory bodies look for. The fieldwork may carry out legal risks if internal auditing checklists are employed instead asking to a forensic accountant and may result serious consultant malpractice risks.

Forensic accountants utilize an understanding of economic theories, business information, financial reporting systems, accounting and auditing standards and procedures, data management & electronic discovery, data analysis techniques for fraud detection, evidence gathering and investigative techniques, and litigation processes and procedures to perform their work. Forensic accountants are also increasingly playing more proactive risk reduction roles by designing and performing extended procedures as part of the statutory audit, acting as advisers to audit committees, fraud deterrence engagements, and assisting in investment analyst research.

Computational Criminology

Computational criminology is an interdisciplinary field which uses computing science methods to formally define criminology concepts, improve our understanding of complex phenomena, and generate solutions for related problems.

Methods

Computing science methods being used include:

- Algorithms
- Data Mining
- Data Structures
- Formal Methods
- Software Development Process

Areas of usage

Computational criminology is interdisciplinary in the sense that both criminologists and computing scientists work together to ensure that computational models properly match their theoretical and real-world counterparts. Areas of criminology for which computational approaches are being used include:

- Environmental Criminology
- Identity Theft
- Justice

Forensics

Computational forensics (CF) is a quantitative approach to the methodology of the forensic sciences. It involves computer-based modeling, computer simulation, analysis, and recognition in studying and solving problems posed in various forensic disciplines. CF integrates expertise from computational science and forensic sciences.

A broad range of objects, substances and processes are investigated, which are mainly based on pattern evidence, such as toolmarks, fingerprints, shoeprints, documents etc., but also physiological and behavioral patterns, DNA, digital evidence and crime scenes.

Computational methods find a place in the forensic sciences in several ways, as for example:

- rigorous quantification of individuality,
- definition and establishment of likelihood ratio,
- increase of efficiency and effectiveness in daily forensic casework.

Algorithms implemented are from the fields of signal and image processing, computer vision, computer graphics, data visualization, statistical pattern recognition, data mining, machine learning, and robotics.

Computer forensics (also referred to as "digital forensics" or "forensic information technology") is one specific discipline that could use computational science to study digital evidence. Computational Forensics examines diverse types of evidence.

Forensic Animation

Forensic animation is a branch of forensic science in which audio-visual reconstructions of incidents or accidents are created to aid investigators. Examples include the use of computer animation, stills, and other audio visual aids. Application of computer animation in courtrooms today is becoming more popular.

The first use of forensic animation was in *Connors v. United States*, both sides used computer re-creations and animations in a case surrounding the crash of Delta Flight 191 on August 2, 1985. The crash resulted in the deaths of 137 people and extensive property damage. In the resulting lawsuit a method was required to explain complicated information and situations to the jury. As part of the plaintiff presentation, a 45-minute computer generated presentation was created to explain the intricacies of the evidence and thus began forensic animation.

The first reported use of computer animation in a U.S. criminal trial was in the 1991 Marin County, CA homicide trial of James Mitchell (of the porno-businessman Mitchell Brothers) The prosecution used the animation to explain the complex details of the shooting incident to the jury. It showed the positions of James Mitchell, Artie Mitchell (the victim), the bullet impact points, and the path taken by bullets as they entered Artie's body. The animation was admitted, over objection by the defense, and the case resulted in a conviction. The use of the animation was upheld on appeal and the success of the forensic animation led to its use in many other trials. In India Prof. T D Dogra at AIIMS New Delhi in 2008 used animation to explain the court of law and investigating agencies first time in two important cases of firearm injuries,case of Murder and Terrorist encounter killings(Batla house encounter case).

Forensic Anthropology

Forensic anthropology is the application of the anatomical science of anthropology and its various subfields, including forensic archaeology and forensic taphonomy, in a legal setting. A forensic anthropologist can assist in the identification of deceased individuals whose remains are decomposed, burned, mutilated or otherwise unrecognizable, as might happen in a plane crash. Forensic anthropologists are also instrumental to the investigation and documentation of genocide and mass graves. Along with forensic pathologists, forensic dentists, and homicide investigators, forensic anthropologists commonly testify in court as expert witnesses. Using physical markers present on a skeleton, a forensic anthropologist can potentially determine a victim's age, sex, stature, and ancestry. In addition to identifying physical characteristics of the individual, forensic anthropologists can use skeletal abnormalities to potentially determine cause of death, past trauma such as broken bones or medical procedures, as well as diseases such as bone cancer.

The methods used to identity a person from a skeleton relies on the past contributions of various anthropologists and the study of human skeletal differences. Through the collection of thousands of specimens and the analysis of differences within a population, estimations can be made based on physical characteristics. Through these, a set of remains can potentially be identified. The field of forensic anthropology grew during the twentieth century into a fully recognized forensic specialty involving trained anthropologists as well as numerous research institutions gathering data on decomposition and the effects it can have on the skeleton.

Modern uses

Today, forensic anthropology is a well established discipline within the forensic field. Anthropologists are called upon to investigate remains and to help identify individuals from bones when other physical characteristics which could be used to identify a body no longer exist. Forensic anthropologists work in conjunction with forensic pathologists to identify remains based on their skeletal characteristics. If the victim is not found for a lengthy period of time or has been eaten by scavengers, flesh markers used for identification would be destroyed, making normal identification difficult if not impossible. Forensic anthropologists can provide physical characteristics of the person to input into missing person databases such as that of the National Crime Information Center in the US or INTERPOL's yellow notice database.

Exhumed bodies of victims of the 1995 Srebrenica Genocide in a mass grave found in 2007.

In addition to these duties, forensic anthropologists often assist in the investigation of war crimes and mass fatality investigations. Anthropologists have been tasked with helping to identify victims of the 9/11 terrorist attacks as well as plane crashes such as the Arrow Air Flight 1285 disaster and the USAir Flight 427 disaster where the flesh had been vaporized or so badly mangled that normal identification was impossible. Anthropologists have also helped identify victims of genocide in countries around the world, often long after the actual event. War crimes anthropologists have helped investigate include the Rwandan Genocide and the Srebrenica Genocide. Organizations such as the Forensic Anthropology Society of Europe, the British Association for Forensic Anthropology, and the American Society of Forensic Anthropologists continue to provide guidelines for the improvement of forensic anthropology and the development of standards within the discipline.

History

Early History

Earnest Hooton, one of the pioneers in the field of physical anthropology.

The use of anthropology in the forensic investigation of remains grew out of the recognition of anthropology as a distinct scientific discipline and the growth of physical anthropology. The field of anthropology began in the United States and struggled to obtain recognition as a legitimate science during the early years of the twentieth century. Earnest Hooton pioneered the field of physical anthropology and became the first physical anthropologist to hold a full-time teaching position in the United States. He was an organizing committee member of the American Association of Physical Anthropologists along with its founder Aleš Hrdlička. Hooton's students created some of the first doctoral programs in physical anthropology during the early 20th century. In addition to physical anthropology, Hooton was a proponent of criminal anthropology. Now considered a pseudoscience, criminal anthropologists believed that phrenology and physiognomy could link a person's behavior to specific physical characteristics. The use of criminal anthropology to try to explain certain criminal behaviors arose out of the eugenics movement, popular at the time. It is because of these ideas that skeletal differences were measured in earnest eventually leading to the development of anthropometry and the Bertillon method of skeletal measurement by Alphonse Bertillon. The study of this information helped shape anthropologists' understanding of the human skeleton and the multiple skeletal differences that can occur.

Another prominent early anthropologist, Thomas Wingate Todd, was primarily responsible for the creation of the first large collection of human skeletons in 1912. In total, Todd acquired 3,300 human skulls and skeletons, 600 anthropoid skulls and skeletons, and 3,000 mammalian skulls and skeletons. Todd's contributions to the field of anthropology remain in use in the modern era and include various studies regarding suture closures on the skull and timing of teeth eruption in the mandible. Todd also developed age estimates based on physical characteristics of the pubic symphysis. Though the standards have been updated, these estimates are still used by forensic anthropologists to narrow down an age range of skeletonized remains. These early pioneers legitimized the field of anthropology, but it was not until the 1940s, with the help of Todd's student, Wilton M. Krogman, that forensic anthropology gained recognition as a legitimate subdiscipline.

The Growth of Forensic Anthropology

During the 1940s, Krogman was the first anthropologist to actively publicize anthropologists' potential forensic value, going as far as placing advertisements in the FBI Law Enforcement Bulletin informing agencies of the ability of anthropologists to assist in the identification of skeletal remains. This period saw the first official use of anthropologists by federal agencies including the FBI. During the 1950s, the U.S. Army Quartermaster Corps employed forensic anthropologists in the identification of war casualties during the Korean War. It was at this time that forensic anthropology officially began. The sudden influx of available skeletons for anthropologists to study, whose identities were eventually confirmed, allowed for the creation of more accurate formulas for the identification of sex, age, and stature based solely on skeletal characteristics. These formulas, developed in the 1940s and refined by war, are still in use by modern forensic anthropologists.

The professionalization of the field began soon after, during the 1950s and 1960s. This move coincided with the replacement of coroners with medical examiners in many locations around the country. It was during this time that the field of forensic anthropology gained recognition as a separate field within the American Academy of Forensic Sciences and the first forensic anthropology research facility and body farm was opened by William M. Bass. Public attention and interest in forensic anthropology began to increase around this time as forensic anthropologists started working on more high-profile cases. One of the major cases of the era involved anthropologist Charles Merbs who helped identify the victims murdered by Ed Gein.

Methods

One of the main tools forensic anthropologists use in the identification of remains is their knowledge of osteology and the various differences that occur within the human skeleton. During the course of an investigation, anthropologists are often tasked with helping to determinate an individual's sex, stature, age, and ancestry. To do this, anthropologists must be aware of how the human skeleton can differ between individuals.

Determination of Sex

Depending on which bones are present, sex can be determined by looking for distinctive sexual dimorphisms. When available, the pelvis is extremely useful in the determination of sex and when properly examined can achieve sex determination with a great level of accuracy. The examination of the pubic arch and the location of the sacrum can help determine sex.

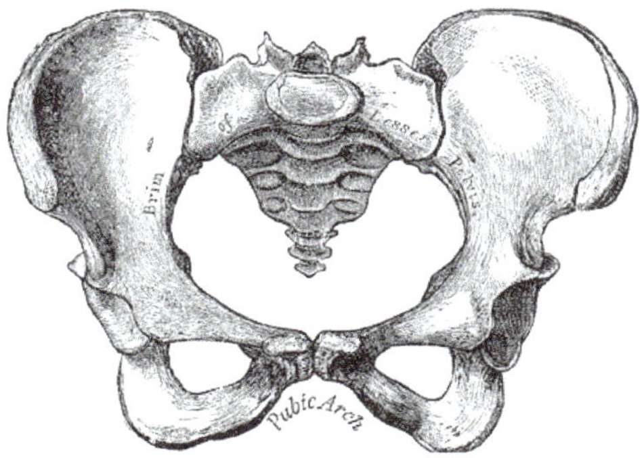

Female pelvis. Note wide pubic arch and shorter, pushed back sacrum

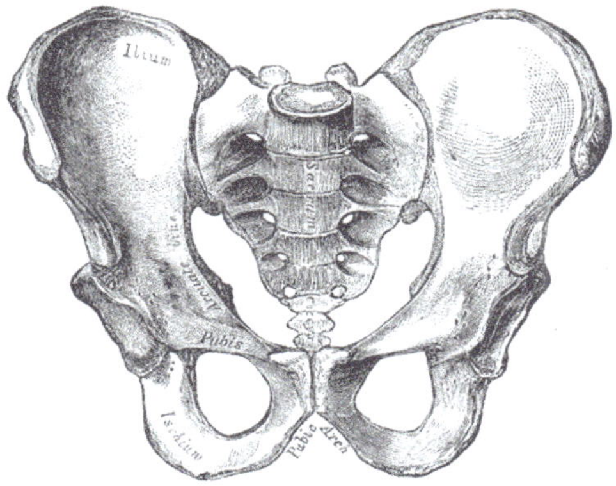

Male pelvis. Note narrow pubic arch and longer sacrum.

However, the pelvis is not always present, so forensic anthropologists must be aware of other areas on the skeleton that have distinct characteristics between sexes. The skull also contains multiple markers that can be used to determine sex. Specific markers on the skull include the temporal line, the eye sockets, the supraorbital ridge, as well as the nuchal lines, and the mastoid process. In general, male skulls tend to be larger and thicker than female skulls, and to have more pronounced ridges.

It is important for forensic anthropologists to take into account all available markers in the determination of sex due to the differences that can occur between individuals of the same sex. For example, it is possible that a female may have a slightly more narrow than normal pubic arch. It is for this reason that anthropologists usually classify sex as one of five possibilities: male, may be male, indeterminate, may be female, or female. In addition, forensic anthropologists are generally unable to make a sex determination unless the individual was an adult at the time of death. The sexual dimorphisms present in the skeleton begin to occur during puberty and are not fully pronounced until after sexual maturation.

Determination of Stature

The determination of stature by anthropologists is based on a series of formulas that have been developed over time by the examination of multiple different skeletons from a multitude of different regions and backgrounds. Stature is given as a range of possible values, in centimeters, and typically computed by measuring the bones of the leg. The three bones that are used are the femur, the tibia, and the fibula. In addition to the leg bones, the bones of the arm, the humerus, ulna, and radius can be used. The formulas that are used to determine stature rely on various information regarding the individual. Sex, ancestry, and age should be determined before attempting to ascertain height, if possible. This is due to the differences that occur between populations, sexes, and age groups. By knowing all the variables associated with height, a more accurate estimate can be made. For example, a male formula for stature estimation using the femur is $2.32 \times$ femur length $+ 65.53 \pm 3.94$ cm. A female of the same ancestry would use the formula, $2.47 \times$ femur length $+ 54.10 \pm 3.72$ cm. It is also important to note an individual's approximate age when determining stature. This is due to the shrinkage of the skeleton that naturally occurs as a person ages. After age 30, a person loses approximately one centimeter of their height every decade.

Determination of Age

The determination of an individual's age by anthropologists depends on whether or not the individual was an adult or a child. The determination of the age of children, under the age of 21, is usually performed by examining the teeth. When teeth are not available, children can be aged based on which growth plates are sealed. The tibia plate seals around age 16 or 17 in girls and around 18 or 19 in boys. The clavicle is the last bone to complete growth and the plate is sealed around age 25. In addition, if a complete skeleton is available anthropologists can count the number of bones. While adults have 206 bones, the bones of a child have not yet fused resulting in a much higher number.

The aging of adult skeletons is not as straightforward as aging a child's skeleton as the skeleton changes little once adulthood is reached. One possible way to estimate the age of an adult skeleton is to look at bone osteons under a microscope. New osteons are constantly formed by bone marrow even after the bones stop growing. Younger adults have fewer and larger osteons while older adults have smaller and more osteon fragments. Another potential method for determining the age of an adult skeleton is to look for arthritis indicators on the bones. Arthritis will cause noticeable rounding of the bones. The degree of rounding from arthritis coupled with the size and number of osteons can help an anthropologist narrow down a potential age range for the individual.

Determination of Ancestry

The determination of an individual's ancestry is typically grouped into three historical groups, Caucasoid, Mongoloid, and Negroid. However, the use of these classifications is becoming much harder as the rate of interancestrial marriages increases and markers become less defined. By measuring distances between landmarks on the skull as well as the size and shape of specific bones anthropologists can use a series of equations to estimate ancestry. Typically, the maxilla is used to help anthropologists determine an individual's ancestry due to the three basic shapes, hyperbolic, parabolic, and rounded, belonging to the three historical ancestries, Negroid, Caucasoid, and Mongoloid respectively. In addition to the maxilla, the zygomatic arch and the nasal opening have been used to narrow down possible ancestry. A program called FORDISC has been created that will calculate the most likely ancestry using complex mathematical formulas. This program is continually updated with new information from known individuals to maintain a database of current populations and their respective measurements.

Other Markers

Anthropologists are also able to see other markers present on the bones. Past fractures will be evident by the presence of bone remodeling. The examination of any fractures on the bones can potentially help determine cause of death as well by determining if a fracture occurred ante-mortem (before death), peri-mortem (at the time of death), or post-mortem (after death). Ante-mortem fractures will show signs of healing while peri- and post-mortem fractures will not. Peri-mortem fractures will usually appear clean while post-mortem breaks will appear brittle. Diseases such as bone cancer might be present in bone marrow samples and can help narrow down the list of possible identifications.

Subfields

Forensic Archaeology

Forensic archaeologists employ their knowledge of proper excavation techniques to ensure that remains are recovered in a controlled and forensically acceptable manner. When remains are found partially or completely buried the proper excavation of the remains will ensure that any evidence present on the bones will remain intact. The difference between forensic archaeologists and forensic anthropologists is that where forensic anthropologists are trained specifically in human osteology and recovery of human remains, forensic archaeologists specialize more broadly in the processes of search and discovery. In addition to remains, archaeologists are trained to look for objects contained in and around the excavation area. These objects can include anything from wedding rings to potentially probative evidence such as cigarette butts or shoe prints. Their training extends further to observing context, association and significance of objects in a crime scene and drawing conclusions that may be useful for locating a victim or suspect. A forensic archaeologist must also be able to utilize a degree of creativity and adaptability during times when crime scenes can not be excavated using traditional archaeological techniques. For example, one particular case study was conducted on the search and recovery of the remains of a missing girl who was found in a septic tank underground. This instance required unique methods unlike those of a typical archeological excavation in order to exhume and preserve the contents of the tank.

Forensic archaeologists are involved within three main areas. Assisting with crime scene research, investigation, and recovery of evidence and/or skeletal remains is only one aspect.

Processing scenes of mass fatality or incidents of terrorism (i.e. homicide, mass graves and war crimes, and other violations of human rights) is a branch of work that forensic archaeologists are involved with as well.

Forensic archaeologists can help determine potential grave sites that might have been overlooked. Differences in the soil can help forensic archaeologists locate these sites. During the burial of a body, a small mound of soil will form from the filling of the grave. The loose soil and increasing nutrients from the decomposing body encourages different kinds of plant growth than surrounding areas. Typically, grave sites will have looser, darker, more organic soil than areas around it. The search for additional grave sites can be useful during the investigation of genocide and mass graves to search for additional burial locations.

One other implement to the career of a forensic archaeologist is teaching and research. Educating law enforcement, crime scene technicians and investigators, as well as undergraduate and graduate students is a critical part of a forensic archaeologist's career in order to spread knowledge of proper excavation techniques to other forensic personnel and to increase awareness of the field in general. Crime scene evidence in the past has been compromised due to improper excavation and recovery by untrained personnel. Forensic anthropologists are then unable to provide meaningful analyses on retrieved skeletal remains due to damage or contamination. Research conducted to improve archaeological field methods, particularly to advance nondestructive methods of search and recovery are also important for the advancement and recognition of the field.

There is an ethical component that must be considered. The capability to uncover information about victims of war crimes or homicide may present a conflict in cases that involve competing interests. Forensic archaeologists are often contracted to assist with the processing of mass graves by larger organisations that have motives related to exposure and prosecution rather than providing peace of mind to families and communities. These projects are at times opposed by smaller, human rights groups who wish to avoid overshadowing memories of the individuals with their violent manner(s) of death. In cases like these, forensic archaeologists must practice caution and recognize the implications behind their work and the information they uncover.

Forensic Taphonomy

The examination of remains can help build a peri and post-mortem profile of the individual.

The examination of skeletal remains often takes into account environmental factors that affect decomposition. Forensic taphonomy is the study of these postmortem changes to human remains caused by soil, water, and the interaction with plants, insects, and other animals. In order to study these effects, body farms have been set up by multiple universities. Students and faculty study various environmental effects on the decomposition of donated cadavers. At these locations, cadavers are placed in various situations and their rate of decomposition along with any other factors related to the decomposition process are studied. Potential research projects can include whether black plastic causes decomposition to occur faster than clear plastic or the effects freezing can have on a dumped body.

Forensic taphonomy is divided into two separate sections, biotaphonomy and geotaphonomy. Biotaphonomy is the study of how the environment affects the decomposition of the body. Specifically it is the examination of biological remains in order to ascertain how decomposition or destruction occurred. This can include factors such as animal scavenging, climate, as well as the size and age of the individual at the time of death. Biotaphonomy must also take into account common mortuary services such as embalming and their effects on decomposition.

Geotaphonomy is the examination of how the decomposition of the body affects the environment. Geotaphonomy examinations can include how the soil was disturbed, pH alteration of the surrounding area, and either the acceleration or deceleration of plant growth around the body. By examining these characteristics, examiners can begin to piece together a timeline of the events during and after death. This can potentially help determine the time since death, whether or not trauma on the skeleton was a result of peri or post-mortem activity, as well as if scattered remains were the result of scavengers or a deliberate attempt to conceal the remains by an assailant.

Education

Forensic Anthropology Lab at the National Museum of National History, Smithsonian Institution, Washington D.C.

Individuals looking to become forensic anthropologists first obtain a bachelor's degree in anthropology from an accredited university. During their studies they should focus on physical anthropology as well as osteology. In addition it is recommended that individuals take courses in a wide range of sciences such as biology, chemistry, anatomy, and genetics.

Once undergraduate education is completed the individual should proceed to graduate level courses. Typically, forensic anthropologists obtain doctorates in physical anthropology and have completed coursework in osteology, forensics, and archaeology. It is also recommended that individuals looking to pursue a forensic anthropology profession get experience in dissection usually through a gross anatomy class as well as useful internships with investigative agencies or practicing anthropologists. Once educational requirements are complete one can become certified by the forensic anthropology society in the region. This can include the IALM exam given by the Forensic Anthropology Society of Europe or the certification exam given by the American Board of Forensic Anthropology.

Typically, most forensic anthropologists perform forensic casework on a part-time basis, however there are individuals who work in the field full-time usually with federal or international agencies. Forensic anthropologists are usually employed in academia either at a university or a research facility.

Ethics

Like other forensic fields, forensic anthropologists are held to a high level of ethical standards due to their work in the legal system. Individuals who purposefully misrepresent themselves or any piece of evidence can be sanctioned, fined, or imprisoned by the appropriate authorities depending on the severity of the violation. Individuals who fail to disclose any conflict of interests or who fail to report all of their findings, regardless of what they may be, can face disciplinary actions. It is important that forensic anthropologists remain impartial during the course of an investigation. Any perceived bias during an investigation could hamper efforts in court to bring the responsible parties to justice.

In addition to the evidentiary guidelines forensic anthropologists should always keep in mind that the remains they are working with were once a person. If possible, local customs regarding dealing with the dead should be observed and all remains should be treated with respect and dignity.

Forensic Facial Reconstruction

Tsar Ivan the Terrible of Russia. Reconstruction by M. Gerasimov, Soviet archaeologist and anthropologist who developed the first technique of forensic sculpture. 1965

Forensic facial reconstruction (or forensic facial approximation) is the process of recreating the face of an individual (whose identity is often not known) from their skeletal remains through an amalgamation of artistry, forensic science, anthropology, osteology, and anatomy. It is easily the most subjective—as well as one of the most controversial—techniques in the field of forensic anthropology. Despite this controversy, facial reconstruction has proved successful frequently enough that research and methodological developments continue to be advanced.

In addition to remains involved in criminal investigations, facial reconstructions are created for remains believed to be of historical value and for remains of prehistoric hominids and humans.

Legal Admissibility

In the U.S., the Daubert Standard is a legal precedent set in 1993 by the Supreme Court regarding the admissibility of expert witness testimony during legal proceedings, set in place to ensure that expert testimony is based on sufficient facts or data, derived from proper application of reliable principles and methods. When multiple forensic artists produce approximations for the same set of skeletal remains, no two reconstructions are ever the same and the data from which approximations are created are largely incomplete. Because of this, forensic facial reconstruction does not uphold the Daubert Standard, is not considered a legally recognized techniques for positive identification, and is not admissible as expert testimony. Currently, reconstructions are only produced to aid the process of positive identification in conjunction with verified methods.

Types of Identification

There are two types of identification in forensic anthropology: circumstantial and positive.

- Circumstantial identification is established when an individual fits the biological profile of a set of skeletal remains. This type of identification does not prove or verify identity because any number of individuals may fit the same biological description.

- Positive identification, one of the foremost goals of forensic science, is established when a unique set of biological characteristics of an individual are matched with a set of skeletal remains. This type of identification requires the skeletal remains to correspond with medical or dental records, unique ante mortem wounds or pathologies, DNA analysis, and still other means.

Facial reconstruction presents investigators and family members involved in criminal cases concerning unidentified remains with a unique alternative when all other identification techniques have failed. Facial approximations often provide the stimuli that eventually lead to the positive identification of remains.

Types of Reconstructions

Two-dimensional Reconstructions

Two-dimensional facial reconstructions are based on ante mortem photographs, and the skull. Occasionally skull radiographs are used but this is not ideal since many cranial structures are not visible or at the correct scale. This method usually requires the collaboration of an artist and a forensic anthropologist. A commonly used method of 2D facial reconstruction was pioneered by Karen T. Taylor of Austin, Texas during the 1980s. Taylor's method involves adhering tissue depth markers on an unidentified skull at various anthropological landmarks, then photographing the skull. Life-size or one-to-one frontal and lateral photographic prints are then used as a foundation for facial drawings done on transparent vellum. Recently developed, the F.A.C.E. and C.A.R.E.S. computer software programs quickly produce two-dimensional facial approximations that can be edited and manipulated with relative ease. These programs may help speed the reconstruction process and allow subtle variations to be applied to the drawing, though they may produce more generic images than hand-drawn artwork.

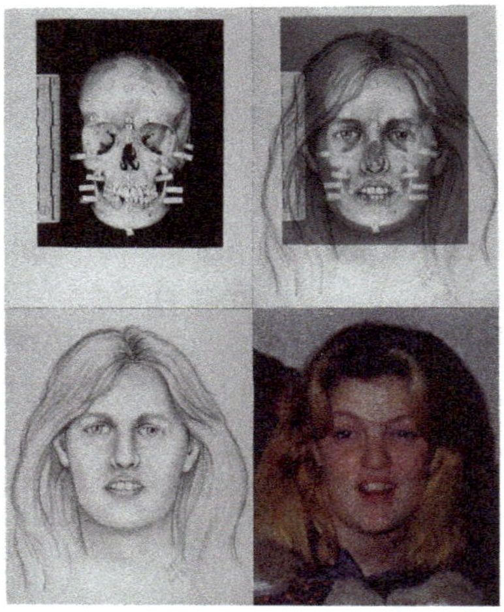

An example of a 2D facial reconstruction conducted by forensic artist Karen T. Taylor, and the subsequent identification, April Dawn Lacy.

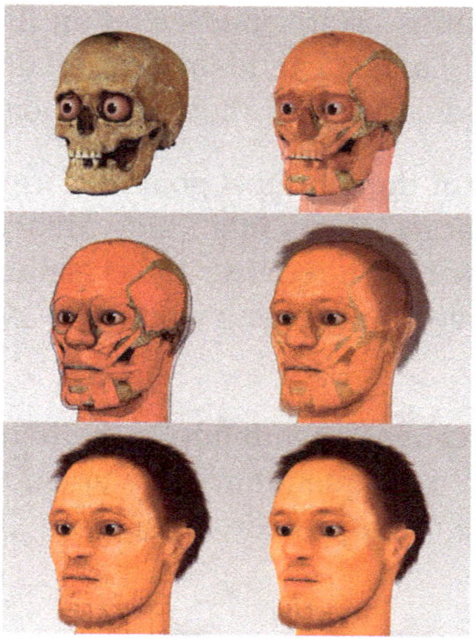

Forensic facial reconstruction of Alberto di Trento by Arc-Team and the 3D artist Cicero Moraes

Three-dimensional Reconstructions

Three-dimensional facial reconstructions are either: 1) sculptures (made from casts of cranial remains) created with modeling clay and other materials or 2) high-resolution, three-dimensional computer images. Like two-dimensional reconstructions, three-dimensional reconstructions usually require both an artist and a forensic anthropologist. Computer programs create three-dimensional reconstructions by manipulating scanned photographs of the unidentified cranial remains, stock photographs of facial features, and other available reconstructions. These computer approximations are usually most effective in victim identification because they do not appear too artificial. This method has been adapted by the National Center for Missing & Exploited Children, which uses this method often to show approximations of an unidentified decedent to release to the public in hopes to identify the subject.

Superimposition

Superimposition is a technique that is sometimes included among the methods of forensic facial reconstruction. It is not always included as a technique because investigators must already have some kind of knowledge about the identity of the skeletal remains with which they are dealing (as opposed to 2D and 3D reconstructions, when the identity of the skeletal remains are generally completely unknown). Forensic superimpositions are created by superimposing a photograph of an individual suspected of belonging to the unidentified skeletal remains over an X-ray of the unidentified skull. If the skull and the photograph are of the same individual, then the anatomical features of the face should align accurately.

History

Hermann Welcker in 1883 and Wilhelm His, Sr. in 1895, were the first to reproduce three-dimensional facial approximations from cranial remains. Most sources, however, acknowledge His as the forerunner in advancing the technique. His also produced the first data on average facial tissue thickness followed by Kollmann and Buchly who later collected additional data and compiled tables that are still referenced in most laboratories working on facial reproductions today.

Facial reconstruction originated in two of the four major subfields of anthropology. In biological anthropology, they were used to approximate the appearance of early hominid forms, while in archaeology they were used to validate the remains of historic figures. In 1964, Mikhail Gerasimov was probably the first to attempt paleo-anthropological facial reconstruction to estimate the appearance of ancient peoples

Although students of Gerasimov later used his techniques to aid in criminal investigations, it was Wilton M. Krogman who popularized facial reconstruction's application to the forensic field. Krogman presented his method for facial reconstruction in his 1962 book, detailing his method for approximation. Others who helped popularize three-dimensional facial reconstruction include Cherry (1977), Angel (1977), Gatliff (1984), Snow (1979), and Iscan (1986).

In 2004 it was noted by Dr. Andrew Nelson of the University of Western Ontario, Department of Anthropology that noted Canadian artist Christian Corbet created the first forensic facial reconstruction of an approximately 2,200-year-old mummy based on CT and laser scans. This reconstruction is known as the Sulman Mummy project.

Technique for Creating a Three-dimensional Clay Reconstruction

Because a standard method for creating three-dimensional forensic facial reconstructions has not been widely agreed upon, multiple methods and techniques are used. The process detailed below reflects the method presented by Taylor and Angel from their chapter in Craniofacial Identification in Forensic

Medicine, pgs 177-185. This method assumes that the sex, age, and race of the remains to undergo facial reconstruction have already been determined through traditional forensic anthropological techniques.

The skull is the basis of facial reconstruction; however, other physical remains that are sometimes available often prove to be valuable. Occasionally, remnants of soft tissue are found on a set of remains. Through close inspection, the forensic artist can easily approximate the thickness of the soft tissue over the remaining areas of the skull based on the presence of these tissues. This eliminates one of the most difficult aspects of reconstruction, the estimation of tissue thickness. Additionally, any other bodily or physical evidence found in association with remains (e.g. jewelry, hair, glasses, etc.) are vital to the final stages of reconstruction because they directly reflect the appearance of the individual in question.

Steps of forensic facial reconstruction of a mummy

Most commonly, however, only the bony skull and minimal or no other soft tissues are present on the remains presented to forensic artists. In this case, a thorough examination of the skull is completed. This examination focuses on, but is not limited to, the identification of any bony pathologies or unusual landmarks, ruggedness of muscle attachments, profile of the mandible, symmetry of the nasal bones, dentition, and wear of the occlusal surfaces. All of these features have an effect on the appearance of an individual's face.

Once the examination is complete, the skull is cleaned and any damaged or fragmented areas are repaired with wax. The mandible is then reattached, again with wax, according to the alignment of teeth, or, if no teeth are present, by averaging the vertical dimensions between the mandible and maxilla. Undercuts (like the nasal openings) are filled in with modeling clay and prosthetic eyes are inserted into the orbits centered between the superior and inferior orbital rims. At this point, a plaster cast of the skull is prepared.

After the cast is set, colored plastics or the colored ends of safety matches are attached at twenty-one specific "landmark" areas that correspond to the reference data. These sites represent the average facial tissue thickness for persons of the same sex, race, and age as that of the remains. From this point on, all features are added using modeling clay.

First, the facial muscles are layered onto the cast in the following order: temporalis, masseter, buccinator and occipito-frontals, and finally the soft tissues of the neck. Next, the nose and lips are reconstructed before any of the other muscles are formed. The lips are approximately as wide as the interpupillary distance. However, this distance varies significantly with age, sex, race, and occlusion. The nose is one of the most difficult facial features to reconstruct because the underlying bone is limited and the possibility of variation is expansive. The nasal profile is constructed by first measuring the width of the nasal aperture and the nasal spine. Using a calculation of three times the length of the spine plus the depth of tissue marker number five will yield the approximate nose length. Next, the pitch of the nose is determined by examining the direction of the nasal spine - down, flat, or up. A block of clay that is the proper length is then placed on the nasal spine and the remaining nasal tissue is filled in using tissue markers two and three as a guide for the bridge of the nose. The alae are created by first marking a point five millimeters below the bottom of the nasal aperture. After the main part of the nose is constructed, the alae are created as small egg-shaped balls of clay, that are five millimeters in diameter at the widest point, these are positioned on the sides of the nose corresponding with the mark made previously. The alae are then blended to the nose and the overall structure of the nose is rounded out and shaped appropriately.

The muscles of facial expression and the soft tissue around the eyes are added next. Additional measurements are made according to race (especially for those with eye folds characteristic of Asian descent) during this stage. Next, tissues are built up to within one millimeter of the tissue thickness markers and the ears (noted as being extremely complicated to reproduce) are added. Finally, the face is "fleshed," meaning clay is added until the tissue thickness markers are covered, and any specific characterization is added (for example, hair, wrinkles in the skin, noted racial traits, glasses, etc.). The skull of Mozart was the basis of his facial reconstruction from anthropological data. The bust was unveiled at the "Salon du Son", Paris, in 1991.

Problems with Facial Reconstruction

There are multiple outstanding problems associated with forensic facial reconstruction.

Insufficient Tissue Thickness Data

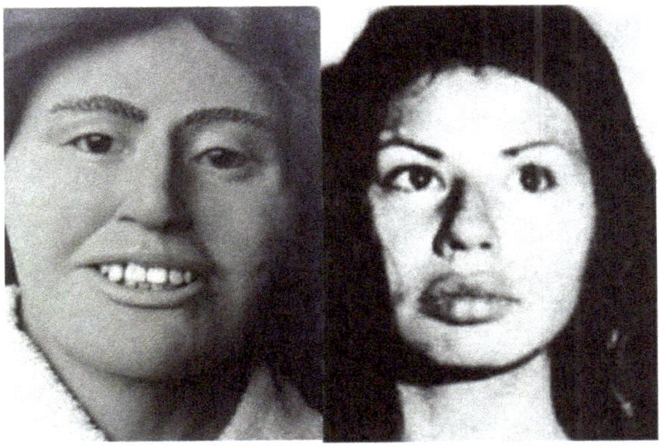

Reconstruction and actual photograph of Green River victim Gail Mathews. The victim had distinctive lips, which could not be represented in the reconstruction, as her body was decomposed.

The most pressing issue relates to the data used to average facial tissue thickness. The data available to forensic artists are still very limited in ranges of ages, sexes, and body builds. This disparity greatly affects the accuracy of reconstructions. Until this data is expanded, the likelihood of producing the most accurate reconstruction possible is largely limited.

In many cases, the subject's hairstyle is unknown, which causes an artist to guess possible solutions, such as this unidentified woman found in Ontario, Canada.

Lack of Methodological Standardization

A second problem is the lack of a methodological standardization in approximating facial features. A single, official method for reconstructing the face has yet to be recognized. This also presents major setback in facial approximation because facial features like the eyes and nose and individuating characteristics like hairstyle - the features most likely to be recalled by witnesses - lack a standard way of being reconstructed. Recent research on computer-assisted methods, which take advantage of digital image processing, pattern recognition, promises to overcome current limitations in facial reconstruction and linkage.

Subjectivity

Reconstructions only reveal the type of face a person *may* have exhibited because of artistic subjectivity. The position and general shape of the main facial features are mostly accurate because they are greatly determined by the skull.

In Popular Culture

The facial reconstruction of Tutankhamun as shown on the cover of *National Geographic* in 2005.

In recent years, the presence of forensic facial reconstructions in the entertainment industry and the media has increased. The way the fictional criminal investigators and forensic anthropologists utilize forensics and facial reconstructions are, however, often misrepresented (an influence known as the "CSI effect"). For example, the fictional forensic investigators will often call for the creation of a facial reconstruction as soon as a set of skeletal remains is discovered. In reality, facial reconstructions are widely used as a last resort to stimulate the possibility of identifying a victim.

Facial reconstruction has been featured as part of an array of forensic science methods in fictional TV shows like *CSI: Crime Scene Investigation* and *NCIS* and their respective spinoffs in the *CSI* and *NCIS* franchises.

In *Bones*, a long-running TV series centered around forensic analysis of decomposed and skeletal human remains, facial reconstruction is featured in the majority of episodes, used much like a police artist sketch in police procedurals. Regular cast character Angela Montenegro, the Bones team's facial reconstruction specialist, employs 3D software and holographic projection to "give victims back their faces" (as noted in the episode, "A Boy in a Bush").

In the *MacGyver* episode "The Secret Of Parker House", MacGyver reconstructs the skull of Penny's aunt Betty while investigating her house.

The facial reconstruction of Egypt's Tutankhamun, popularly known as King Tut, made the June 2005 cover of National Geographic Magazine.

A variety of facial reconstruction kits toys are available, with "crime scene" versions, also, reconstructions of famous historical figures, like King Tut and the dinosaur T-Rex.

Recently, facial reconstruction has been part of the process used by researchers attempting to identify human remains of two Canadian Army soldiers lost in World War I. One soldier was identified through DNA analysis in 2007, but due to DNA deterioration, identifying the second using the same techniques failed. In 2011, the second of the soldiers' remains discovered at Avion, France were identified through a combination of 3-D printing software, reconstructive sculpture and use of isotopic analysis of bone.

Forensic Arts

Forensic art is any art used in law enforcement or legal proceedings. Within this field are such skills as composite drawing, crime scene sketching, image modification and image identification, courtroom drawings, demonstrative evidence, and postmortem and facial approximation aids. Not every forensic artist uses all of these skills.

The term *forensic* comes from the Roman forum where law and politics were debated. From this beginning, the word *forensic* now means anything pertaining to law or law enforcement or debate.

The skill of facial approximation is closely associated and related to forensic anthropology in that an artist specializes in the reconstruction of the remains of a human body. Generally this discipline focuses on the human face for identification purposes. The forensic artist can create a facial approximation in a number of ways to include 2D (drawing), 3D (sculpture) and by methods using new computerized technology. Forensic artists generally can add greater character and make their subjects come back to "life".

Most forensic artists do the job as a collateral duty to their "regular" job in law enforcement, such as police officer, crime scene tech, etc. They do the work on salary, and normally are not paid extra for it. There are extremely few full-time forensic artist jobs to be had. Most full-time artists work in large cities, or in state or federal agencies. "Freelancing" in forensic art is extremely difficult to build as a career, as ties to law enforcement are a necessary part of the job, and agencies have limited budgets to pay contractors.

A well known (fictional) Forensic Artist is Angela Montenegro from the television series Bones.

References

- Riggs, Robert (11 September 2011). "Robert Riggs Reports Forensic Artist Reconstructs Victims Faces May 2004". Retrieved 13 January 2015
- Crumbley, D. Larry; Heitger, Lester E.; Smith, G. Stevenson (2005-08-05). Forensic and Investigative Accounting. CCH Group. ISBN 0-8080-1365-3
- Spencer, Frank (1981). "The Rise of Academic Physical Anthropology in the United States (1880-1980)". American Journal of Physical Anthropology. 56: 353–364. doi:10.1002/ajpa.1330560407
- "Reconstruction of Scene by Forensic Animation Two Case Reports" (PDF). J Indian Acad Forensic Med.Vol. 36, No. 1. January 2014. Retrieved 24 June 2014
- Cicchella, Denise (2005). Construction audit guide: overview, monitoring, and auditing. Altamonte Springs, FL: IIA Research Foundation. ISBN 0-89413-587-2
- Golda, Stephanie (2010). "A Look at the History of Forensic Anthropology: Tracing My Academic Genealogy". Journal of Contemporary Anthropology. 1
- Elson, Rachel (May 9, 2004). "Piecing together the victims of genocide / Forensic anthropologist identifies remains, but questions about their deaths remain". SFGate. Retrieved August 18, 2015
- Steele, Caroline (2008-08-20). "Archaeology and the Forensic Investigation of Recent Mass Graves: Ethical Issues for a New Practice of Archaeology". Archaeologies. 4 (3): 414–428. ISSN 1555-8622. doi:10.1007/s11759-008-9080-x
- Parr, Russell L.; Smith, Gordon V. (2010). Intellectual property: valuation, exploitation, and infringement damages. Hoboken, N.J.: Wiley. pp. Chapter 33. ISBN 0-470-45703-1
- Trotter, M.; Gleser, G.C. (1952). "Estimation of Stature from Long Bones of American Whites and Negroes". American Journal of Physical Anthropology. 10: 463–514. doi:10.1002/ajpa.1330100407
- McFadden, Robert (May 16, 2014). "Clyde Snow, Sleuth Who Read Bones From King Tut's to Kennedy's, Dies at 86". Retrieved September 28, 2015
- Nigrini, Mark (June 2011). "Forensic Analytics: Methods and Techniques for Forensic Accounting Investigations". Hoboken, NJ: John Wiley & Sons Inc. ISBN 978-0-470-89046-2
- "Quick Tips: How To Estimate The Chronological Age Of A Human Skeleton — The Basics". All Things AAFS!. August 20, 2013. Retrieved August 20, 2015
- Snow, Clyde Collins (1982). "Forensic Anthropology". Annual Review of Anthropology. 11: 97–131. doi:10.1146/annurev.an.11.100182.000525
- Quiring, Tami (March 22, 2011). "3D Printing Technology Helped Identify Canadian WW1 Soldier". Village Gamer. Aldergrove, British Columbia. Retrieved 23 June 2012

4

An Introduction to Forensic Engineering

Forensic engineering is the study of the objects that cause injury to any person or property due of a technical error in the product. This subject can be applied to both criminal and civil legal cases. Unexpected structural failures are a key event to which forensic engineering is applied. The chapter strategically encompasses and incorporates the major components and key concepts of forensic engineering, providing a complete understanding.

Forensic Engineering

Forensic engineering is the investigation of materials, products, structures or components that fail or do not operate or function as intended, causing personal injury or damage to property. The consequences of failure are dealt with by the law of product liability. The field also deals with retracing processes and procedures leading to accidents in operation of vehicles or machinery. The subject is applied most commonly in civil law cases, although it may be of use in criminal law cases. Generally, the purpose of a forensic engineering investigation is to locate cause or causes of failure with a view to improve performance or life of a component, or to assist a court in determining the facts of an accident. It can also involve investigation of intellectual property claims, especially patents.

History

As the field of engineering has evolved over time, so has the field of forensic engineering. Early examples include investigation of bridge failures such as the Tay rail bridge disaster of 1879 and the Dee bridge disaster of 1847. Many early rail accidents prompted the invention of tensile testing of samples and fractography of failed components.

Investigation

Vital to the field of forensic engineering is the process of investigating and collecting data related to the materials, products, structures or components that failed. This involves inspections, collecting evidence, measurements, developing models, obtaining exemplar products, and performing experiments. Often testing and measurements are conducted in an Independent testing laboratory or other reputable unbiased laboratory.

Analysis

Failure mode and effects analysis (FMEA) and fault tree analysis methods also examine product or process failure in a structured and systematic way, in the general context of safety engineering. However, all such techniques rely on accurate reporting of failure rates, and precise identification, of the failure modes involved.

There is some common ground between forensic science and forensic engineering, such as scene of crime and scene of accident analysis, integrity of the evidence and court appearances. Both disciplines make extensive use of optical and scanning electron microscopes, for example. They also share common use of spectroscopy (infrared, ultraviolet, and nuclear magnetic resonance) to examine critical evidence. Radiography using X-rays (such as X-ray computed tomography), or neutrons is also very useful in examining thick products for their internal defects before destructive examination is attempted. Often, however, a simple hand lens may reveal the cause of a particular problem.

Trace evidence is sometimes an important factor in reconstructing the sequence of events in an accident. For example, tire burn marks on a road surface can enable vehicle speeds to be estimated, when the brakes were applied and so on. Ladder feet often leave a trace of movement of the ladder during a slipaway, and may show how the accident occurred. When a product fails for no obvious reason, SEM and Energy-dispersive Xray spectroscopy (EDX) performed in the microscope can reveal the presence of aggressive chemicals that have left traces on the fracture or adjacent surfaces. Thus an acetal resin water pipe joint suddenly failed and caused substantial damages to a building in which it was situated. Analysis of the joint showed traces of chlorine, indicating a stress corrosion cracking failure mode. The failed fuel pipe junction mentioned above showed traces of sulfur on the fracture surface from the sulfuric acid, which had initiated the crack.

Extracting physical evidence from digital photography is a major technique used in forensic accident reconstruction. Camera matching, photogrammetry, and photo rectification techniques are used to create three-dimensional and top-down views from the two-dimensional photos typically taken at an accident scene. Overlooked or undocumented evidence for accident reconstruction can be retrieved and quantified as long as photographs of such evidence are available. By using photographs of the accident scene including the vehicle, "lost" evidence can be recovered and accurately determined.

Forensic materials engineering involves methods applied to specific materials, such as metals, glasses, ceramics, composites and polymers.

Examples

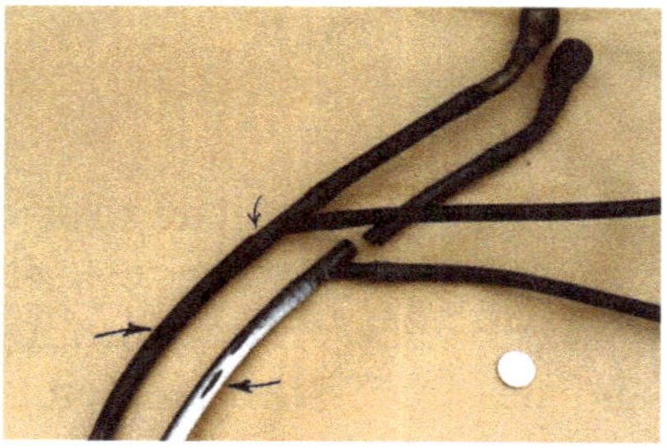

Failed fuel pipe at right from a road traffic accident.

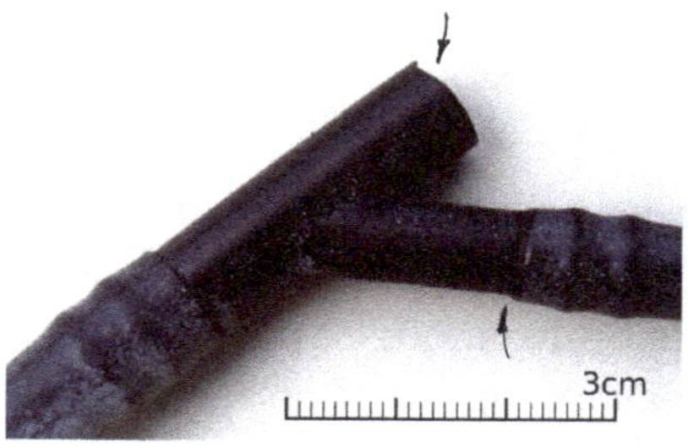

Close-up of the broken fuel pipe from a road traffic accident.

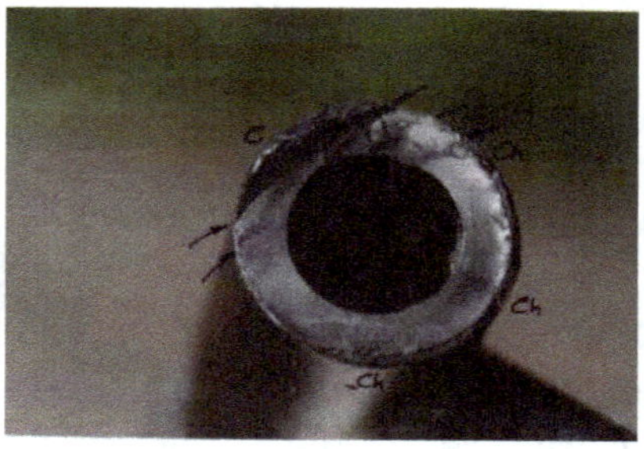

Close-up of the broken fuel pipe.

The broken fuel pipe shown at left caused a serious accident when diesel fuel poured out from a van onto the road. A following car skidded and the driver was seriously injured when she collided with an oncoming lorry. Scanning electron microscopy or SEM showed that the nylon connector had fractured by stress corrosion cracking (SCC) due to a small leak of battery acid. Nylon is susceptible to hydrolysis when in contact with sulfuric acid, and only a small leak of acid would have sufficed to start a brittle crack in the injection moulded nylon 6,6 connector by SCC. The crack took about 7 days to grow across the diameter of the tube. The fracture surface showed a mainly brittle surface with striations indicating progressive growth of the crack across the diameter of the pipe. Once the crack had penetrated the inner bore, fuel started leaking onto the road.

The nylon 6,6 had been attacked by the following reaction, which was catalyzed by the acid:

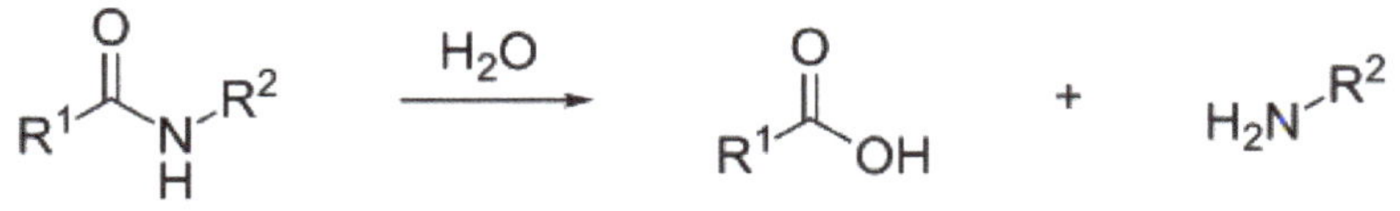

Diesel fuel is especially hazardous on road surfaces because it forms a thin, oily film that cannot be easily seen by drivers. It is much like black ice in its slipperiness, so skids are common when diesel leaks occur. The insurers of the van driver admitted liability and the injured driver was compensated.

Applications

Most manufacturing models will have a forensic component that monitors early failures to improve quality or efficiencies. Insurance companies use forensic engineers to prove liability or non-liability. Most engineering disasters (structural failures such as bridge and building collapses) are subject to forensic investigation by engineers experienced in forensic methods of investigation. Rail crashes, aviation accidents, and some automobile accidents are investigated by forensic engineers in particular where component failure is suspected. Furthermore, appliances, consumer products, medical devices, structures, industrial machinery, and even simple hand tools such as hammers or chisels can warrant investigations upon incidents causing injury or property damages. The failure of medical devices is often safety-critical to the user, so reporting failures and analysing them is particularly important. The environment of the body is complex, and implants must both survive this environment, and not leach potentially toxic impurities. Problems have been reported with breast implants, heart valves, and catheters, for example.

Failures that occur early in the life of a new product are vital information for the manufacturer to improve the product. New product development aims to eliminate defects by testing in the factory before launch, but some may occur during its early life. Testing products to simulate their behavior in the external environment is a difficult skill, and may involve accelerated life testing for example. The worst kind of defect to occur after launch is a safety-critical defect, a defect that can endanger life or limb. Their discovery usually leads to a product recall or even complete withdrawal of the product from the market. Product defects often follow the bathtub curve, with high initial failures, a lower rate during regular life, followed by another rise due to wear-out. National standards, such as those of ASTM and the British Standards Institute, and International Standards can help the designer in increasing product integrity.

Historic Examples

There are many examples of forensic methods used to investigate accidents and disasters, one of the earliest in the modern period being the fall of the Dee bridge at Chester, England. It was built using cast iron girders, each of which was made of three very large castings dovetailed together. Each girder was strengthened by wrought iron bars along the length. It was finished in September 1846, and opened for local traffic after approval by the first Railway Inspector, General Charles Pasley. However, on 24 May 1847, a local train to Ruabon fell through the bridge. The accident resulted in five deaths (three passengers, the train guard, and the locomotive fireman) and nine serious injuries. The bridge had been designed by Robert Stephenson, and he was accused of negligence by a local inquest.

Dee bridge disaster.

Although strong in compression, cast iron was known to be brittle in tension or bending. On the day of the accident, the bridge deck was covered with track ballast to prevent the oak beams supporting the track from catching fire, imposing a heavy extra load on the girders supporting the bridge and probably exacerbating the accident. Stephenson took this precaution because of a recent fire on the Great Western Railway at Uxbridge, London, where Isambard Kingdom Brunel's bridge caught fire and collapsed.

One of the first major inquiries conducted by the newly formed Railway Inspectorate was conducted by Captain Simmons of the Royal Engineers, and his report suggested that repeated flexing of the girder weakened it substantially. He examined the broken parts of the main girder, and confirmed that the girder had broken in two places, the first break occurring at the center. He tested the remaining girders by driving a locomotive across them, and found that they deflected by several inches under the moving load. He concluded that the design was flawed, and that the wrought iron trusses fixed to the girders did not reinforce the girders at all, which was a conclusion also reached by the jury at the inquest. Stephenson's design had depended on the wrought iron trusses to strengthen the final structures, but they were anchored on the cast iron girders themselves, and so deformed with any load on the bridge. Others (especially Stephenson) argued that the train had derailed and hit the girder, the impact force causing it to fracture. However, eyewitnesses maintained that the girder broke first and the fact that the locomotive remained on the track showed otherwise.

Forensic Materials Engineering

Forensic materials engineering, a branch of forensic engineering, focuses on the material evidence from crime or accident scenes, seeking defects in those materials which might explain why an accident occurred, or the source of a specific material to identify a criminal. Many analytical methods used for material identification may be used in investigations, the exact set being determined by the nature of the material in question, be it metal, glass, ceramic, polymer or composite. An important aspect is the analysis of trace evidence such as skid marks on exposed surfaces, where contact between dissimilar materials leaves material traces of one left on the other. Provided the traces can be analysed successfully, then an accident or crime can often be reconstructed. Another aim will be to determine the cause of a broken component using the technique of fractography.

Metals and Alloys

Crankshaft fatigue fracture

Metal and alloy surfaces can be analyzed in a number of ways, including by spectroscopy and EDX used during scanning electron microscopy. The nature and composition of the metal can normally be established by sectioning and polishing the bulk, and examining the flat section using optical microscopy after etching solutions have been used to provide contrast in the section between alloy constituents. Such solutions (often an acid) attack the surface preferentially, so isolating features or inclusions of one composition, enabling them to be seen much more clearly than in the polished but untreated surface. Metallography is a routine technique for examining the microstructure of metals, but can also be applied to ceramics, glasses and polymers. SEM can often be critical in determining failures modes by examining fracture surfaces. The origin of a crack can be found and the way it grew assessed, to distinguish, for example, overload failure from fatigue. Often however, fatigue fractures are easy to distinguish from overload failures by the lack of ductility, and the existence of a fast crack growth region and the slow crack growth area on the fracture surface. Crankshaft fatigue for example is a common failure mode for engine parts. The example shows just two such zones, the slow crack at the base, the fast at the top.

Ceramics and Glasses

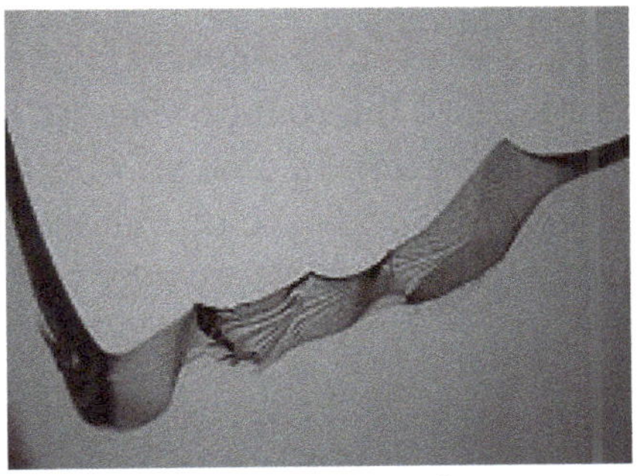

Brittle fracture in glass

Hard products like ceramic pottery and glass windscreens can be studied using the same SEM methods used for metals, especially ESEM conducted at low vacuum. Fracture surfaces are especially valuable sources of information because surface features like hachures can enable the origin or origins of the cracks to be found. Analysis of the surface features is carried out using fractography.

The position of the origin can then be matched with likely loads on the product to show how an accident occurred, for example. Inspection of bullet holes can often show the direction of travel and energy of the impact, and the way common glass products like bottles can be analysed to show whether deliberately or accidentally broken in a crime or accident. Defects such as foreign particles will often occur near or at the origin of the critical crack, and can be readily identified by ESEM.

Polymers and Composites

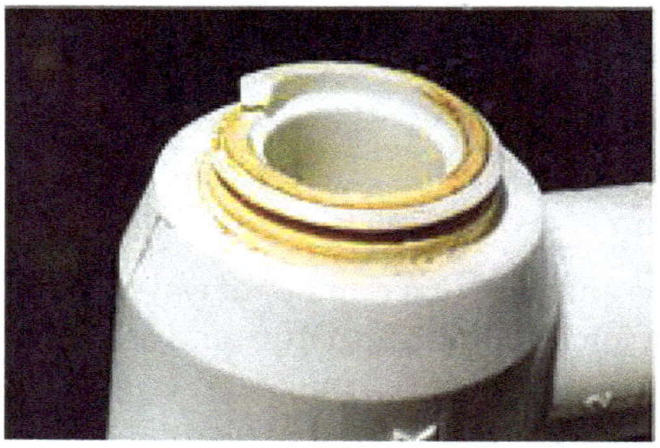

chlorine attack of acetal resin plumbing joint

Thermoplastics, thermosets, and composites can be analyzed using FTIR and UV spectroscopy as well as NMR and ESEM. Failed samples can either be dissolved in a suitable solvent and examined directly (UV, IR and NMR sepctroscopy) or as a thin film cast from solvent or cut using microtomy from the solid product. The slicing method is preferable since there are no complications from solvent absorption, and the integrity of the sample is partly preserved. Fractured products can be examined using fractography, an especially useful method for all fractured components using macrophotography and optical microscopy. Although polymers usually possess quite different properties to metals and ceramics, they are just as susceptible to failure from mechanical overload, fatigue and stress corrosion cracking if products are poorly designed or manufactured. Many plastics are susceptible to attack by active chemicals like chlorine, present at low levels in potable water supplies, especially if the injection mouldings are faulty.

ESEM is especially useful for providing elemental analysis from viewed parts of the sample being investigated. It is effectively a technique of microanalysis and valuable for examination of trace evidence. On the other hand, colour rendition is absent, and there is no information provided about the way in which those elements are bonded to one another. Specimens will be exposed to a vacuum, so any volatiles may be removed, and surfaces may be contaminated by substances used to attach the sample to the mount.

Elastomers

Rubber products are often safety-critical parts of machines, so that failure can often cause accidents or loss of function. Failed products can be examined with many of the generic polymer methods, although it is more difficult if the sample is vulcanized or cross-linked. Attenuated total reflectance infra-red spectroscopy is useful because the product is usually flexible so can be pressed against the selenium crystal used for analysis. Simple swelling tests can also help to identify the specific elastomer used in a product. Often the best technique is ESEM using the X-ray elemental analysis facility on the microscope. Although the method only provides elemental analysis, it can provide clues as to the identity of the elastomer being examined. Thus the presence of substantial amounts of chlorine indicates polychloroprene while the presence of nitrogen indicates nitrile rubber. The method is also useful in confirming ozone cracking by the large amounts of oxygen present on cracked surfaces. Ozone attacks susceptible elastomers such as natural rubber, nitrile rubber and polybutadiene and associated copolymers. Such elastomers possess double bonds in their main chains, the group which is attacked during ozonolysis.

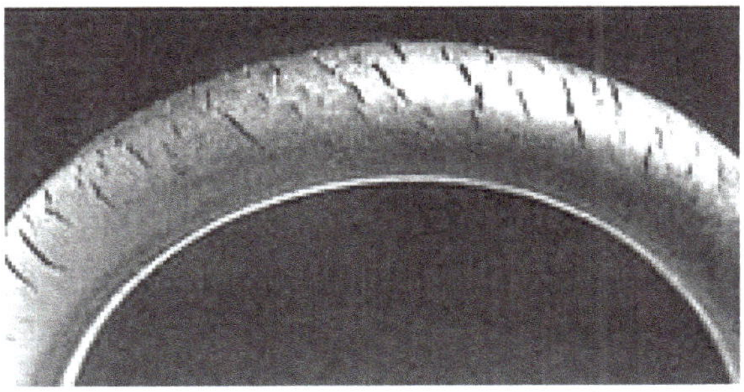

Ozone cracking in Natural rubber tubing

The problem occurs when small concentrations of ozone gas are present near to exposed elastomer surfaces, such as O-rings and diaphragm seals. The product must be in tension, but only very low strains are sufficient to cause degradation.

Forensic Electrical Engineering

Forensic electrical engineering is a branch of forensic engineering, and is concerned with investigating electrical failures and accidents in a legal context. Many forensic electrical engineering investigations apply to fires suspected to be caused by electrical failures. Forensic electrical engineers are most commonly retained by insurance companies or attorneys representing insurance companies, or by manufacturers or contractors defending themselves against subrogation by insurance companies. Other areas of investigation include accident investigation involving electrocution, and intellectual property disputes such as patent actions. Additionally, since electrical fires are most often cited as the cause for "suspect" fires an electrical engineer is often employed to evaluate the electrical equipment and systems to determine whether the cause of the fire was electrical in nature.

Goals

The ultimate goal of these investigations is often to determine the legal liability for a fire or other accident for purposes of insurance subrogation or an injury lawsuit. Some examples include:

- *Defective appliances*: If a property fire was caused by an appliance which had a manufacturing or design defect (for example, a coffee maker overheating and igniting), making it unreasonably hazardous, the insurance company might attempt to collect the cost of the fire damage ("subrogate") from the manufacturer; if the fire caused personal injury or death, the injured party might also attempt an injury lawsuit against the manufacturer, in addition to the carrier of health or life insurance attempting subrogation.

- *Improper workmanship*: If, for example, an electrician made an improper installation in a house, leading to an electrical fault and fire, he or she could likewise be the target of subrogation or an injury lawsuit (for this reason, electricians are required to carry liability insurance).
- *Electrical injury*: If an electrical fault or unreasonably hazardous electrical system causes an electrical injury ("electrocution" if the injury is fatal), the party responsible for the electrical accident can be the target of insurance subrogation or an injury lawsuit.
- *Equipment failure*: if electrical equipment stops functioning, it can cause a loss of income (such as a factory losing productivity due to inoperative equipment) or additional damage (such as food products spoiling due to loss of refrigeration), and again be the subject of a subrogation or liability case. Liability in such a case can also include the cost of repairing or replacing the equipment, which can be substantial.

Applications

Forensic electrical engineers are also involved in some arson and set-fire investigations; while it is not common for arsonists to cause electrical failures to ignite fires, the presence of electrical appliances and systems in many fires scenes often requires them to be evaluated as possible accidental causes of the fire. Some electrical means of ignition, when discovered, are fairly obvious to an origin and cause investigator and most likely do not require consulting with a forensic electrical engineer. (Note that "arson" refers specifically to a criminal act, subject to criminal prosecution; a more general term is a "set fire". A homeowner setting a fire deliberately in order to defraud an insurance company might be prosecuted for arson by a government body; however, the insurance company would concern itself only with denying the insurance claim, possibly leading to a civil lawsuit.)

Patent disputes may also require the expert opinion of an electrical engineer to advise a court. Issues in conflict may include the precise meaning of technical terms, especially in the patent claims, the prior art in a particular product field and the obviousness of various patents.

Liability

Most states have a statute of ultimate repose that limits the length of time after which a party can legally be held liable for their negligent act or defective product. Many states have a "useful life" statute of ultimate repose. Therefore, a determination of the length of time the product would normally be expected to be used before wearing out needs to be made. For example, a refrigerator might have a longer "useful life" than an electric fan; an airplane might have a longer useful life than a car. Some states pick an arbitrary number of years for the statute of ultimate repose. It may be short (six or seven years) or longer 15 or 25 years. If a coffee maker starts on fire after the statute of ultimate repose has expired, the manufacturer can no longer be held liable for manufacturing or design defects. The statute of ultimate repose is different from the statute of limitations. In a state with a short statute of ultimate repose, it is common that a person's right to bring a claim in court expires before their injury ever occurs. Thus, if a defective product (for example a car) caused a collision when the steering failed, but the collision occurred after the expiration of a statute of ultimate repose, no claim could be brought against the manufacturer for selling a defective product. The right to bring the claim expired before the claim even occurred.

References

- Evans, Ralph A. (January 5, 1976). Engineering Design Handbook Design for Reliability (PDF). US Army Materiel Command. AMCP-706-196. Retrieved 2014-05-17
- Kmenta, Steven; Ishii, Koshuke (2004). "Scenario-Based Failure Modes and Effects Analysis Using Expected Cost". Journal of Mechanical Design. 126 (6): 1027. doi:10.1115/1.1799614
- Center for Chemical Process Safety (April 2008). Guidelines for Hazard Evaluation Procedures (3rd ed.). Wiley. ISBN 978-0-471-97815-2
- Benner, Ludwig (1975). "Accident Theory and Accident Investigation". Proceedings of the Society of Air Safety Investigators Annual Seminar. Retrieved 2010-01-17
- Tay K. M.; Lim C.P. "n On the use of fuzzy inference techniques in assessment models: part II: industrial applications". Fuzzy Optimization and Decision Making. 7: 283–302. doi:10.1007/s10700-008-9037-y
- Kerk Y.W.; Tay K. M.; Lim C.P. "n Analytical Interval Fuzzy Inference System for Risk Evaluation and Prioritization in Failure Mode and Effect Analysis". IEEE Systems Journal: 1–12. doi:10.1109/JSYST.2015.2478150
- Center for Chemical Process Safety (October 1999). Guidelines for Chemical Process Quantitative Risk Analysis (2nd ed.). American Institute of Chemical Engineers. ISBN 978-0-8169-0720-5
- "7.9 Fault Tree Analysis". Electronic Reliability Design Handbook (pdf). B. U.S. Department of Defense. 1998. MIL–HDBK–338B. Retrieved 2010-01-17
- Chang, Wui Lee; Pang, Lie Meng; Tay, Kai Meng (March 2017). "Application of Self-Organizing Map to Failure Modes and Effects Analysis Methodology". Neurocomputing. PP: PP. doi:10.1016/j.neucom.2016.04.073

5

Methods of Evidence Collection

Fingerprints are detailed and are almost unique. Fingerprint analysis is used to identify people, making it easier to solve crimes. The other methods of evidence collection are blood residue, forensic footwear evidence, DNA profiling, skid mark, MABMAT and trace evidence. The topics discussed in the chapter are of great importance to broaden the existing knowledge on the methods used in evidence collection.

Fingerprint

A fingerprint in its narrow sense is an impression left by the friction ridges of a human finger. The recovery of fingerprints from a crime scene is an important method of forensic science. Fingerprints are easily deposited on suitable surfaces (such as glass or metal or polished stone) by the natural secretions of sweat from the eccrine glands that are present in epidermal ridges. These are sometimes referred to as "Chanced Impressions".

In a wider use of the term, fingerprints are the traces of an impression from the friction ridges of any part of a human or other primate hand. A print from the sole of the foot can also leave an impression of friction ridges.

Deliberate impressions of fingerprints may be formed by ink or other substances transferred from the peaks of friction ridges on the skin to a relatively smooth surface such as a fingerprint card. Fingerprint records normally contain impressions from the pad on the last joint of fingers and thumbs, although fingerprint cards also typically record portions of lower joint areas of the fingers.

Human fingerprints are detailed, nearly unique, difficult to alter, and durable over the life of an individual, making them suitable as long-term markers of human identity. They may be employed by police or other authorities to identify individuals who wish to conceal their identity, or to identify people who are incapacitated or deceased and thus unable to identify themselves, as in the aftermath of a natural disaster. Fingerprint analysis, in use since the early 20th century, has led to many crimes being solved. This means that many criminals consider gloves essential. In 2015, the identification of sex by use of a fingerprint test has been reported.

Biology

A friction ridge is a raised portion of the epidermis on the digits (fingers and toes), the palm of the hand or the sole of the foot, consisting of one or more connected ridge units of friction ridge skin. These are sometimes known as "epidermal ridges" which are caused by the underlying interface between the dermal papillae of the dermis and the interpapillary (rete) pegs of the epidermis. These epidermal ridges serve to amplify vibrations triggered, for example, when fingertips brush across an uneven surface, better transmitting the signals to sensory nerves involved in fine texture perception. These ridges may also assist in gripping rough surfaces and may improve surface contact in wet conditions.

Classifying

Before computerisation, manual filing systems were used in large fingerprint repositories. Manual classification systems were based on the general ridge patterns of several or all fingers (such as the presence or absence of circular patterns). This allowed the filing and retrieval of paper records in large collections based on friction ridge patterns alone. The most popular systems used the pattern class of each finger to form a key (a number) to assist lookup in a filing system. Classification systems include the Roscher system, the Juan Vucetich system, and the Henry Classification System. The Roscher system was developed in Germany and implemented in both Germany and Japan, the Vucetich system (developed by a Croatian-born Buenos Aires Police Officer) was developed in Argentina and implemented throughout South America, and the Henry system was developed in India and implemented in most English-speaking countries.

In the Henry system of classification, there are three basic fingerprint patterns: loop, whorl, and arch, which constitute 60–65%, 30–35%, and 5% of all fingerprints respectively. There are also more complex classification systems that break down patterns even further, into plain arches or tented arches, and into loops that may be radial or ulnar, depending on the side of the hand toward which the tail points. Ulnar loops start on the pinky-side of the finger, the side closer to the ulna, the lower arm bone. Radial loops start on the thumb-side of the finger, the side closer to the radius. Whorls may also have sub-group classifications including plain whorls, accidental whorls, double loop whorls, peacock's eye, composite, and central pocket loop whorls.

Other common fingerprint patterns include the tented arch, the plain arch, and the central pocket loop.

The system used by most experts, although complex, is similar to the Henry System of Classification. It consists of five fractions, in which *R* stands for right, *L* for left, *i* for index finger, *m* for middle finger, *t* for thumb, *r* for ring finger and *p*(pinky) for little finger. The fractions are as follows: $Ri/Rt + Rr/Rm + Lt/Rp + Lm/Li + Lp/Lr$. The numbers assigned to each print are based on whether or not they are whorls. A whorl in the first fraction is given a 16, the second an 8, the third a 4, the fourth a 2, and 0 to the last fraction. Arches and loops are assigned values of 0. Lastly, the numbers in the numerator and denominator are added up, using the scheme:

$$(Ri + Rr + Lt + Lm + Lp)/(Rt + Rm + Rp + Li + Lr)$$

and a 1 is added to both top and bottom, to exclude any possibility of division by zero. For example, if the right ring finger and the left index finger have whorls, the fractions would look like this:

> $0/0 + 8/0 + 0/0 + 0/2 + 0/0 + 1/1$, and the calculation: $(0 + 8 + 0 + 0 + 0 + 1)/(0 + 0 + 0 + 2 + 0 + 1) = 9/3 = 3$.

Using this system reduces the number of prints that the print in question needs to be compared to. For example, the above set of prints would only need to be compared to other sets of fingerprints with a value of 3.

		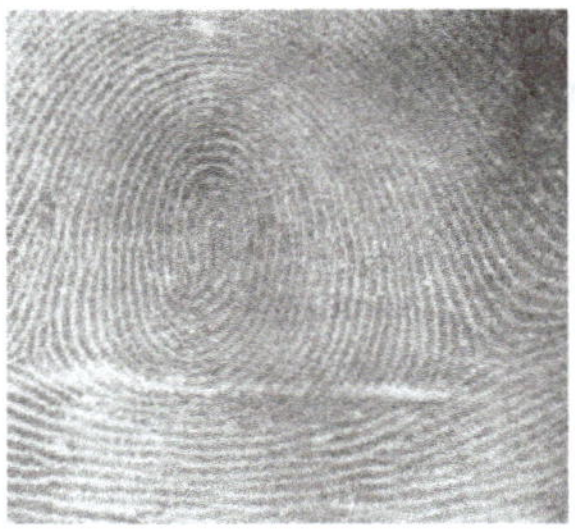	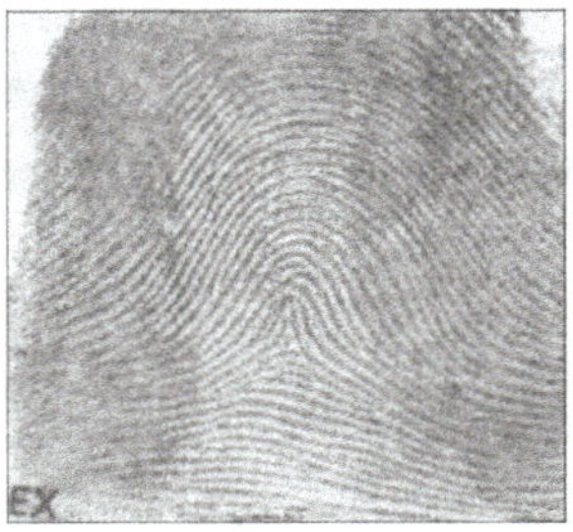
Arch	Loop (Right Loop)	Whorl	Arch (Tented Arch)

Identification and Classification of Individual Fingerprints

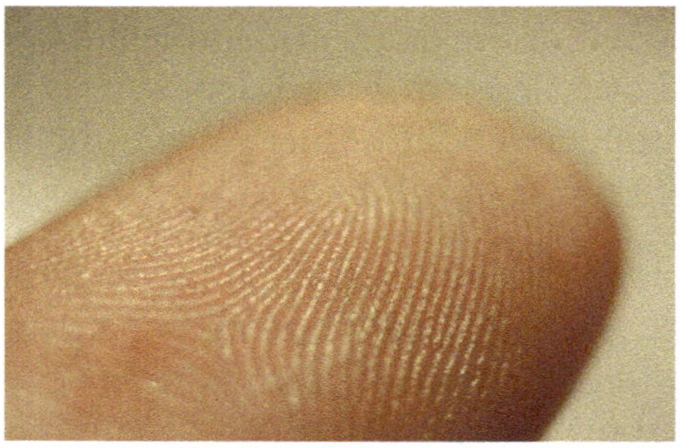

The friction ridges on a finger

Fingerprint identification, known as dactyloscopy, or hand print identification, is the process of comparing two instances of friction ridge skin impressions, from human fingers or toes, or even the palm of the hand or sole of the foot, to determine whether these impressions could have come from the same individual. The flexibility of friction ridge skin means that no two finger or palm prints are ever exactly alike in every detail; even two impressions recorded immediately after each other from the same hand may be slightly different. Fingerprint identification, also referred to as individualization, involves an expert, or an expert computer system operating under threshold scoring rules, determining whether two friction ridge impressions are likely to have originated from the same finger or palm (or toe or sole).

An image of a fingerprint created by the friction ridge structure

An intentional recording of friction ridges is usually made with black printer's ink rolled across a contrasting white background, typically a white card. Friction ridges can also be recorded

digitally, usually on a glass plate, using a technique called Live Scan. A "latent print" is the chance recording of friction ridges deposited on the surface of an object or a wall. Latent prints are invisible to the naked eye, whereas "patent prints" or "plastic prints" are viewable with the unaided eye. Latent prints are often fragmentary and require the use of chemical methods, powder, or alternative light sources in order to be made clear. Sometimes an ordinary bright flashlight will make a latent print visible.

When friction ridges come into contact with a surface that will take a print, material that is on the friction ridges such as perspiration, oil, grease, ink or blood, will be transferred to the surface. Factors which affect the quality of friction ridge impressions are numerous. Pliability of the skin, deposition pressure, slippage, the material from which the surface is made, the roughness of the surface and the substance deposited are just some of the various factors which can cause a latent print to appear differently from any known recording of the same friction ridges. Indeed, the conditions surrounding every instance of friction ridge deposition are unique and never duplicated. For these reasons, fingerprint examiners are required to undergo extensive training. The scientific study of fingerprints is called dermatoglyphics.

Types

Exemplar

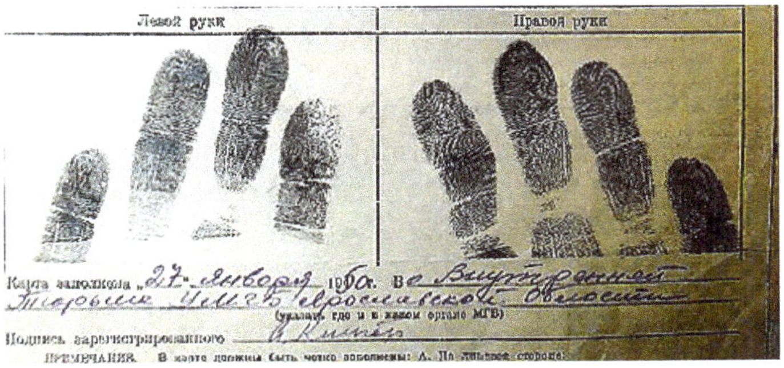

Exemplar prints on paper using ink

Exemplar prints, or known prints, is the name given to fingerprints deliberately collected from a subject, whether for purposes of enrollment in a system or when under arrest for a suspected criminal offense. During criminal arrests, a set of exemplar prints will normally include one print taken from each finger that has been rolled from one edge of the nail to the other, plain (or slap) impressions of each of the four fingers of each hand, and plain impressions of each thumb. Exemplar prints can be collected using live scan or by using ink on paper cards.

Latent

Although the word latent means hidden or invisible, in modern usage for forensic science the term latent prints means any chance or accidental impression left by friction ridge skin on a surface, regardless of whether it is visible or invisible at the time of deposition. Electronic, chemical and physical processing techniques permit visualization of invisible latent print residues whether they are from natural sweat on the skin or from a contaminant such as motor oil, blood, ink, paint or some other form of dirt. The different types of fingerprint patterns, such as arch, loop and whorl, will be described below.

Barely visible latent prints on a knife

Although the word latent means hidden or invisible, in modern usage for forensic science the term latent prints means any chance or accidental impression left by friction ridge skin on a surface, regardless of whether it is visible or invisible at the time of deposition. Electronic, chemical and physical processing techniques permit visualization of invisible latent print residues whether they are from natural sweat on the skin or from a contaminant such as motor oil, blood, ink, paint or some other form of dirt. The different types of fingerprint patterns, such as arch, loop and whorl, will be described below.

Latent prints may exhibit only a small portion of the surface of a finger and this may be smudged, distorted, overlapped by other prints from the same or from different individuals, or any or all of these in combination. For this reason, latent prints usually present an "inevitable source of error in making comparisons", as they generally "contain less clarity, less content, and less undistorted information than a fingerprint taken under controlled conditions, and much, much less detail compared to the actual patterns of ridges and grooves of a finger."

Patent

Patent prints are chance friction ridge impressions which are obvious to the human eye and which have been caused by the transfer of foreign material from a finger onto a surface. Some obvious examples would be impressions from flour and wet clay. Because they are already visible and have no need of enhancement they are generally photographed rather than being lifted in the way that latent prints are. An attempt to preserve the actual print is always made for later presentation in court, and there are many techniques used to do this. Patent prints can be left on a surface by materials such as ink, dirt, or blood.

Plastic

A plastic print is a friction ridge impression left in a material that retains the shape of the ridge detail. Although very few criminals would be careless enough to leave their prints in a lump of wet clay, this would make a perfect plastic print. Commonly encountered examples are melted candle wax, putty removed from the perimeter of window panes and thick grease deposits on car parts. Such prints are already visible and need no enhancement, but investigators must not overlook the potential that invisible latent prints deposited by accomplices may also be on such surfaces. After photographically recording such prints, attempts should be made to develop other non-plastic impressions deposited from sweat or other contaminants.

Electronic Recording

There has been a newspaper report of a man selling stolen watches sending images of them on a mobile phone, and those images included parts of his hands in enough detail for police to be able to identify fingerprint patterns.

Recent studies found that the improving cameras with increasing resolution of smartphones might have a high impact on users' security: The back-facing camera of a device can be used to capture an image of the user's index finger, which on smartphones using biometric means of authentication is often used to authenticate a user against the smartphone.

At the 31st Chaos Communication Congress, hardware hacker starbug presented how DSLRs with high resolution and equipped with a long focus lens can be used to capture images of hands, or more specifically, fingers in order to use them for spoofing.

Footprints

Friction ridge skin present on the soles of the feet and toes (plantar surfaces) is as unique in its ridge detail as are the fingers and palms (palmar surfaces). When recovered at crime scenes or on items of evidence, sole and toe impressions can be used in the same manner as finger and palm prints to effect identifications. The footprints of infants, along with the thumb or index finger prints of mothers, are still commonly recorded in hospitals to assist in verifying the identity of infants. It is not uncommon for military records of flight personnel to include bare foot inked impressions. Friction ridge skin protected inside flight boots tends to survive the trauma of a plane crash (and accompanying fire) better than fingers.

Capture and Detection

Livescan Devices

Fingerprint image acquisition is considered to be the most critical step in an automated fingerprint authentication system, as it determines the final fingerprint image quality, which has a drastic effect on the overall system performance. There are different types of fingerprint readers on the market, but the basic idea behind each is to measure the physical difference between ridges and valleys.

Fingerprint being scanned

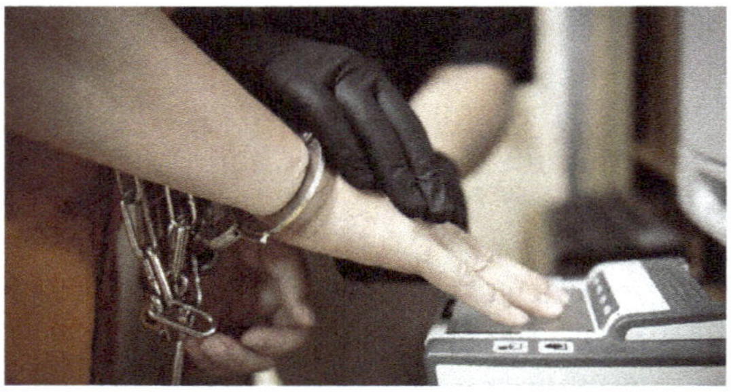

Prisoner being fingerprinted.

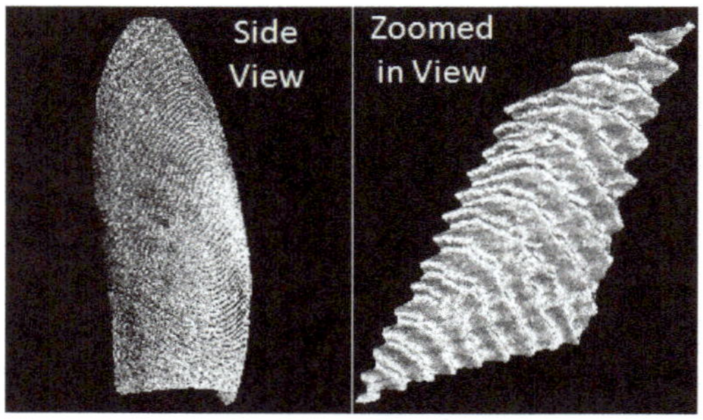

3D fingerprint

All the proposed methods can be grouped into two major families: solid-state fingerprint readers and optical fingerprint readers. The procedure for capturing a fingerprint using a sensor consists of rolling or touching with the finger onto a sensing area, which according to the physical principle in use (optical, ultrasonic, capacitive or thermal) captures the difference between valleys and ridges. When a finger touches or rolls onto a surface, the elastic skin deforms. The quantity and direction of the pressure applied by the user, the skin conditions and the projection of an irregular 3D object (the finger) onto a 2D flat plane introduce distortions, noise and inconsistencies in the captured fingerprint image. These problems result in inconsistent, irreproducible and non-uniform irregularities in the image. During each acquisition, therefore, the results of the imaging are different and uncontrollable. The representation of the same fingerprint changes every time the finger is placed on the sensor plate, increasing the complexity of any attempt to match fingerprints, impairing the system performance and consequently, limiting the widespread use of this biometric technology.

In order to overcome these problems, as of 2010, non-contact or touchless 3D fingerprint scanners have been developed. Acquiring detailed 3D information, 3D fingerprint scanners take a digital approach to the analog process of pressing or rolling the finger. By modelling the distance between neighboring points, the fingerprint can be imaged at a resolution high enough to record all the necessary detail.

Scanning Dead or Unconscious People

Placing the hand of a dead or unconscious person on a scanner to gain unauthorized access has become a common plot device. However, a *MythBusters* episode revealed that this doesn't work (at least with the scanners available to the program). But Adam Savage and Jamie Hyneman found a way to convert fingerprints lifted from the hand to a photographic form that the sensor would accept. For obvious reasons, they refuse to reveal the technique.

Latent Detection

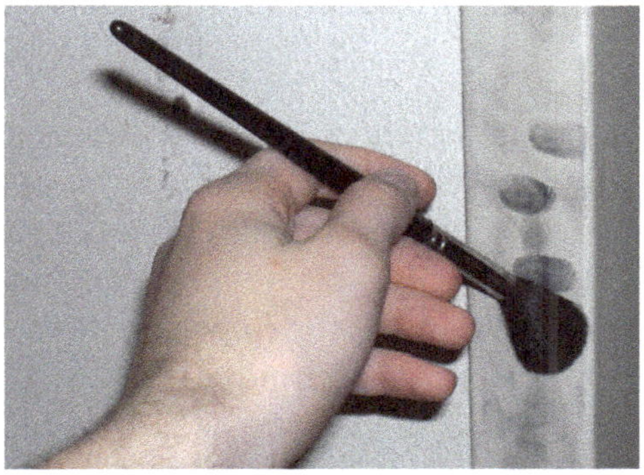

Use of fine powder and brush to reveal latent fingerprints

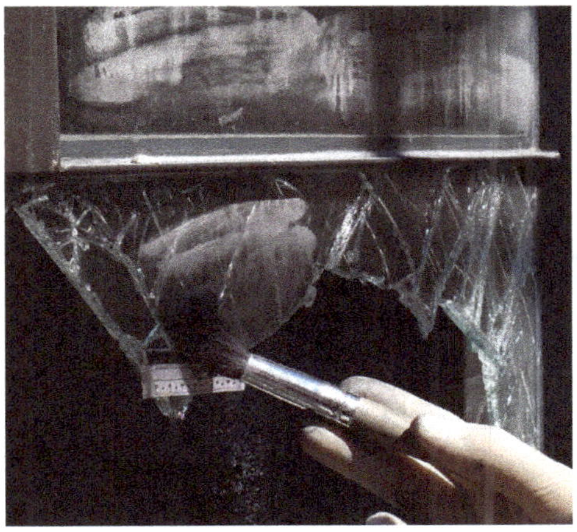

Fingerprints dusting of a burglary scene

In the 1930s criminal investigators in the United States first discovered the existence of latent fingerprints on the surfaces of fabrics, most notably on the insides of gloves discarded by perpetrators.

Since the late nineteenth century, fingerprint identification methods have been used by police agencies around the world to identify suspected criminals as well as the victims of crime. The basis of the traditional fingerprinting technique is simple. The skin on the palmar surface of the hands and feet forms ridges, so-called papillary ridges, in patterns that are unique to each individual and which do not change over time. Even identical twins (who share their DNA) do not have identical fingerprints. The best way to render latent fingerprints visible, so that they can be photographed, can be complex and may depend, for example, on the type of surfaces on which they have been left. It is generally necessary to use a 'developer', usually a powder or chemical reagent, to produce a high degree of visual contrast between the ridge patterns and the surface on which a fingerprint has been deposited.

Developing agents depend on the presence of organic materials or inorganic salts for their effectiveness, although the water deposited may also take a key role. Fingerprints are typically formed from the aqueous-based secretions of the eccrine glands of the fingers and palms with additional material from sebaceous glands primarily from the forehead. This latter contamination results from the common human behaviors of touching the face and hair. The resulting latent fingerprints consist usually of a substantial proportion of water with small traces of amino acids and chlorides mixed with a fatty, sebaceous component which contains a number of fatty acids and triglycerides. Detection of a small proportion of reactive organic substances such as urea and amino acids is far from easy.

Fingerprints at a crime scene may be detected by simple powders, or by chemicals applied *in situ*. More complex techniques, usually involving chemicals, can be applied in specialist laboratories to appropriate articles removed from a crime scene. With advances in these more sophisticated techniques, some of the more advanced crime scene investigation services from around the world were, as of 2010, reporting that 50% or more of the fingerprints recovered from a crime scene had been identified as a result of laboratory-based techniques.

A city fingerprint identification room.

Laboratory Techniques

Although there are hundreds of reported techniques for fingerprint detection, many of these are only of academic interest and there are only around 20 really effective methods which are currently in use in the more advanced fingerprint laboratories around the world. Some of these techniques, such as ninhydrin, diazafluorenone and vacuum metal deposition, show great sensitivity and are used operationally. Some fingerprint reagents are specific, for example ninhydrin or diazafluorenone reacting with amino acids. Others such as ethyl cyanoacrylate polymerisation, work apparently by water-based catalysis and polymer growth. Vacuum metal deposition using gold and zinc has been shown to be non-specific, but can detect fat layers as thin as one molecule. More mundane methods, such as the application of fine powders, work by adhesion to sebaceous deposits and possibly aqueous deposits in the case of fresh fingerprints. The aqueous component of a fingerprint, whilst initially sometimes making up over 90% of the weight of the fingerprint, can evaporate quite quickly and may have mostly gone after 24 hours. Following work on the use of argon ion lasers for fingerprint detection, a wide range of fluorescence techniques have been introduced, primarily for the enhancement of chemically developed fingerprints; the inherent fluorescence of some latent fingerprints may also be detected. Fingerprints can for example be visualized three-dimensionally and without chemicals by the use of infrared lasers. A comprehensive manual of the operational methods of fingerprint enhancement was last published by the UK Home Office Scientific Development Branch in 2013 and is used widely around the world.

A technique proposed in 2007 aims to identify an individual's ethnicity, gender, and dietary patterns.

Research

The International Fingerprint Research Group (IFRG) which meets biennially, consists of members of the leading fingerprint research groups from Europe, the US, Canada, Australia and Israel and leads the way in the development, assessment and implementation of new techniques for operational fingerprint detection.

One problem for the early twenty-first century is the fact that the organic component of any deposited material is readily destroyed by heat, such as occurs when a gun is fired or a bomb is detonated, when the temperature may reach as high as 500 °C. Encouragingly, however, the non-volatile inorganic component of eccrine secretion has been shown to remain intact even when exposed to temperatures as high as 600 °C.

A technique has been developed that enables fingerprints to be visualised on metallic and electrically conductive surfaces without the need to develop the prints first. This technique involves the use of an instrument called a scanning Kelvin probe (SKP), which measures the voltage, or electrical potential, at pre-set intervals over the surface of an object on which a fingerprint may have been deposited. These measurements can then be mapped to produce an image of the fingerprint. A higher resolution image can be obtained by increasing the number of points sampled, but at the expense of the time taken for the process. A sampling frequency of 20 points per mm is high enough to visualise a fingerprint in sufficient detail for identification purposes and produces a voltage map in 2–3 hours. As of 2010, this technique had been shown to work effectively on a wide range of forensically important metal surfaces including iron, steel and aluminium. While initial experiments were performed on flat surfaces, the technique has been further developed to cope with irregular or curved surfaces, such as the warped cylindrical surface of fired cartridge cases. Research during 2010 at Swansea University has found that physically removing a fingerprint from a metal surface, for example by rubbing with a tissue, does not necessarily result in the loss of all fingerprint information from that surface. The reason for this is that the differences in potential that are the basis of the visualisation are caused by the interaction of inorganic salts in the fingerprint deposit and the metal surface and begin to occur as soon as the finger comes into contact with the metal, resulting in the formation of metal-ion complexes that cannot easily be removed.

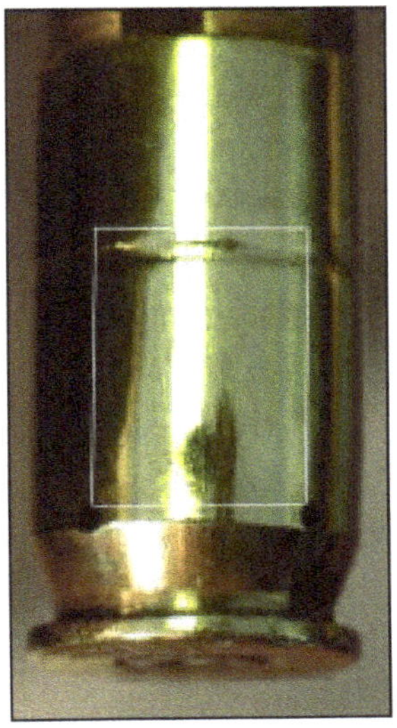

Cartridge case with an applied fingerprint

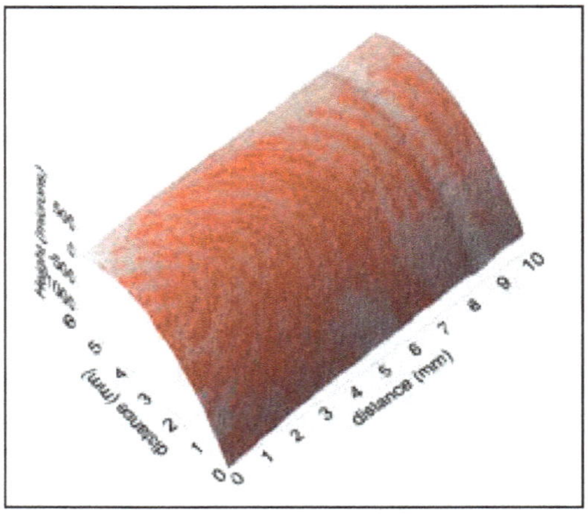

Scanning Kelvin probe scan of the same cartridge case with the fingerprint detected. The Kelvin probe can easily cope with the 3D curvature of the cartridge case, increasing the versatility of the technique.

Another problem for the early twenty-first century is that during crime scene investigations, a decision has to be made at an early stage whether to attempt to retrieve fingerprints through the use of developers or whether to swab surfaces in an attempt to salvage material for DNA profiling. The two processes are mutually incompatible, as fingerprint developers destroy material that could potentially be used for DNA analysis, and swabbing is likely to make fingerprint identification impossible.

The application of the new scanning Kelvin probe (SKP) fingerprinting technique, which makes no physical contact with the fingerprint and does not require the use of developers, has the potential to allow fingerprints to be recorded whilst still leaving intact material that could subsequently be subjected to DNA analysis. A forensically usable prototype was under development at Swansea University during 2010, in research that was generating significant interest from the British Home Office and a number of different police forces across the UK, as well as internationally. The hope is that this instrument could eventually be manufactured in sufficiently large numbers to be widely used by forensic teams worldwide.

Disappearance of Children's Latent Prints

In 1995, researchers at the Oak Ridge National Laboratory, at the instigation of Detective Art Bohanan of the Knoxville Police Department, discovered that children's fingerprints are considerably more short-lived than adult fingerprints. The rapid disappearance of children's fingerprints was attributed to a lack of the more waxy oils that become present at the onset of puberty. The lighter fatty acids of children's fingerprints evaporate within a few hours. As of 2010, researchers at Oak Ridge National Laboratory are investigating techniques to capture these lost fingerprints.

Detection of Drug Use

The secretions, skin oils and dead cells in a human fingerprint contain residues of various chemicals and their metabolites present in the body. These can be detected and used for forensic purposes. For example, the fingerprints of tobacco smokers contain traces of cotinine, a nicotine metabolite; they also contain traces of nicotine itself. Caution should be used, as its presence may be caused by mere contact of the finger with a tobacco product. By treating the fingerprint with gold nanoparticles with attached cotinine antibodies, and then subsequently with a fluorescent agent attached to cotinine antibodies, the fingerprint of a smoker becomes fluorescent; non-smokers' fingerprints stay dark. The same approach, as of 2010, is being tested for use in identifying heavy coffee drinkers, cannabis smokers, and users of various other drugs. In 2008, British researchers developed methods of identifying users of marijuana, cocaine and methadone from their fingerprint residues.

United States Databases and Compression

In the United States, the FBI manages a fingerprint identification system and database called the Integrated Automated Fingerprint Identification System, or IAFIS, which currently holds the fingerprints and criminal records of over 51 million criminal record subjects and over 1.5 million civil (non-criminal) fingerprint records. US Visit currently holds a repository of the fingerprints of over 50 million people, primarily in the form of two-finger records. In 2008, US Visit hoped to have changed over to a system recording FBI-standard ten-print records.

Most American law enforcement agencies use Wavelet Scalar Quantization (WSQ), a wavelet-based system for efficient storage of compressed fingerprint images at 500 pixels per inch (ppi). WSQ was developed by the FBI, the Los Alamos National Lab, and the National Institute for Standards and Technology (NIST). For fingerprints recorded at 1000 ppi spatial resolution, law enforcement (including the FBI) uses JPEG 2000 instead of WSQ.

A city fingerprint identification office

Validity

The validity of forensic fingerprint evidence has been challenged by academics, judges and the media. While fingerprint identification was an improvement on earlier anthropometric systems, the subjective nature of matching, despite a very low error rate, has made this forensic practice controversial.

Certain specific criticisms are now being accepted by some leaders of the forensic fingerprint community, providing an incentive to improve training and procedures.

Criticism

The words "reliability" and "validity" have specific meanings to the scientific community. Reliability means that successive tests bring the same results. Validity means that these results are judged to accurately reflect the external criteria being measured.

Although experts are often more comfortable relying on their instincts, this reliance does not always translate into superior predictive ability. For example, in the popular Analysis, Comparison, Evaluation, and Verification (ACE-V) paradigm for fingerprint identification, the verification stage, in which a second examiner confirms the assessment of the original examiner, may increase the consistency of the assessments. But while the verification stage has implications for the reliability of latent print comparisons, it does not assure their validity.

—Sandy L Zabell,

The few tests that have been made of the validity of forensic fingerprinting have not been supportive of the method.

"Despite the absence of objective standards, scientific validation, and adequate statistical studies, a natural question to ask is how well fingerprint examiners actually perform. Proficiency tests do not validate a procedure per se, but they can provide some insight into error rates. In 1995, the Collaborative Testing Service (CTS) administered a proficiency test that, for the first time, was "designed, assembled, and reviewed" by the International Association for Identification (IAI). The results were disappointing. Four suspect cards with prints of all ten fingers were provided together with seven latents. Of 156 people taking the test, only 68 (44%) correctly classified all seven latents. Overall, the tests contained a total of 48 incorrect identifications. David Grieve, the editor of the Journal of Forensic Identification, describes the reaction of the forensic community to the results of the CTS test as ranging from "shock to disbelief", and added:

'Errors of this magnitude within a discipline singularly admired and respected for its touted absolute certainty as an identification process have produced chilling and mind-numbing realities. Thirty-four participants, an incredible 22% of those involved, substituted presumed but false certainty for truth. By any measure, this represents a profile of practice that is unacceptable and thus demands positive action by the entire community.'

What is striking about these comments is that they do not come from a critic of the fingerprint community, but from the editor of one of its premier publications."

—Sandy L Zabell,

Investigations have been conducted into whether experts can objectively focus on feature information in fingerprints without being misled by extraneous information, such as context. Fingerprints that have previously been examined and assessed by latent print experts to make a positive identification of suspects have then been re-presented to those same experts in a new context which makes it likely that there will be no match. Within this new context, most of the fingerprint experts made different judgments, thus contradicting their own previous identification decisions.

Complaints have been made that there have been no published, peer-reviewed studies directly examining the extent to which people can correctly match fingerprints to one another. Experiments have been carried out using naïve undergraduates to match images of fingerprints. The results of these experiments demonstrate that people can identify fingerprints quite well, and that matching accuracy can vary as a function of both source finger type and image similarity.

Defense

Fingerprints collected at a crime scene, or on items of evidence from a crime, have been used in forensic science to identify suspects, victims and other persons who touched a surface. Fingerprint identification emerged as an important system within police agencies in the late 19th century, when it replaced anthropometric measurements as a more reliable method for identifying persons having a prior record, often under a false name, in a criminal record repository. The science of fingerprint identification has been able to assert its standing amongst forensic sciences for many reasons. In modern times, researchers can find traces of addictive drugs on just a fingerprint.

Track Record

Fingerprinting has served all governments worldwide during the past 100 years or so to provide accurate identification of criminals. No two identical fingerprints have ever been found in many billions of human and automated computer comparisons. Fingerprints are the fundamental tool in every police agency for the identification of people with a criminal history. They remain the most commonly gathered forensic evidence worldwide, and in most jurisdictions fingerprint examination is more common than all other forensic examination casework combined. Moreover, it continues to expand, with tens of thousands of people added to fingerprint repositories daily in America alone — far more than other forensic databases.

Professional Standing and Certification

Fingerprinting was the basis upon which the first forensic professional organization was formed, the International Association for Identification (IAI), in 1915. The first professional certification program for forensic scientists was established in 1977, the IAI's Certified Latent Print Examiner program, which issued certificates to those meeting stringent criteria and had the power to revoke certification where an individual's performance warranted it. Other forensic disciplines have followed suit and established their own certification programs.

Instances of Error

Brandon Mayfield and the Madrid Bombing

Brandon Mayfield is an Oregon lawyer who was identified as a participant in the 2004 Madrid train bombings based on a fingerprint match by the FBI. The FBI Latent Print Unit processed a fingerprint collected in Madrid and reported a "100 percent positive" match against one of the 20 fingerprint candidates returned in a search response from their Integrated Automated Fingerprint Identification System. The FBI initially called it an "absolutely incontrovertible match". Subsequently, however, Spanish National Police examiners suggested that the print did not match Mayfield and after two weeks, identified another man whom they claimed the fingerprint did belong to. The FBI acknowledged their error, and a judge released Mayfield, who had spent two weeks in police custody, in May 2004. In January 2006, a U.S. Justice Department report was released which criticized the FBI for sloppy work but exonerated them of some more serious allegations. The report found that the misidentification had been due to a misapplication of methodology by the examiners involved: Mayfield is an American-born convert to Islam and his wife is an Egyptian immigrant, but these are not factors that should have affected fingerprint search technology.

On November 29, 2006, the FBI agreed to pay Brandon Mayfield US$2 million in compensation. The judicial settlement allowed Mayfield to continue a suit regarding certain other government practices surrounding his arrest and detention. The formal apology stated that the FBI, which erroneously linked him to the 2004 Madrid bombing through a fingerprinting mistake, had taken steps to "ensure that what happened to Mr. Mayfield and the Mayfield family does not happen again."

René Ramón Sánchez

René Ramón Sánchez, a legal Dominican Republic immigrant to the US, was arrested on July 15, 1995, on a charge of driving while intoxicated. His fingerprints were mistakenly placed on a card containing the name, Social Security number and other data for one Leo Rosario, who was being processed at the same time. Leo Rosario had been arrested for selling cocaine to an undercover police officer. On October 11, 2000, while returning from a visit to relatives in the Dominican Republic, René was misidentified as Leo Rosario at John F. Kennedy International Airport in New York and arrested. Even though he did not match the physical description of Rosario, the erroneously cataloged fingerprints were considered to be more reliable.

Shirley McKie

Shirley McKie was a police detective in 1997 when she was accused of leaving her thumb print inside a house in Kilmarnock, Scotland, where Marion Ross had been murdered. Although McKie denied having been inside the house, she was arrested in a dawn raid the following year and charged with perjury. The only evidence the prosecution had was this thumb print allegedly found at the murder scene. Two American experts testified on her behalf at her trial in May 1999 and she was found not guilty. The Scottish Criminal Record Office (SCRO) would not admit any error, although Scottish first minister Jack McConnell later said it had been an "honest mistake".

On February 7, 2006, McKie was awarded £750,000 in compensation from the Scottish Executive and the Scottish Criminal Record Office. Controversy continued to surround the McKie case and the Fingerprint Inquiry into the affair finished taking evidence in November 2009. The Inquiry Report was published on 11 December 2011.

Stephan Cowans

Stephan Cowans was convicted of attempted murder in 1997 after he was accused of shooting a police officer whilst fleeing a robbery in Roxbury, Massachusetts. He was implicated in the crime by the testimony of two witnesses, one of whom was the victim. There was also a fingerprint on a glass mug from which the assailant had drunk some water and experts testified that the fingerprint belonged to Cowans. He was found guilty and sent to prison for 35 years. Whilst in prison, Cowans earned money cleaning up biohazards until he could afford to have the evidence against him tested for DNA. The DNA did not match his and he was released. He had already served six years in prison when he was released on January 23, 2004. Cowans died on October 25, 2007.

Craig D. Harvey

In April 1993, in the New York State Police Troop C scandal, Craig D. Harvey, a New York State Police trooper, was charged with fabricating evidence. Harvey admitted he and another trooper lifted fingerprints from items the suspect, John Spencer, touched while in Troop C headquarters during booking. He attached the fingerprints to evidence cards and later claimed that he had pulled the fingerprints from the scene of the murder. The forged evidence was presented during John Spencer's trial and his subsequent conviction resulted in a term of 50 years to life in prison at his sentencing. Three state troopers were found guilty of fabricating fingerprint evidence and served prison sentences.

History

Antiquity and the Medieval Period

Fingerprints have been found on ancient Babylonian clay tablets, seals, and pottery. They have also been found on the walls of Egyptian tombs and on Minoan, Greek, and Chinese pottery, as well as on bricks and tiles from ancient Babylon and Rome. Some of these fingerprints were deposited unintentionally by the potters and masons as a natural consequence of their work, and others were made in the process of adding decoration. However, on some pottery, fingerprints have been impressed so deeply into the clay that they were possibly intended to serve as an identifying mark by the maker.

Fingerprints were used as signatures in ancient Babylon in the second millennium BCE. In order to protect against forgery, parties to a legal contract would impress their fingerprints into a clay tablet on which the contract had been written. By 246 BCE, Chinese officials were impressing their fingerprints into the clay seals used to seal documents. With the advent of silk and paper in China, parties to a legal contract impressed their handprints on the document. Sometime before 851 CE, an Arab merchant in China, Abu Zayd Hasan, witnessed Chinese merchants using fingerprints to authenticate loans. By 702, Japan allowed illiterate petitioners seeking a divorce to "sign" their petitions with a fingerprint.

Although ancient peoples probably did not realize that fingerprints could uniquely identify individuals, references from the age of the Babylonian king Hammurabi (reigned 1792-1750 BCE) indicate that law officials would take the fingerprints of people who had been arrested. During China's Qin Dynasty, records have shown that officials took hand prints, foot prints as well as finger prints as evidence from a crime scene. In China, around 300 CE, handprints were used as evidence in a trial for theft. By 650, the Chinese historian Kia Kung-Yen remarked that fingerprints could be used as a means of authentication. In his *Jami al-Tawarikh* (Universal History), the Persian physician Rashid-al-Din Hamadani (also known as "Rashideddin", 1247–1318) refers to the Chinese practice of identifying people via their fingerprints, commenting: "Experience shows that no two individuals have fingers exactly alike." In Persia at this time, government documents may have been authenticated with thumbprints.

Europe in the 17th and 18th Centuries

In 1665, the Italian physician Marcello Malpighi (1628–1694) briefly mentioned the existence of patterns of ridges and sweat glands on the fingertips. In 1684, the English physician, botanist, and microscopist Nehemiah Grew (1641–1712) published the first scientific paper to describe the ridge structure of the skin covering the fingers and palms. In 1685, the Dutch physician Govard Bidloo (1649–1713) published a book on anatomy which also illustrated the ridge structure of the fingers.

A century later, in 1788, the German anatomist Johann Christoph Andreas Mayer (1747–1801) recognized that fingerprints are unique to each individual.

Modern Era

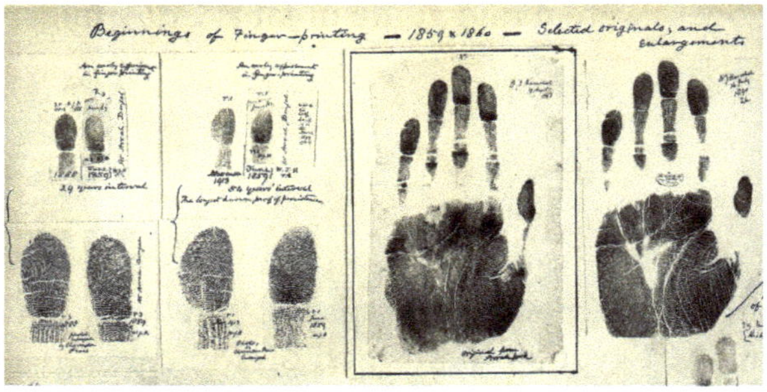

Fingerprints taken by William Herschel 1859/60

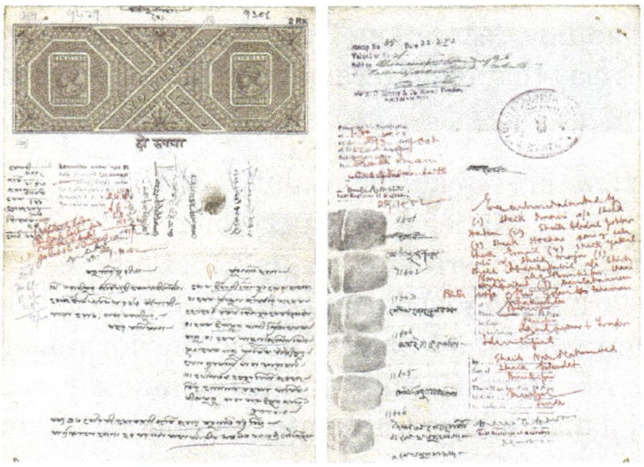

Fingerprints used instead of signatures on an Indian legal document of 1952.

Jan Evangelista Purkyně or Purkinje (1787–1869), a Czech physiologist and professor of anatomy at the University of Breslau, published a thesis in 1823 discussing 9 fingerprint patterns, but he did not mention any possibility of using fingerprints to identify people. In 1840, following the murder of Lord William Russell, a provincial doctor, Robert Blake Overton, wrote to Scotland Yard suggesting checking for fingerprints but the suggestion, though followed up, did not lead to their routine use by the police for another 50 years. Some years later, the German anatomist Georg von Meissner (1829–1905) studied friction ridges, and five years after this, in 1858, Sir William James Herschel initiated fingerprinting in India. In 1877 at Hooghly (near Calcutta) he instituted the use of fingerprints on contracts and deeds to prevent the then-rampant repudiation of signatures and he registered government pensioners' fingerprints to prevent the collection of money by relatives after a pensioner's death. Herschel also fingerprinted prisoners upon sentencing to prevent various frauds that were attempted in order to avoid serving a prison sentence.

In 1863, Paul-Jean Coulier (1824–1890), professor for chemistry and hygiene at the medical and pharmaceutical school of the Val-de-Grâce military hospital in Paris, discovered that iodine fumes can reveal fingerprints on paper.

In 1880, Dr. Henry Faulds, a Scottish surgeon in a Tokyo hospital, published his first paper on the subject in the scientific journal *Nature*, discussing the usefulness of fingerprints for identification and proposing a method to record them with printing ink. He also established their first classification and was also the first to identify fingerprints left on a vial. Returning to the UK in 1886, he offered the concept to the Metropolitan Police in London but it was dismissed at that time. Faulds wrote to Charles Darwin with a description of his method but, too old and ill to work on it, Darwin gave the information to his cousin, Francis Galton, who was interested in anthropology. Having been thus inspired to study fingerprints for ten years, Galton published a detailed statistical model of fingerprint analysis and identification and encouraged its use in forensic science in his book *Finger Prints*. He had calculated that the chance of a "false positive" (two different individuals having the same fingerprints) was about 1 in 64 billion.

Juan Vucetich, an Argentine chief police officer, created the first method of recording the fingerprints of individuals on file, associating these fingerprints to the anthropometric system of Alphonse Bertillon, who had created, in 1879, a system to identify individuals by anthropometric photographs and associated quantitative descriptions. In 1892, after studying Galton's pattern types, Vucetich set up the world's first fingerprint bureau. In that same year, Francisca Rojas of Necochea, was found in a house with neck injuries, whilst her two sons were found dead with their throats cut. Rojas accused a neighbour, but despite brutal interrogation, this neighbour would not confess to the crimes. Inspector Alvarez, a colleague of Vucetich, went to the scene and found a bloody thumb mark on a door. When it was compared with Rojas' prints, it was found to be identical with her right thumb. She then confessed to the murder of her sons.

Women clerical employees of the Los Angeles Police Department being fingerprinted and photographed in 1928.

A Fingerprint Bureau was established in Calcutta (Kolkata), India, in 1897, after the Council of the Governor General approved a committee report that fingerprints should be used for the classification of criminal records. Working in the Calcutta Anthropometric Bureau, before it became the first Fingerprint Bureau in the world, were Azizul Haque and Hem Chandra Bose. Haque and Bose were Indian fingerprint experts who have been credited with the primary development of a fingerprint classification system eventually named after their supervisor, Sir Edward Richard Henry. The Henry Classification System, co-devised by Haque and Bose, was accepted in England and Wales when the first United Kingdom Fingerprint Bureau was founded in Scotland Yard, the Metropolitan Police headquarters, London, in 1901. Sir Edward Richard Henry subsequently achieved improvements in dactyloscopy.

In the United States, Dr. Henry P. DeForrest used fingerprinting in the New York Civil Service in 1902, and by 1906, New York City Police Department Deputy Commissioner Joseph A. Faurot, an expert in the Bertillon system and a finger print advocate at Police Headquarters, introduced the fingerprinting of criminals to the United States.

The Scheffer case of 1902 is the first case of the identification, arrest and conviction of a murderer based upon fingerprint evidence. Alphonse Bertillon identified the thief and murderer Scheffer, who had previously been arrested and his fingerprints filed some months before, from the fingerprints found on a fractured glass showcase, after a theft in a dentist's apartment where the dentist's employee was found dead. It was able to be proved in court that the fingerprints had been made after the showcase was broken. A year later, Alphonse Bertillon created a method of getting fingerprints off smooth surfaces and took a further step in the advance of dactyloscopy.

Many criminals wear gloves to avoid leaving fingerprints. However, the gloves themselves can leave prints that are as unique as human fingerprints. After collecting glove prints, law enforcement can match them to gloves that they have collected as evidence or to prints collected at other crime scenes. In many jurisdictions the act of wearing gloves itself while committing a crime can be prosecuted as an inchoate offense.

As many offenses are crimes of opportunity, assailants do not always possess gloves when they commit their illegal activities. Thus, assailants have been observed using pulled-down sleeves, pieces of clothing, and other fabrics to handle objects and touch surfaces while committing crimes.

Privacy Issues

Fingerprinting of Children

Various schools have implemented fingerprint locks or made a record of children's fingerprints. In the United Kingdom there have been fingerprint locks in Holland Park School in London, and children's fingerprints are stored on databases. There have also been instances in Belgium, at the école Marie-José in Liège, in France and in Italy. The non-governmental organization (NGO) Privacy International in 2002 made the cautionary announcement that tens of thousands of UK school children were being fingerprinted by schools, often without the knowledge or consent of their parents. That same year, the supplier Micro Librarian Systems, which uses a technology similar to that used in US prisons and the German military, estimated that 350 schools throughout Britain were using such systems to replace library cards. By 2007, it was estimated that 3,500 schools were using such systems. Under the United Kingdom Data Protection Act, schools in the UK do not have to ask parental consent to allow such practices to take place. Parents opposed to fingerprinting may only bring individual complaints against schools. In response to a complaint which they are continuing to pursue, in 2010 the European Commission expressed 'significant concerns' over the proportionality and necessity of the practice and the lack of judicial redress, indicating that the practice may break the European Union data protection directive.

In Belgium, the practice of taking fingerprints from children gave rise to a question in Parliament on February 6, 2007, by Michel de La Motte (Humanist Democratic Centre) to the Education Minister Marie Arena, who replied that it was legal provided that the school did not use them for external purposes, or to survey the private life of children. At Angers in France, Carqueiranne College in the Var won the Big Brother Award for 2005 and the Commission nationale de l'informatique et des libertés (CNIL), the official organisation in charge of the protection of privacy in France, declared the measures it had introduced "disproportionate."

In March 2007, the British government was considering fingerprinting all children aged 11 to 15 and adding the prints to a government database as part of a new passport and ID card scheme and disallowing opposition for privacy concerns. All fingerprints taken would be cross-checked against prints from 900,000 unsolved crimes. Shadow Home secretary David Davis called the plan "sinister". An Early Day Motion which called on the UK Government to conduct a full and open consultation with stakeholders about the use of biometrics in schools, secured the support of 85 Members of Parliament (Early Day Motion 686). Following the establishment in the United Kingdom of a Conservative and Liberal Democratic coalition government in May 2010, the ID card scheme was scrapped.

Serious concerns about the security implications of using conventional biometric templates in schools have been raised by a number of leading IT security experts, one of whom has voiced the opinion that "it is absolutely premature to begin using 'conventional biometrics' in schools". The vendors of biometric systems claim that their products bring benefits to schools such as improved reading skills, decreased wait times in lunch lines and increased revenues. They do not cite independent research to support this view. One education specialist wrote in 2007: "I have not been able to find a single piece of published research which suggests that the use of biometrics in schools promotes healthy eating or improves reading skills amongst children... There is absolutely no evidence for such claims". The Ottawa Police in Canada have advised parents who fear their children may be kidnapped, to fingerprint their children.

Other Uses

Welfare Claimants

It has been alleged that taking the fingerprints of welfare recipients as identification serves as a social stigma that evokes cultural images associated with the processing of criminals.

Log-in Authentication and other Locks

Since 2000, electronic fingerprint readers have been introduced for security applications such as log-in authentication for the identification of computer users. However, some less sophisticated devices have been discovered to be vulnerable to quite simple methods of deception, such as fake fingerprints cast in gels. In 2006, fingerprint sensors gained popularity in the notebook PC market. Built-in sensors in laptops, such as ThinkPads, VAIO, HP Pavilion and EliteBook laptops, and others also double as motion detectors for document scrolling, like the scroll wheel.

Following the release of the iPhone 5S model, a group of German hackers announced on September 21, 2013, that they had bypassed Apple's new Touch ID fingerprint sensor by photographing a fingerprint from a glass surface and using that captured image as verification. The spokesman for the group stated: "We hope that this finally puts to rest the illusions people have about fingerprint biometrics. It is plain stupid to use something that you can't change and that you leave everywhere every day as a security token."

Electronic Registration and Library Access

Fingerprints and, to a lesser extent, iris scans can be used to validate electronic registration, cashless catering, and library access. By 2007, this practice was particularly widespread in UK schools, and it was also starting to be adopted in some states in the US.

Absence or Mutilation of Fingerprints

A very rare medical condition, adermatoglyphia, is characterized by the absence of fingerprints. Affected persons have completely smooth fingertips, palms, toes and soles, but no other medical signs or symptoms. A 2011 study indicated that adermatoglyphia is caused by the improper expression of the protein SMARCAD1. The condition has been called *immigration delay disease* by the researchers describing it, because the congenital lack of fingerprints causes delays when affected persons attempt to prove their identity while traveling. Only five families with this condition have been described as of 2011.

People with Naegeli–Franceschetti–Jadassohn syndrome and dermatopathia pigmentosa reticularis, which are both forms of ectodermal dysplasia, also have no fingerprints. Both of these rare genetic syndromes produce other signs and symptoms as well, such as thin, brittle hair.

The anti-cancer medication capecitabine may cause the loss of fingerprints. Swelling of the fingers, such as that caused by bee stings, will in some cases cause the temporary disappearance of fingerprints, though they will return when the swelling recedes.

Since the elasticity of skin decreases with age, many senior citizens have fingerprints that are difficult to capture. The ridges get thicker; the height between the top of the ridge and the bottom of the furrow gets narrow, so there is less prominence.

Fingerprints can be erased permanently and this can potentially be used by criminals to reduce their chance of conviction. Erasure can be achieved in a variety of ways including simply burning the fingertips, using acids and advanced techniques such as plastic surgery. John Dillinger burned his fingers with acid, but prints taken during a previous arrest and upon death still exhibited almost complete relation to one another.

In other Species

Some other animals have evolved their own unique prints, especially those whose lifestyle involves climbing or grasping wet objects; these include many primates, such as gorillas and chimpanzees, Australian koalas and aquatic mammal species such as the North American fisher. According to one study, even with an electron microscope, it can be quite difficult to distinguish between the fingerprints of a koala and a human. Koalas' independent development of fingerprints is an example of convergent evolution.

In Fiction

Mark Twain

Mark Twain's memoir *Life on the Mississippi* (1883), notable mainly for its account of the author's time on the river, also recounts parts of his later life, and includes tall tales and stories allegedly told to him. Among them is an involved, melodramatic account of a murder in which the killer is identified by a thumbprint. Twain's novel *Pudd'nhead Wilson*, published in 1893, includes a courtroom drama that turns on fingerprint identification.

Crime Fiction

The use of fingerprints in crime fiction has, of course, kept pace with its use in real-life detection. Sir Arthur Conan Doyle wrote a short story about his celebrated sleuth Sherlock Holmes which features a fingerprint: "The Norwood Builder" is a 1903 short story set in 1894 and involves the discovery of a bloody fingerprint which helps Holmes to expose the real criminal and free his client.

The British detective writer R. Austin Freeman's first Thorndyke novel *The Red Thumb-Mark* was published in 1907 and features a bloody fingerprint left on a piece of paper together with a parcel of diamonds inside a safe-box. These become the center of a medico-legal investigation led by Dr. Thorndyke, who defends the accused whose fingerprint matches that on the paper, after the diamonds are stolen.

Film and Television

On the television series Bonanza (1959–1973), the first episode with the ethnic Chinese character, Hop Sing, #316 The Mark of Guilt was about fingerprinting and its relationship to Chinese culture. Hop Sing uses his Oriental knowledge of "chops" (unique prints from fingers) to free Little Joe from a murder charge.

The movie *Men in Black*, a popular 1997 science fiction thriller, required Agent J, played by Will Smith, to remove his ten fingerprints by putting his hands on a metal ball, an action deemed necessary by the MIB agency to remove the identity of its agents.

In a 2009 science fiction movie starring Paul Giamatti, *Cold Souls*, a mule who is paid to smuggle souls across borders, wears latex fingerprints to frustrate airport security terminals. She can change her identity by changing her wig, and switching latex fingerprints from the privacy of a restroom, storing extra fingerprints in a ziploc bag, so she can assume an alias that is suitable to her undertaking.

Other Reliable Identifiers

Other forms of biometric identification utilizing a physical attribute that is nearly unique to humans include iris recognition, the tongue and DNA profiling, also known as genetic fingerprinting. Forensic dentistry has also been used as an identifier, but bite mark analysis is notable for being unreliable.

Glove Prints

Glove prints, also sometimes described as gloveprints or glove marks, are latent, fingerprint-like impressions that are transferred to a surface or object by an individual who is wearing gloves.

Many criminals often wear gloves to avoid leaving fingerprints, which makes the crime investigation more difficult. Although the gloves act as a protective covering for the wearer's prints, the gloves themselves can leave prints that are just as unique as human fingerprints, thus betraying the wearer. After collecting glove prints, law enforcement can then match them to gloves that they have collected as evidence as well as glove prints retrieved from other crime scenes.

History

Since the advent of fingerprint detection, many criminals have resorted to the wearing of gloves during the commission of their crimes in order to avoid leaving their fingerprints as evidence. In the era prior to contemporary advances in forensic science, the simple act of covering the hands often assured criminal assailants their anonymity if no witnesses were present during their offenses; thus a pair of gloves became the most essential and crucial tool for any successful perpetrator.

In earlier decades, investigators would dust for fingerprints only to find smears and smudges caused by gloves. Often in earlier decades these smudges were ignored because very little of their detail was retrievable. With the advent of latent fingerprint detection in the late 20th century, investigators started to collect, analyze, and record prints left at crime scenes that were created by the wearing of gloves. Glove prints can be as simple as marks caused by seams or folds in fabric of a glove, or they can be as complex as marks left behind by the grain or texture of the fabric of a glove. When gloves are collected as evidence their prints can be taken and compared to glove prints that were taken at crime scenes or from evidence.

Offenders who wear gloves tend to use their hands and fingers very freely, and thus, because their gloves give them a false sense of protection, leave easily distinguishable glove prints on the surfaces they handle. If when either a fingerprint is able to pass through a glove, or when, because of holes in a glove, finger and glove prints appear together, investigators are now able to better distinguish between prints made by friction ridges and prints made by gloves. Many times this also happens because criminals also opt to wear gloves that are both tight-fitting and relatively short, which makes the occurrence of prints being made by the butt of the palm and the wrist (palm prints) more common as the gloves may slip, thus exposing areas of the skin that may leave prints. Also, many times criminals would discard their gloves at crime scenes or hide them nearby. Today, latent fingerprints (first discovered on the surfaces of fabrics by investigators in the 1930s), as well as DNA and incriminating bacteria can also be recovered from the inside of these discarded gloves.

In many jurisdictions the act of wearing gloves itself while committing a crime can be prosecuted as an inchoate offense.

By the 1950s, after over a half century of frustration due to the wearing of gloves by assailants, fingerprint experts began studies to determine how it may be feasible to detect and compare glove prints found at crime scenes.

In 1971, the Metropolitan Police Service of London, England claims the first (or one of the very first) convictions based on glove print-evidence. Glove-prints were found on a broken window and were later matched to the gloves of a suspect.

Starting in early 2009, law enforcement in Derbyshire, East Midlands, England began uploading hundreds of files of collected glove prints into their criminal database. The Glove Mark Working Group in Derbyshire includes the Derbyshire Police Department, the Home Office Scientific Development Branch, and Nottingham Trent University.

With the belief that individual offenders possess preferences for specific types of gloves (style and fabric/material), forensic scientists have also used glove print databases to create complex computations and charts that isolate, geographically, "hot spots" where prints taken from specific types of gloves are matched against similar types of crimes. Forensic scientists have even had success matching partial glove prints by using these databases and related software. Offenders may prefer a specific type of glove depending on its perceived inherent benefits. Latex, nitrile, plastic, rubber, or vinyl gloves are worn because they are thin and cling to the wearer's skin which in turn provides a level of dexterity to the wearer. Leather gloves possess pores that provides the wearer with an enhanced gripping ability. Leather gloves that are thin and tight-fitting provide both enhanced gripping and dexterity to the wearer.

Prints from Different Glove Types

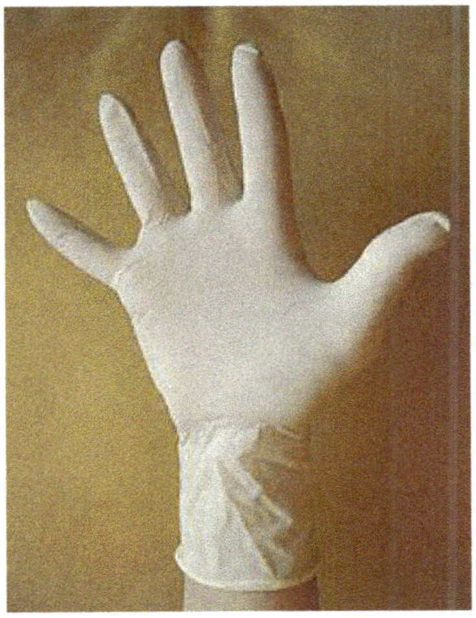

Assailants may prefer thin latex gloves because their snug fit helps to maintain dexterity.
This same thin and snugness may allow the wearer's fingerprints to pass through the material.
When discovered by authorities, latent fingerprints may also be recovered from the inside of these gloves.

- Thin, latex, rubber, plastic, vinyl or nitrile gloves: These gloves are worn by criminals because of their tight, thin fit that allows the hands to remain dexterous. Because of the thinness of these gloves, fingerprints may pass through the material, thus transferring the wearer's prints onto whatever surface is touched or handled.

Lined leather gloves may leave a print that is as unique as a human fingerprint.
When discovered by authorities, latent fingerprints may also be recovered from the inside of these gloves.

- Leather gloves: These gloves are worn by criminals because the tactile properties of the leather allow for good grip and dexterity. These properties are the result of the grain present on the surface of the glove. The grain makes the surface of the leather unique to each glove.

Over time, the pores and grain of leather gloves will pick up dirt and grease from surfaces that they have touched or handled. The dirt and grease can in return help to create prints on surfaces. Also, unlined gloves provide the most dexterity but can over time become saturated with the oils and sweat of the wearer's hands. This helps to increase the gripping properties of the gloves but causes the gloves to leave prints. A print that contains the glove wearer's sweat and oils will contain their DNA, which can incriminate them. Investigators are able to dust for the marks left behind from leather the same way they dust for fingerprints.

- Woolen, cotton, or other fabric gloves: These gloves are worn by criminals because they are typically inexpensive and readily available as well. Weave patterns of fabric gloves may also be unique to that glove and when collected at a crime scene, can be compared to gloves that are taken in as evidence. Like leather gloves, these gloves will over time pick up dirt and grease as well.

Notable Instances

Batting gloves usually include an unlined leather palm and a nylon or cotton back. For the same reason baseball players wear these gloves, to improve their grip while maintaining dexterity while batting, assailants wear these gloves as to maintain dexterity and be able to grip easily during their offenses.

- In 1993, Rochester, New York law enforcement was responding to a reported burglary when they arrested a suspect who was fleeing the burglarized home. On his person, investigators found a yellow rubber glove that was later found to match glove prints that were found on property that was known to have been stolen from the home.
- In 2001, Cobb County, Georgia, US, law enforcement responded to a break-in and burglary of an under-construction condominium development and found glove marks on a window that had been pushed open by the perpetrator. Law enforcement later found the perpetrator hiding in the complex and collected items that the perpetrator was hiding with him. Investigators were able to match the texture and weave pattern of the palms of the pair of construction/work-type gloves that the perpetrator had to the glove prints found on the window.
- In 2002, Grand Rapids, Michigan law enforcement was investigating a string of burglaries in the area. No fingerprints were found but latent glove prints were found with the use of fingerprint powder. A particularly detailed hand print of a leather glove became visible at the break-in point of one burglary. After a group of suspected burglars were brought in, the investigators received a warrant to search a vehicle that was linked the suspects. A brown leather

batting glove was recovered that seemed to match the stitch detail on the glove prints taken from the break-in point. After scanning both the palm of the leather glove and the recovered glove print into a computer, the investigators used Adobe Photoshop software to compare the grain detail of the glove with the grain detail of the glove print. The investigators were thus able to match the stitching and grain detail of both, thus incriminating the suspects.

- In 2009, a teenager was arrested in Royal Oak, Michigan for obstructing police near the location of a recently reported burglary. While in custody investigators compared the gloves that the suspect had in his possession to glove prints that were found at several break-in locations. Investigators were able to link marks left on a window to his gloves.
- In 2011, the Maricopa County, Arizona Sherriff's Office began investigating a string of robberies, dating to at least 1993, of high-end homes in the vicinity of Paradise Valley, Arizona. Investigators noted that the assailant (or assailants) wore fabric/cloth gardening gloves with rubber grips that had left unique prints on many surfaces in the burglarized locations. Upon arresting a 58-year-old suspect near a home that was under surveillance by the sheriff's office, authorities found amongst burglary tools in his possession, gardening gloves that matched the unique prints found at the burglarized locations.
- In 2012, law enforcement in Newton County, Indiana found unique glove prints at a home that was recently burglarized. The impressions left by the gloves seemed to possess indentations made by letters "M", "e", and "c" which would have been present on the surface of the gloves. Authorities were later able to match these unique impressions to Mechanix-brand gloves that were found at the residence of a suspect.
- On December 7, 2013 the Toronto Sun reported that the Royal Canadian Mounted Police seized hundreds of firearms that they found while searching homes in High River, Alberta that were temporarily deserted due to the 2013 Alberta floods. Residents who had their firearms seized also found glove marks on conspicuous places such as bedroom furniture, where guns were thought to be stored.

Blood Residue

In forensic science, blood residue – wet and dry remnants of blood, as well the discoloration of surfaces on which blood has been shed – can help investigators identify weapons, reconstruct a criminal action, and link suspects to the crime. Analysis of blood residue is also an important technique in archeology.

Forensic Significance

Blood constitutes about eight percent of a person's weight (normally about five liters), and it circulates near the surface of the skin. Almost all trauma to the body, therefore, results in the shedding of blood. Its red color makes it readily apparent at crime scenes, and its residues are very difficult to completely remove. Blood residue has even been recovered from 100,000-year-old stone tools.

Laboratory testing can reveal whether a substance is indeed blood, whether the blood is of animal or human origin, and the blood group to which it belongs. This allows investigators to include or exclude persons as perpetrators or victims. The antigens that allow blood group testing, however, deteriorate with age or improper storage. The DNA contained in blood, on the other hand, is less subject to deterioration, and allows near-certain matching of blood residue to individuals with DNA profiling techniques. Through bloodstain pattern analysis, information about events can also be gained from the spatial distribution of bloodstains.

Forensic Procedure

Finding and Documenting Blood Residue

Freshly dried bloodstains are a glossy reddish-brown in color. Under the influence of sunlight, the weather or removal attempts, the color eventually disappears and the stain turns gray. The surface on which it is found may also influence the stain's color.

Crime scenes are normally carefully searched for blood residue. Flashlights held at an angle to the surfaces under examination assist in this, as do luminol sprays which can detect even trace amounts of blood. Presumptive tests exist with which blood can be distinguished from other reddish stains, such as of ketchup or rust, found at the scene. The search includes areas beyond the immediate crime scene where blood might have been wiped off or bloody fingerprints left, such as towels or doorknobs. At outdoor crime scenes, bloodstains may be recovered from the ground or from plant surfaces.

The standard documentation of blood residue includes photographs and descriptions of form, color, size and position of each stain found. Overall photographs and sketches are also produced to show the relationship of the blood residue to other elements of the scene and to enable pattern analysis. Recently 3D imaging techniques have been tried for documenting and investigating bloodstains.

Collection and Preservation

To collect samples for analysis, wet blood is collected with a syringe and stored in a tube with anticoagulant, or collected with absorbent fabric that is allowed to air-dry. Dried blood is scraped off with a blade, or collected with a moistened cotton-tipped applicator, a gel lifter or fingerprint tape. Bloodstained clothing and other items are generally wrapped in paper and shipped whole to the laboratory. To prevent deterioration, blood residue samples are stored under refrigeration and, in the case of stains, air-dried.

Forensic Footwear Evidence

Forensic footwear evidence can be used in legal proceedings to help prove that a shoe was at a crime scene. Footwear evidence is often the most abundant form of evidence at a crime scene and in some cases can prove to be as specific as a fingerprint. Initially investigators will look to identify the make and model of the shoe or trainer which made an impression. This can be done visually or by comparison with evidence in a database; both methods focus heavily on pattern recognition and brand or logo marks. Information about the footwear can be gained from the analysis of wear patterns which are dependent on angle of footfall and weight distribution. Detailed examination of footwear impressions can help to link a specific piece of footwear to a footwear imprint as each shoe will have unique characteristics.

Types of Footwear Evidence

Footwear evidence can come in at least three forms, footwear outsole impressions, footwear insole impressions and footwear trace evidence.

Footwear Outsole Impressions

Footwear outsole impressions are impressions left on an object that was caused by contact with a piece of footwear. These can be left on the ground or raised surface by persons treading over it, left on doors or walls by persons attempting to kick or climb over a wall or even left on other persons after being kicked or stomped on.

There can also be latent impressions not easily visible to the naked eye, on many different surfaces such as floor tiles, concrete or even carpet. Detection may require the use of additional specialized light sources such as portable ultraviolet lighting. Recovery typically includes photography as well as lifting with "gel" or "electrostatic" dust lifters.

Footwear Insole Imprints

Imprints of a person's foot can be left on the insole's inside footwear. The size and arrangement of foot and toe imprints can be used to determine whether a person has worn a piece of footwear. The analysis and comparisons of foot imprints is part of the discipline of forensic podiatry.

Footwear Trace Evidence

Footwear trace evidence is trace evidence that is recovered from footwear. Types of trace evidence that could be recovered include skin, glass fragments, body hair, fibers from clothing or carpets, soil particles, dust and bodily fluids. The study of this trace evidence could be used to link a piece of footwear to a location or owner. DNA can be one of the contributing factors in forensic footwear evidence.

Detection of Footwear Evidence

Footwear impressions can be detected with a variety of methods including:

- Using artificial light sources to provide oblique, coaxial, and polarized light for detection of visible and latent impressions.
- Using electrostatic lifting devices to lift dusty impressions.
- Using physical or chemical enhancement methods to develop or enhance faint impressions.

Recovery of Footwear Impression Evidence

Footwear evidence occurs most often as either footwear impressions left in a soft surface, such as mud or as dust deposits, which are difficult for the human eye to detect. At violent crimescenes footmarks can be left as a result of a person standing in blood and subsequently trailing it as they move around the scene.

Lifting

Footwear impressions can be lifted from surfaces with tools such as adhesive lifters, gelatin lifters or electrostatic lifting devices.

Casting

Evidence left via impressions can generally be recovered utilizing a plaster cast. Initially the impression is isolated by framing the area with a solid boundary. Following this a plaster mix can be gently poured inside the frame; it is generally considered not best practice to pour directly onto the impression. In some cases where the surface is not ideal for casting prior techniques can be utilised to gain a better cast of the impression. Sand can often be fixed in place by applying an aerosol resin or glue although hair spray is often used. Wet mud impressions can be dried using a combination of pipetting water from the surface and applying hot air, often in the form of a hair dryer.

3D Scanning

Footwear evidence can be recovered with use of 3D scanners.

There are two types of 3D scanners used in forensics:

- crime scene scanners able to capture a large overview map of the scene;
- 'close-up' 3D scanners able to capture individual objects in high resolution and full colour.

Advantage of 3D scanning over casing is that 3D scanners can scan the object without touching or affecting it – most 3D scanners use lasers to capture 3D information. Some scanners can also capture the colour surface, [null producing] a visually [null accurate] replica of the object. To create a complete and highly detailed 3D model of a footprint less than 15 minutes is required.

Three-dimensional Imaging

Recent approach takes advantage of digital photography. A set of digital images of a footmark or target area of interest, taken in different viewpoints is required to create detailed and accurate 3D model. Appropriate software allows to visualise a 3D model in different ways, make accurate measurements from a 3D trace or perform a comparison of multiple traces.

Examination of Footwear Impressions Evidence

Footwear impression can reveal information that may be of use to forensic investigators. Analysis of impressions found at a crime scene may provide the following information:

Number of people at a crime scene: Different footwear impressions left at a crime scene will indicate more than one person was present at the crimescene.

Approximate height of the wearer: There is statistical correlation between foot/footwear size and height and also stride length and height. The dimensions of the footwear impression and the distance between impressions can be used to provide an estimate of height.

Activity of wearer when impression was made: Plastic footwear impression left on soft surfaces can reveal whether a person was walking, running or carrying a heavy load when the impression was made. An impression made by person running will make impressions that are deeper in the heel and toe sections. A person carrying a heavy load such as a body will leave imprints that are deeper than when not carrying a heavy load.

Manufacture, model and approximate size of footwear: Footwear impression can show the design elements (shapes, patterns, arrangement) that form the outsole design. These can be compared with a footwear outsole database to identify the model of footwear that made the impression. Knowledge of the model of footwear that made the impression can assist in narrowing down the list of suspects and can also be used to link multiple crime scenes to the same perpetrator(s).

Establish link between crime scene impression with a specific piece of footwear: Comparison of crime scene impressions with a specific piece of footwear recovered from a suspect can determine if there is any relationship. A worn piece of footwear will gradually acquire unique wear and tear on the outsoles. These randomly acquired characteristics will be unique to that specific shoe and may show in crime scene impressions.

- If class characteristics and size matches: investigators can determine that footwear could have made the impression, but other footwear with similar design and size could also have made the impression.
- If class characteristics, size match and randomly acquired characteristics found in the footwear outsole can also be found in the crime scene impressions: Investigators can determine that the specific piece created the crime scene impression. This relationship can be used as evidence to prove that the footwear's owner was at the crime scene.

Shoeprints left at a crime scene

Photo of a suspect's shoes

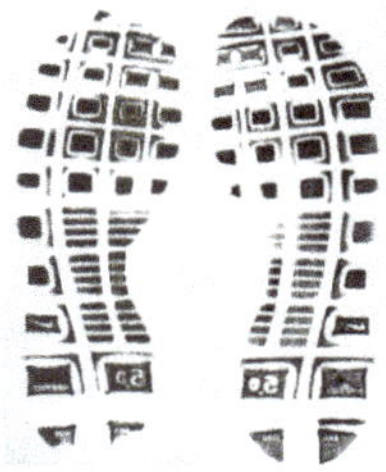

Test impressions made with a suspect's shoes

A suspect's footwear 1

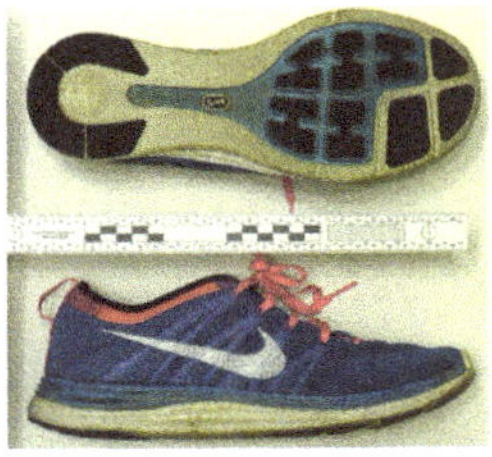

A suspect's footwear 2

Limitations of Footwear Evidence

The Unabomber, Theodore Kaczynski, was known to keep shoes with smaller soles attached to the base in order to confuse investigators about the size of the suspect's feet.

Footwear Databases

Forensic investigators can use computerized footwear databases to quickly compare the class characteristics such as tread design and possibly identify a manufacturer, brand, and model to the ones stored in the database

DNA Profiling

DNA profiling (also called DNA fingerprinting, DNA testing, or DNA typing) is a forensic technique used to identify individuals by characteristics of their DNA. A DNA profile is a small set of DNA variations that is very likely to be different in all unrelated individuals, thereby being as unique to individuals as are fingerprints (hence the alternative name for the technique). DNA profiling should not be confused with full genome sequencing. First developed and used in 1984, DNA profiling is used in, for example, parentage testing and criminal investigation, to identify a person or to place a person at a crime scene, techniques which are now employed globally in forensic science to facilitate police detective work and help clarify paternity and immigration disputes. DNA fingerprinting has also been widely used in the study of animal and floral populations and has revolutionized the fields of zoology, botany, and agriculture.

Although 99.9% of human DNA sequences are the same in every person, enough of the DNA is different that it is possible to distinguish one individual from another, unless they are monozygotic ("identical") twins. DNA profiling uses repetitive ("repeat") sequences that are highly variable, called variable number tandem repeats (VNTRs), in particular short tandem repeats (STRs), also known as microsatellites, and minisatellites. VNTR loci are very similar between closely related individuals, but are so variable that unrelated individuals are extremely unlikely to have the same VNTRs.

The modern process of DNA profiling was developed in 1984 by Sir Alec Jeffreys while working in the Department of Genetics at the University of Leicester.

DNA Profiling Process

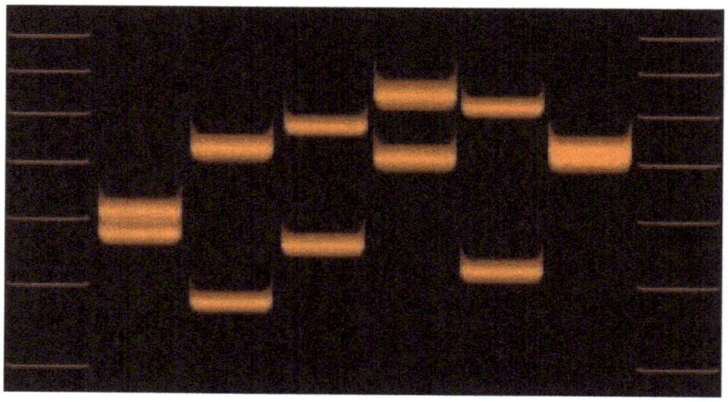

Variations of VNTR allele lengths in 6 individuals.

Developed by Professor of Genetics Sir Alec Jeffreys, the process begins with a sample of an individual's DNA (typically called a "reference sample"). A common method of collecting a reference sample is the use of a buccal swab, which is easy, non-invasive and cheap. When this is not available (e.g. because a court order is needed but not obtainable) other methods may need to be used to collect a sample of blood, saliva, semen, vaginal lubrication, or other appropriate fluid or tissue from personal items (e.g. a toothbrush, razor) or from stored samples (e.g. banked sperm or biopsy tissue). Samples obtained from blood relatives (related by birth, not marriage) can provide an indication of an individual's profile, as could human remains that had been previously profiled.

A reference sample is then analyzed to create the individual's DNA profile using one of a number of techniques, discussed below. The DNA profile is then compared against another sample to determine whether there is a genetic match.

RFLP Analysis

The first methods for finding out genetics used for DNA profiling involved RFLP analysis. DNA is collected from cells, such as a blood sample, and cut into small pieces using a restriction enzyme (a restriction digest). This generates thousands of DNA fragments of differing sizes as a consequence of variations between DNA sequences of different individuals. The fragments are then separated on the basis of size using gel electrophoresis.

The separated fragments are then transferred to a nitrocellulose or nylon filter; this procedure is called a Southern blot. The DNA fragments within the blot are permanently fixed to the filter, and the DNA strands are denatured. Radiolabeled probe molecules are then added that are complementary to sequences in the genome that contain repeat sequences. These repeat sequences tend to vary in length among different individuals and are called variable number tandem repeat sequences or VNTRs. The probe molecules hybridize to DNA fragments containing the repeat sequences and excess probe molecules are washed away. The blot is then exposed to an X-ray film. Fragments of DNA that have bound to the probe molecules appear as dark bands on the film.

The Southern blot technique is laborious, and requires large amounts of undegraded sample DNA. Also, Karl Brown's original technique looked at many minisatellite loci at the same time, increasing the observed variability, but making it hard to discern individual alleles (and thereby precluding paternity testing). These early techniques have been supplanted by PCR-based assays.

Polymerase Chain Reaction(PCR) Analysis

Developed by Kary Mullis in 1983, a process was reported by which specific portions of the sample DNA can be amplified almost indefinitely (Saiki et al. 1985, 1988). This has revolutionized the whole field of DNA study. The process, the polymerase chain reaction (PCR), mimics the biological process of DNA replication, but confines it to specific DNA sequences of interest. With the invention of the PCR technique, DNA profiling took huge strides forward in both discriminating power and the ability to recover information from very small (or degraded) starting samples.

PCR greatly amplifies the amounts of a specific region of DNA. In the PCR process, the DNA sample is denatured into the separate individual polynucleotide strands through heating. Two oligonucleotide DNA primers are used to hybridize to two corresponding nearby sites on opposite DNA strands in such a fashion that the normal enzymatic extension of the active terminal of each primer (that is, the 3' end) leads toward the other primer. PCR uses replication enzymes that are tolerant of high temperatures, such as the thermostable Taq polymerase. In this fashion, two new copies of the sequence of interest are generated. Repeated denaturation, hybridization, and extension in this fashion produce an exponentially growing number of copies of the DNA of interest. Instruments that perform thermal cycling are readily available from commercial sources. This process can produce a million-fold or greater amplification of the desired region in 2 hours or less.

Early assays such as the HLA-DQ alpha reverse dot blot strips grew to be very popular due to their ease of use, and the speed with which a result could be obtained. However, they were not as discriminating as RFLP analysis. It was also difficult to determine a DNA profile for mixed samples, such as a vaginal swab from a sexual assault victim.

However, the PCR method was readily adaptable for analyzing VNTR, in particular STR loci. In recent years, research in human DNA quantitation has focused on new "real-time" quantitative PCR (qPCR) techniques. Quantitative PCR methods enable automated, precise, and high-throughput measurements. Inter-laboratory studies have demonstrated the importance of human DNA quantitation on achieving reliable interpretation of STR typing and obtaining consistent results across laboratories.

STR Analysis

The system of DNA profiling used today is based on PCR and uses simple sequences or short tandem repeats (STR). This method uses highly polymorphic regions that have short repeated sequences of DNA (the most common is 4 bases repeated, but there are other lengths in use, including 3 and 5 bases). Because unrelated people almost certainly have different numbers of repeat units, STRs can be used to discriminate between unrelated individuals. These STR loci (locations on a chromosome) are targeted with sequence-specific primers and amplified using PCR. The DNA fragments that result are then separated and detected using electrophoresis. There are two common methods of separation and detection, capillary electrophoresis (CE) and gel electrophoresis.

Each STR is polymorphic, but the number of alleles is very small. Typically each STR allele will be shared by around 5 - 20% of individuals. The power of STR analysis comes from looking at multiple STR loci simultaneously. The pattern of alleles can identify an individual quite accurately. Thus STR analysis provides an excellent identification tool. The more STR regions that are tested in an individual the more discriminating the test becomes.

From country to country, different STR-based DNA-profiling systems are in use. In North America, systems that amplify the CODIS 20 core loci are almost universal, whereas in the United Kingdom the DNA-17 17 loci system (which is compatible with The National DNA Database) is in use. Whichever system is used, many of the STR regions used are the same. These DNA-profiling systems are based on multiplex reactions, whereby many STR regions will be tested at the same time.

The true power of STR analysis is in its statistical power of discrimination. Because the 20 loci that are currently used for discrimination in CODIS are independently assorted (having a certain number of repeats at one locus does not change the likelihood of having any number of repeats at any other locus), the product rule for probabilities can be applied. This means that, if someone has the DNA type of ABC, where the three loci were independent, we can say that the probability of having that DNA type is the probability of having type A times the probability of having type B times the probability of having type C. This has resulted in the ability to generate match probabilities of 1 in a quintillion ($1x10^{18}$) or more. However, DNA database searches showed much more frequent than expected false DNA profile matches. Moreover, since there are about 12 million monozygotic twins on Earth, the theoretical probability is not accurate.

In practice, the risk of contaminated-matching is much greater than matching a distant relative, such as contamination of a sample from nearby objects, or from left-over cells transferred from a prior test. The risk is greater for matching the most common person in the samples: Everything collected from, or in contact with, a victim is a major source of contamination for any other samples brought into a lab. For that reason, multiple control-samples are typically tested in order to ensure that they stayed clean, when prepared during the same period as the actual test samples. Unexpected matches (or variations) in several control-samples indicates a high probability of contamination for the actual test samples. In a relationship test, the full DNA profiles should differ (except for twins), to prove that a person was not actually matched as being related to their own DNA in another sample.

AmpFLP

Another technique, AmpFLP, or amplified fragment length polymorphism was also put into practice during the early 1990s. This technique was also faster than RFLP analysis and used PCR to amplify DNA samples. It relied on variable number tandem repeat (VNTR) polymorphisms to distinguish various alleles, which were separated on a polyacrylamide gel using an allelic ladder (as opposed to a molecular weight ladder). Bands could be visualized by silver staining the gel. One popular focus for fingerprinting was the D1S80 locus. As with all PCR based methods, highly degraded DNA or very small amounts of DNA may cause allelic dropout (causing a mistake in thinking a heterozygote is a homozygote) or other stochastic effects. In addition, because the analysis is done on a gel, very high number repeats may bunch together at the top of the gel, making it difficult to resolve. AmpFLP analysis can be highly automated, and allows for easy creation of phylogenetic trees based on comparing individual samples of DNA. Due to its relatively low cost and ease of set-up and operation, AmpFLP remains popular in lower income countries.

DNA Family Relationship Analysis

Using PCR technology, DNA analysis is widely applied to determine genetic family relationships such as paternity, maternity, siblingship and other kinships.

During conception, the father's sperm cell and the mother's egg cell, each containing half the amount of DNA found in other body cells, meet and fuse to form a fertilized egg, called a zygote. The zygote contains a complete set of DNA molecules, a unique combination of DNA from both parents. This zygote divides and multiplies into an embryo and later, a full human being.

At each stage of development, all the cells forming the body contain the same DNA—half from the father and half from the mother. This fact allows the relationship testing to use all types of all samples including loose cells from the cheeks collected using buccal swabs, blood or other types of samples.

There are predictable inheritance patterns at certain locations (called loci) in the human genome, which have been found to be useful in determining identity and biological relationships. These loci contain specific DNA markers that scientists use to identify individuals. In a routine DNA paternity test, the markers used are Short Tandem Repeats (STRs), short pieces of DNA that occur in highly differential repeat patterns among individuals.

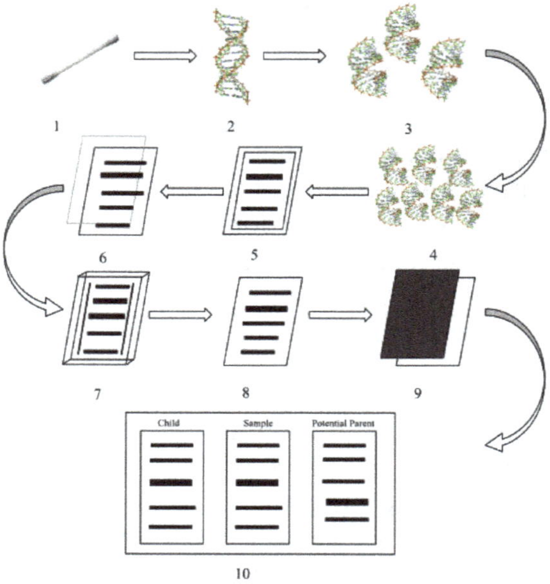

1: A cell sample is taken- usually a cheek swab or blood test
2: DNA is extracted from sample
3: Cleavage of DNA by restriction enzyme- the DNA is broken into small fragments
4: Small fragments are amplified by the Polymerase Chain Reaction- results in many more fragments
5: DNA fragments are separated by electrophoresis
6: The fragments are transferred to an agar plate
7: On the Agar Plate specific DNA fragments are bound to a radioactive DNA probe
8: The Agar Plate is washed free of excess probe
9: An x-ray film is used to detect a radioactive pattern
10: The DNA is compared to other DNA samples

There are predictable inheritance patterns at certain locations (called loci) in the human genome, which have been found to be useful in determining identity and biological relationships. These loci contain specific DNA markers that scientists use to identify individuals. In a routine DNA paternity test, the markers used are Short Tandem Repeats (STRs), short pieces of DNA that occur in highly differential repeat patterns among individuals.

Each person's DNA contains two copies of these markers—one copy inherited from the father and one from the mother. Within a population, the markers at each person's DNA location could differ in length and sometimes sequence, depending on the markers inherited from the parents.

The combination of marker sizes found in each person makes up his/her unique genetic profile. When determining the relationship between two individuals, their genetic profiles are compared to see if they share the same inheritance patterns at a statistically conclusive rate.

For example, the following sample report from this commercial DNA paternity testing laboratory Universal Genetics signifies how relatedness between parents and child is identified on those special markers:

DNA Marker	***Mother***	***Child***	***Alleged father***
D21S11	*28, 30*	*28, 31*	*29, 31*

D7S820	*9, 10*	*10, 11*	*11, 12*
TH01	*14, 15*	*14, 16*	*15, 16*
D13S317	*7, 8*	*7, 9*	*8, 9*
D19S433	*14, 16.2*	*14, 15*	*15, 17*

The partial results indicate that the child and the alleged father's DNA match among these five markers. The complete test results show this correlation on 16 markers between the child and the tested man to enable a conclusion to be drawn as to whether or not the man is the biological father.

Each marker is assigned with a Paternity Index (PI), which is a statistical measure of how powerfully a match at a particular marker indicates paternity. The PI of each marker is multiplied with each other to generate the Combined Paternity Index (CPI), which indicates the overall probability of an individual being the biological father of the tested child relative to a randomly selected man from the entire population of the same race. The CPI is then converted into a Probability of Paternity showing the degree of relatedness between the alleged father and child.

The DNA test report in other family relationship tests, such as grandparentage and siblingship tests, is similar to a paternity test report. Instead of the Combined Paternity Index, a different value, such as a Siblingship Index, is reported.

The report shows the genetic profiles of each tested person. If there are markers shared among the tested individuals, the probability of biological relationship is calculated to determine how likely the tested individuals share the same markers due to a blood relationship.

Y-chromosome Analysis

Recent innovations have included the creation of primers targeting polymorphic regions on the Y-chromosome (Y-STR), which allows resolution of a mixed DNA sample from a male and female or cases in which a differential extraction is not possible. Y-chromosomes are paternally inherited, so Y-STR analysis can help in the identification of paternally related males. Y-STR analysis was performed in the Sally Hemings controversy to determine if Thomas Jefferson had sired a son with one of his slaves. The analysis of the Y-chromosome yields weaker results than autosomal chromosome analysis. The Y male sex-determining chromosome, as it is inherited only by males from their fathers, is almost identical along the patrilineal line. This leads to a less precise analysis than if autosomal chromosomes were testing, because of the random matching that occurs between pairs of chromosomes as zygotes are being made.

Mitochondrial Analysis

For highly degraded samples, it is sometimes impossible to get a complete profile of the 13 CODIS STRs. In these situations, mitochondrial DNA (mtDNA) is sometimes typed due to there being many copies of mtDNA in a cell, while there may only be 1-2 copies of the nuclear DNA. Forensic scientists amplify the HV1 and HV2 regions of the mtDNA, and then sequence each region and compare single-nucleotide differences to a reference. Because mtDNA is maternally inherited, directly linked maternal relatives can be used as match references, such as one's maternal grandmother's daughter's son. In general, a difference of two or more nucleotides is considered to be an exclusion. Heteroplasmy and poly-C differences may throw off straight sequence comparisons, so some expertise on the part of the analyst is required. mtDNA is useful in determining clear identities, such as those of missing people when a maternally linked relative can be found. mtDNA testing was used in determining that Anna Anderson was not the Russian princess she had claimed to be, Anastasia Romanov.

mtDNA can be obtained from such material as hair shafts and old bones/teeth. Control mechanism based on interaction point with data. This can be determined by tooled placement in sample.

DNA Databases

An early application of a DNA database was the compilation of A Mitochondrial DNA Concordance, prepared by Kevin W. P. Miller and John L. Dawson at the University of Cambridge from 1996 to 1998 from data collected as part of Miller's PhD thesis. There are now several DNA databases in existence around the world. Some are private, but most of the largest databases are government controlled. The United States maintains the largest DNA database, with the Combined DNA Index System (CODIS) holding over 5 million records as of 2007. The United Kingdom maintains the National DNA Database (NDNAD), which is of similar size, despite the UK's smaller population. The size of this database, and its rate of growth, are giving concern to civil liberties groups in the UK, where police have wide-ranging powers to take samples and retain them even in the event of acquittal.

The U.S. Patriot Act of the United States provides a means for the U.S. government to get DNA samples from other countries if they are either a division of or a head office of a company operating in the U.S. Under the act; the American offices of the company may not divulge to their subsidiaries/offices in other countries the reasons that these DNA samples are sought or by whom.

When a match is made from a National DNA Databank to link a crime scene to an offender having provided a DNA Sample to a databank that link is often referred to as a *cold hit*. A cold hit is of value in referring the police agency to a specific suspect but is of less evidential value than a DNA match made from outside the DNA Databank.

FBI agents cannot legally store DNA of a person not convicted of a crime. DNA collected from a suspect not later convicted must be disposed of and not entered into the database. In 1998, a man residing in the UK was arrested on accusation of burglary. His DNA was taken and tested, and he was later released. Nine months later, this man's DNA was accidentally and illegally entered in the DNA database. New DNA is automatically compared to the DNA found at cold cases and, in this case, this man was found to be a match to DNA found at a rape and assault case one year earlier. The government then prosecuted him for these crimes. During the trial the DNA match was requested to be removed from the evidence because it had been illegally entered into the database. The request was carried out.

The DNA collected from victims of rape are often stored for years until matched with the perpetrator's, usually when committing another crime. In 2014, Congress extended a bill that helps states deal with "a backlog" of unexamined evidence.

Considerations when Evaluating DNA Evidence

In the early days of the use of genetic fingerprinting as criminal evidence, juries were often swayed by spurious statistical arguments by defense lawyers along these lines: Given a match that had a

1 in 5 million probability of occurring by chance, the lawyer would argue that this meant that in a country of say 60 million people there were 12 people who would also match the profile. This was then translated to a 1 in 12 chance of the suspect's being the guilty one. This argument is not sound unless the suspect was drawn at random from the population of the country. In fact, a jury should consider how likely it is that an individual matching the genetic profile would also have been a suspect in the case for other reasons. Also, different DNA analysis processes can reduce the amount of DNA recovery if the procedures are not properly done. Therefore, the number of times a piece of evidence is sampled can diminish the DNA collection efficiency. Another spurious statistical argument is based on the false assumption that a 1 in 5 million probability of a match automatically translates into a 1 in 5 million probability of innocence and is known as the prosecutor's fallacy.

When using RFLP, the theoretical risk of a coincidental match is 1 in 100 billion (100,000,000,000), although the practical risk is actually 1 in 1000 because monozygotic twins are 0.2% of the human population. Moreover, the rate of laboratory error is almost certainly higher than this, and often actual laboratory procedures do not reflect the theory under which the coincidence probabilities were computed. For example, the coincidence probabilities may be calculated based on the probabilities that markers in two samples have bands in *precisely* the same location, but a laboratory worker may conclude that similar—but not precisely identical—band patterns result from identical genetic samples with some imperfection in the agarose gel. However, in this case, the laboratory worker increases the coincidence risk by expanding the criteria for declaring a match. Recent studies have quoted relatively high error rates, which may be cause for concern. In the early days of genetic fingerprinting, the necessary population data to accurately compute a match probability was sometimes unavailable. Between 1992 and 1996, arbitrary low ceilings were controversially put on match probabilities used in RFLP analysis rather than the higher theoretically computed ones. Today, RFLP has become widely disused due to the advent of more discriminating, sensitive and easier technologies.

Since 1998, the DNA profiling system supported by The National DNA Database in the UK is the SGM+ DNA profiling system that includes 10 STR regions and a sex-indicating test. STRs do not suffer from such subjectivity and provide similar power of discrimination (1 in 10^{13} for unrelated individuals if using a full SGM+ profile). Figures of this magnitude are not considered to be statistically supportable by scientists in the UK; for unrelated individuals with full matching DNA profiles a match probability of 1 in a billion is considered statistically supportable. However, with any DNA technique, the cautious juror should not convict on genetic fingerprint evidence alone if other factors raise doubt. Contamination with other evidence (secondary transfer) is a key source of incorrect DNA profiles and raising doubts as to whether a sample has been adulterated is a favorite defense technique. More rarely, chimerism is one such instance where the lack of a genetic match may unfairly exclude a suspect.

Evidence of Genetic Relationship

It is also possible to use DNA profiling as evidence of genetic relationship, although such evidence varies in strength from weak to positive. Testing that shows no relationship is absolutely certain.

While almost all individuals have a single and distinct set of genes, ultra-rare individuals, known as "chimeras", have at least two different sets of genes. There have been two cases of DNA profiling that falsely suggested that a mother was unrelated to her children. This happens when two eggs are fertilized at the same time and fuse together to create one individual instead of twins.

Fake DNA Evidence

In one case, a criminal planted fake DNA evidence in his own body: John Schneeberger raped one of his sedated patients in 1992 and left semen on her underwear. Police drew what they believed to be Schneeberger's blood and compared its DNA against the crime scene semen DNA on three occasions, never showing a match. It turned out that he had surgically inserted a Penrose drain into his arm and filled it with foreign blood and anticoagulants.

The functional analysis of genes and their coding sequences (open reading frames [ORFs]) typically requires that each ORF be expressed, the encoded protein purified, antibodies produced, phenotypes examined, intracellular localization determined, and interactions with other proteins sought. In a study conducted by the life science company Nucleix and published in the journal Forensic Science International, scientists found that an In vitro synthesized sample of DNA matching any desired genetic profile can be constructed using standard molecular biology techniques without obtaining any actual tissue from that person. Nucleix claims they can also prove the difference between non-altered DNA and any that was synthesized.

In the case of the Phantom of Heilbronn, police detectives found DNA traces from the same woman on various crime scenes in Austria, Germany, and France—among them murders, burglaries and robberies. Only after the DNA of the "woman" matched the DNA sampled from the burned body of a *male* asylum seeker in France, detectives began to have serious doubts about the DNA evidence. In that case, DNA traces were already present on the cotton swabs used to collect the samples at the crime scene, and the swabs had all been produced at the same factory in Austria. The company's product specification said that the swabs were guaranteed to be sterile, but not DNA-free.

DNA Evidence as Evidence in Criminal Trials

Familial DNA Searching

Familial DNA searching (sometimes referred to as "Familial DNA" or "Familial DNA Database Searching") is the practice of creating new investigative leads in cases where DNA evidence found at the scene of a crime (forensic profile) strongly resembles that of an existing DNA profile (offender profile) in a state DNA database but there is not an exact match. After all other leads have been exhausted, investigators may use specially developed software to compare the forensic profile to all profiles taken from a state's DNA database to generate a list of those offenders already in the database who are most likely to be a very close relative of the individual whose DNA is in the forensic profile. To eliminate the majority of this list when the forensic DNA is a man's, crime lab technicians conduct Y-STR analysis. Using standard investigative techniques, authorities are then able to build a family tree. The family tree is populated from information gathered from public records and criminal justice records. Investigators rule out family members' involvement in the crime by finding excluding factors such as sex, living out of state or being incarcerated when the crime was committed. They may also use other leads from the case, such as witness or victim statements, to identify a suspect. Once a suspect has been identified, investigators seek to legally obtain a DNA sample from the suspect. This suspect DNA profile is then compared to the sample found at the crime scene to definitively identify the suspect as the source of the crime scene DNA.

Familial DNA database searching was first used in an investigation leading to the conviction of Craig Harman of manslaughter in the United Kingdom on April 19, 2004. Craig Harman was convicted using familial DNA because of the partial matches from Harman's brother. When the police questioned Harman's brother, the police noticed Harman lived very close to the original crime scene. Harman confessed when his DNA isolated from the DNA found on the brick, matched. Currently, familial DNA database searching is not conducted on a national level in the United States, where states determine how and when to conduct familial searches. The first familial DNA search with a subsequent conviction in the United States was conducted in Denver, Colorado, in 2008, using software developed under the leadership of Denver District Attorney Mitch Morrissey and Denver Police Department Crime Lab Director Gregg LaBerge. California was the first state to implement a policy for familial searching under then Attorney General, now Governor, Jerry Brown. In his role as consultant to the Familial Search Working Group of the California Department of Justice, former Alameda County Prosecutor Rock Harmon is widely considered to have been the catalyst in the adoption of familial search technology in California. The technique was used to catch the Los Angeles serial killer known as the "Grim Sleeper" in 2010. It wasn't a witness or informant that tipped off law enforcement to the identity of the "Grim Sleeper" serial killer, who had eluded police for more than two decades, but DNA from the suspect's own son. The suspect's son was arrested and convicted in a felony weapons charge and swabbed for DNA last year. When his DNA was entered into the database of convicted felons, detectives were alerted to a partial match to evidence found at the "Grim Sleeper" crime scenes. David Franklin Jr., also known as the Grim Sleeper, was charged with ten counts of murder and one count of attempted murder. More recently, familial DNA, led to the arrest of 21-year-old Elvis Garcia on charges of sexual assault and false imprisonment of a woman in Santa Cruz in 2008. In March 2011 Virginia Governor Bob McDonnell announced that Virginia would begin using familial DNA searches. Other states are expected to follow.

At a press conference in Virginia on March 7, 2011, regarding the East Coast Rapist, Prince William County prosecutor Paul Ebert and Fairfax County Police Detective John Kelly said the case would have been solved years ago if Virginia had used familial DNA searching. Aaron Thomas, the suspected East Coast Rapist, was arrested in connection with the rape of 17 women from Virginia to Rhode Island, but familial DNA was not used in the case.

Critics of familial DNA database searches argue that the technique is an invasion of an individual's 4th Amendment rights. Privacy advocates are petitioning for DNA database restrictions, arguing that the only fair way to search for possible DNA matches to relatives of offenders or arrestees would be to have a population-wide DNA database. Some scholars have pointed out that the privacy concerns surrounding familial searching are similar in some respects to other police search techniques, and most have concluded that the practice is constitutional. The Ninth Circuit Court of Appeals in *United States v. Pool* (vacated as moot) suggested that this practice is somewhat analogous to a witness looking at a photograph of one person and stating that it looked like the perpetrator, which leads law enforcement to show the witness photos of similar looking individuals, one of whom is identified as the perpetrator. Regardless of whether familial DNA searching was the method used to identify the suspect, authorities always conduct a normal DNA test to match the suspect's DNA with that of the DNA left at the crime scene.

Critics also claim that racial profiling could occur on account of Familial DNA testing. In the United States, the conviction rates of racial minorities are much higher than that of the overall population. It is unclear whether this is due to discrimination from police officers and the courts, as opposed to a simple higher rate of offence among minorities. Arrest-based databases, which are found in the majority of the United States, lead to an even greater level of racial discrimination. An arrest, as opposed to conviction, relies much more heavily on police discretion.

For instance, investigators with Denver District Attorney's Office successfully identified a suspect in a property theft case using a familial DNA search. In this example, the suspect's blood left at the scene of the crime strongly resembled that of a current Colorado Department of Corrections prisoner. Using publicly available records, the investigators created a family tree. They then eliminated all the family members who were incarcerated at the time of the offense, as well as all of the females (the crime scene DNA profile was that of a male). Investigators obtained a court order to collect the suspect's DNA, but the suspect actually volunteered to come to a police station and give a DNA sample. After providing the sample, the suspect walked free without further interrogation or detainment. Later confronted with an exact match to the forensic profile, the suspect pleaded guilty to criminal trespass at the first court date and was sentenced to two years probation.

In Italy a familiar DNA search has been done to solve the case of the murder of Yara Gambirasio whose body was found in the bush three months after her disappearance. A DNA trace was found on the underwear of the murdered teenage near and a DNA sample was requested from a person who lived near the municipality of Brembate di Sopra and a common male ancestor was found in the DNA sample of a young man not involved in the murder. After a long investigation the father of the supposed killer was identified in Giuseppe Guerinoni a deceased man but his two sons born from his wife were not related with the DNA samples found on the body of Yara. After 3 and a half years the DNA found on the underwear of the deceased girl was matched with Massimo Giuseppe Bosetti who was arrested and accused of the murder of the 13-year-old girl. In the summer of 2016 Bosetti was found guilty and sentenced to life by the Corte d'assise of Bergamo.

Partial Matches

Partial DNA matches are not searches themselves, but are the result of moderate stringency CODIS searches that produce a potential match that shares at least one allele at every locus. Partial matching does not involve the use of familial search software, such as those used in the UK and United States, or additional Y-STR analysis, and therefore often misses sibling relationships. Partial matching has been used to identify suspects in several cases in the UK and United States, and has also been used as a tool to exonerate the falsely accused. Darryl Hunt was wrongly convicted in connection with the rape and murder of a young woman in 1984 in North Carolina. Hunt was exonerated in 2004 when a DNA database search produced a remarkably close match between a convicted felon and the forensic profile from the case. The partial match led investigators to the felon's brother, Willard E. Brown, who confessed to the crime when confronted by police. A judge then signed an order to dismiss the case against Hunt.

Surreptitious DNA Collecting

Police forces may collect DNA samples without the suspects' knowledge, and use it as evidence. Legality of this mode of proceeding has been questioned in Australia.

In the United States, it has been accepted, courts often claiming that there was no expectation of privacy, citing *California v. Greenwood* (1985), in which the Supreme Court held that the Fourth Amendment does not prohibit the warrantless search and seizure of garbage left for collection outside the curtilage of a home. Critics of this practice underline that this analogy ignores that "most people have no idea that they risk surrendering their genetic identity to the police by, for instance, failing to destroy a used coffee cup. Moreover, even if they do realize it, there is no way to avoid abandoning one's DNA in public."

In the UK, the Human Tissue Act 2004 prohibited private individuals from covertly collecting biological samples (hair, fingernails, etc.) for DNA analysis, but excluded medical and criminal investigations from the offence.

The U.S. Supreme Court ruled 5–4 on June 3, 2013, in the case of *Maryland v. King*, that DNA sampling of prisoners arrested for serious crimes is constitutional.

England and Wales

Evidence from an expert who has compared DNA samples must be accompanied by evidence as to the sources of the samples and the procedures for obtaining the DNA profiles. The judge must ensure that the jury must understand the significance of DNA matches and mismatches in the profiles. The judge must also ensure that the jury does not confuse the 'match probability' (the probability that a person that is chosen at random has a matching DNA profile to the sample from the scene) with the probability that a person with matching DNA committed the crime. In 1996 *R v. Doheny* Phillips LJ gave this example of a summing up, which should be carefully tailored to the particular facts in each case:

Members of the Jury, if you accept the scientific evidence called by the Crown, this indicates that there are probably only four or five white males in the United Kingdom from whom that semen stain could have come. The Defendant is one of them. If that is the position, the decision you have to reach, on all the evidence, is whether you are sure that it was the Defendant who left that stain or whether it is possible that it was one of that other small group of men who share the same DNA characteristics.

Juries should weigh up conflicting and corroborative evidence, using their own common sense and not by using mathematical formulae, such as Bayes' theorem, so as to avoid "confusion, misunderstanding and misjudgment".

Presentation and Evaluation of Evidence of Partial or Incomplete DNA profiles

In *R v Bates*, Moore-Bick LJ said:

We can see no reason why partial profile DNA evidence should not be admissible provided that the jury are made aware of its inherent limitations and are given a sufficient explanation to enable them to evaluate it. There may be cases where the match probability in relation to all the samples tested is so great that the judge would consider its probative value to be minimal and decide to exclude the evidence in the exercise of his discretion, but this gives rise to no new question of principle and can be left for decision on a case by case basis. However, the fact that there exists in the case of all partial profile evidence the possibility that a "missing" allele might exculpate the accused altogether does not provide sufficient grounds for rejecting such evidence. In many there is a possibility (at least in theory) that evidence that would assist the accused and perhaps even exculpate him altogether exists, but that does not provide grounds for excluding relevant evidence that is available and otherwise admissible, though it does make it important to ensure that the jury are given sufficient information to enable them to evaluate that evidence properly.

DNA Testing in the United States

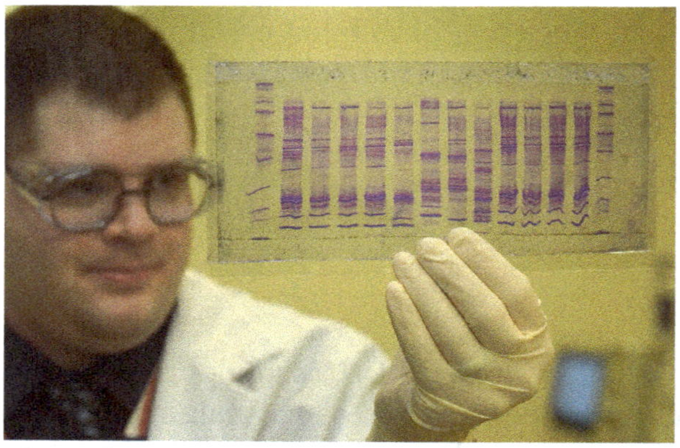

CBP chemist reads a DNA profile to determine the origin of a commodity.

There are state laws on DNA profiling in all 50 states of the United States. Detailed information on database laws in each state can be found at the National Conference of State Legislatures website.

Development of Artificial DNA

In August 2009, scientists in Israel raised serious doubts concerning the use of DNA by law enforcement as the ultimate method of identification. In a paper published in the journal *Forensic Science International: Genetics*, the Israeli researchers demonstrated that it is possible to manufacture DNA in a laboratory, thus falsifying DNA evidence. The scientists fabricated saliva and blood samples, which originally contained DNA from a person other than the supposed donor of the blood and saliva.

The researchers also showed that, using a DNA database, it is possible to take information from a profile and manufacture DNA to match it, and that this can be done without access to any actual DNA from the person whose DNA they are duplicating. The synthetic DNA oligos required for the procedure are common in molecular laboratories.

The New York Times quoted the lead author, Daniel Frumkin, saying, "You can just engineer a crime scene...any biology undergraduate could perform this". Frumkin perfected a test that can differentiate real DNA samples from fake ones. His test detects epigenetic modifications, in particular, DNA methylation. Seventy percent of the DNA in any human genome is methylated, meaning it contains methyl group modifications within a CpG dinucleotide context. Methylation at the promoter region is associated with gene silencing. The synthetic DNA lacks this epigenetic modification, which allows the test to distinguish manufactured DNA from genuine DNA.

It is unknown how many police departments, if any, currently use the test. No police lab has publicly announced that it is using the new test to verify DNA results.

Cases

- In 1986, Richard Buckland was exonerated, despite having admitted to the rape and murder of a teenager near Leicester, the city where DNA profiling was first developed. This was the first use of DNA fingerprinting in a criminal investigation, and the first to prove a suspect's innocence. The following year Colin Pitchfork was identified as the perpetrator of the same murder, in addition to another, using the same techniques that had cleared Buckland.
- In 1987, genetic fingerprinting was used in criminal court for the first time in the trial of a man accused of unlawful intercourse with a mentally handicapped 14-year-old female who gave birth to a baby.
- In 1987, Florida rapist Tommie Lee Andrews was the first person in the United States to be convicted as a result of DNA evidence, for raping a woman during a burglary; he was convicted on November 6, 1987, and sentenced to 22 years in prison.
- In 1988, Timothy Wilson Spencer was the first man in Virginia to be sentenced to death through DNA testing, for several rape and murder charges. He was dubbed "The South Side Strangler" because he killed victims on the south side of Richmond, Virginia. He was later charged with rape and first-degree murder and was sentenced to death. He was executed on April 27, 1994. David Vasquez, initially convicted of one of Spencer's crimes, became the first man in America exonerated based on DNA evidence.
- In 1989, Chicago man Gary Dotson was the first person whose conviction was overturned using DNA evidence.
- In 1991, Allan Legere was the first Canadian to be convicted as a result of DNA evidence, for four murders he had committed while an escaped prisoner in 1989. During his trial, his defense argued that the relatively shallow gene pool of the region could lead to false positives.
- In 1992, DNA evidence was used to prove that Nazi doctor Josef Mengele was buried in Brazil under the name Wolfgang Gerhard.
- In 1992, DNA from a palo verde tree was used to convict Mark Alan Bogan of murder. DNA from seed pods of a tree at the crime scene was found to match that of seed pods found in Bogan's truck. This is the first instance of plant DNA admitted in a criminal case.
- In 1993, Kirk Bloodsworth was the first person to have been convicted of murder and sentenced to death, whose conviction was overturned using DNA evidence.
- The 1993 rape and murder of Mia Zapata, lead singer for the Seattle punk band The Gits was unsolved nine years after the murder. A database search in 2001 failed, but the killer's DNA was collected when he was arrested in Florida for burglary and domestic abuse in 2002.
- The science was made famous in the United States in 1994 when prosecutors heavily relied on DNA evidence allegedly linking O. J. Simpson to a double murder. The case also brought to light the laboratory difficulties and handling procedure mishaps that can cause such evidence to be significantly doubted.
- In 1994, Royal Canadian Mounted Police (RCMP) detectives successfully tested hairs from

a cat known as Snowball, and used the test to link a man to the murder of his wife, thus marking for the first time in forensic history the use of non-human animal DNA to identify a criminal (Plant DNA was used in 1992).

- In 1994, the claim that Anna Anderson was Grand Duchess Anastasia Nikolaevna of Russia was tested after her death using samples of her tissue that had been stored at a Charlottesville, Virginia hospital following a medical procedure. The tissue was tested using DNA fingerprinting, and showed that she bore no relation to the Romanovs.
- In 1994, Earl Washington, Jr., of Virginia had his death sentence commuted to life imprisonment a week before his scheduled execution date based on DNA evidence. He received a full pardon in 2000 based on more advanced testing. His case is often cited by opponents of the death penalty.
- In 1995, the British Forensic Science Service carried out its first mass intelligence DNA screening in the investigation of the Naomi Smith murder case.
- In 1998, Richard J. Schmidt was convicted of attempted second-degree murder when it was shown that there was a link between the viral DNA of the human immunodeficiency virus (HIV) he had been accused of injecting in his girlfriend and viral DNA from one of his patients with AIDS. This was the first time viral DNA fingerprinting had been used as evidence in a criminal trial.
- In 1999, Raymond Easton, a disabled man from Swindon, England, was arrested and detained for seven hours in connection with a burglary. He was released due to an inaccurate DNA match. His DNA had been retained on file after an unrelated domestic incident some time previously.
- In 2000 Frank Lee Smith was proved innocent by DNA profiling of the murder of an eight-year-old girl after spending 14 years on death row in Florida, USA. However he had died of cancer just before his innocence was proven. In view of this the Florida state governor ordered that in future any death row inmate claiming innocence should have DNA testing.
- In May 2000 Gordon Graham murdered Paul Gault at his home in Lisburn, Northern Ireland. Graham was convicted of the murder when his DNA was found on a sports bag left in the house as part of an elaborate ploy to suggest the murder occurred after a burglary had gone wrong. Graham was having an affair with the victim's wife at the time of the murder. It was the first time Low Copy Number DNA was used in Northern Ireland.
- In 2001, Wayne Butler was convicted for the murder of Celia Douty. It was the first murder in Australia to be solved using DNA profiling.
- In 2002, the body of James Hanratty, hanged in 1962 for the "A6 murder", was exhumed and DNA samples from the body and members of his family were analysed. The results convinced Court of Appeal judges that Hanratty's guilt, which had been strenuously disputed by campaigners, was proved "beyond doubt". Paul Foot and some other campaigners continued to believe in Hanratty's innocence and argued that the DNA evidence could have been contaminated, noting that the small DNA samples from items of clothing, kept in a police laboratory for over 40 years "in conditions that do not satisfy modern evidential standards", had had to be subjected to very new amplification techniques in order to yield any genetic profile.

However, no DNA other than Hanratty's was found on the evidence tested, contrary to what would have been expected had the evidence indeed been contaminated.

- In 2002, DNA testing was used to exonerate Douglas Echols, a man who was wrongfully convicted in a 1986 rape case. Echols was the 114th person to be exonerated through post-conviction DNA testing.
- In August 2002, Annalisa Vincenzi was shot dead in Tuscany. Bartender Peter Hamkin, 23, was arrested, in Merseyside, in March 2003 on an extradition warrant heard at Bow Street Magistrates' Court in London to establish whether he should be taken to Italy to face a murder charge. DNA "proved" he shot her, but he was cleared on other evidence.
- In 2003, Welshman Jeffrey Gafoor was convicted of the 1988 murder of Lynette White, when crime scene evidence collected 12 years earlier was re-examined using STR techniques, resulting in a match with his nephew. This may be the first known example of the DNA of an innocent yet related individual being used to identify the actual criminal, via "familial searching".
- In March 2003, Josiah Sutton was released from prison after serving four years of a twelve-year sentence for a sexual assault charge. Questionable DNA samples taken from Sutton were retested in the wake of the Houston Police Department's crime lab scandal of mishandling DNA evidence.
- In June 2003, because of new DNA evidence, Dennis Halstead, John Kogut and John Restivo won a re-trial on their murder conviction, their convictions were struck down and they were released. The three men had already served eighteen years of their thirty-plus-year sentences.
- The trial of Robert Pickton (convicted in December 2003) is notable in that DNA evidence is being used primarily to identify the *victims*, and in many cases to prove their existence.
- In 2004, DNA testing shed new light into the mysterious 1912 disappearance of Bobby Dunbar, a four-year-old boy who vanished during a fishing trip. He was allegedly found alive eight months later in the custody of William Cantwell Walters, but another woman claimed that the boy was her son, Bruce Anderson, whom she had entrusted in Walters' custody. The courts disbelieved her claim and convicted Walters for the kidnapping. The boy was raised and known as Bobby Dunbar throughout the rest of his life. However, DNA tests on Dunbar's son and nephew revealed the two were not related, thus establishing that the boy found in 1912 was not Bobby Dunbar, whose real fate remains unknown.
- In 2005, Gary Leiterman was convicted of the 1969 murder of Jane Mixer, a law student at the University of Michigan, after DNA found on Mixer's pantyhose was matched to Leiterman. DNA in a drop of blood on Mixer's hand was matched to John Ruelas, who was only four years old in 1969 and was never successfully connected to the case in any other way. Leiterman's defense unsuccessfully argued that the unexplained match of the blood spot to Ruelas pointed to cross-contamination and raised doubts about the reliability of the lab's identification of Leiterman.
- In December 2005, Evan Simmons was proven innocent of a 1981 attack on an Atlanta woman after serving twenty-four years in prison. Mr. Clark is the 164th person in the United States and the fifth in Georgia to be freed using post-conviction DNA testing.

- In November 2008, Anthony Curcio was arrested for masterminding one of the most elaborately planned armored car heists in history. DNA evidence linked Curcio to the crime.
- In March 2009, Sean Hodgson—convicted of 1979 killing of Teresa De Simone, 22, in her car in Southampton—was released after tests proved DNA from the scene was not his. It was later matched to DNA retrieved from the exhumed body of David Lace. Lace had previously confessed to the crime but was not believed by the detectives. He served time in prison for other crimes committed at the same time as the murder and then committed suicide in 1988.

Skid Mark

Skid marks on an asphalt road.

A skid mark is the visible mark left by any solid which moves against another, and is an important aspect of trace evidence analysis in forensic science and forensic engineering. Skid marks caused by tires on roads occur when a vehicle wheel stops rolling and slides or spins on the surface of the road. Skid marks can be analyzed to find the maximum and minimum vehicle speed prior to an impact or incident. Skidding can also occur on black ice or diesel deposits on the road and may not leave a mark at all.

Characteristics

Skid marks are divided into "acceleration marks" created on acceleration, if the engine provides more power than the tire can transmit; "braking marks," if the brakes "lock up" and cause the tire to slide; or "yaw marks", if the tire slides sideways. Each has a characteristic appearance, and an experienced accident reconstructor or forensic engineer can often determine what the vehicle was doing by examining the marks left by the tire.

Skid mark from a faulty ladder.

Contrary to popular belief, skid marks are not caused by pieces of rubber from the tire being deposited on the road because friction heats up the tire. Skid marks are actually bituminous oils in the asphalt that are heated because of the friction of breaking or accelerating and rise to the surface, leaving dark marks. This is why the marks fade. Within one hour, 3-4% of the mark has already faded.

Skid marks will vary depending on whether the car uses ABS or not. If not, there will be two lines. The darker marks on the outside are from the front wheels, while the back tires leave thinner marks. This is because the force exerted on them makes the wheels take on a conical shape. If the car uses ABS, the marks will be much fainter as less heat is produced by the release-stop mechanism of ABS. Scuff marks may be visible however with ABS.

Ladder Accidents

Skid marks can also be formed where a ladder suddenly slips and the user falls to the ground, especially if the ladder feet are faulty or absent. Loss of the rubber feet or foot causes the aluminum stile to make contact with the ground, and if a hard surface like concrete or tiling, a skid mark shows how and why the ladder slipped. Unless fixed to the wall upon which they are leaning, ladders can slip down easily especially if leant at an angle lower than about 75 degrees. Such slip accidents tend to happen when the user is near the top, so increasing his or her chances of serious personal injury.

Accident Reconstruction

Such marks are important evidence for vehicular accident reconstruction, when their size and shape can reveal much about vehicle speed and forces of acceleration or deceleration. They are one form of trace evidence. They represent a form of contact evidence produced according to Locard's exchange principle. The length of the skid mark is usually closely related to the vehicle speed at the instant of braking, so measuring the marks yields an estimate of original speed.

MABMAT (Rover)

MABMAT (rover) is a robotic imaging system designed to capture photographs and videos of crime scenes and map locations in 360 degrees. This robot's main feature is taking the 360-degree photos and videos and converting them to virtual crime scene data which can be used with virtual reality headsets to examine the captured scene.

The MABMAT was not invented by robotics engineers; however, it was created by a forensic science expert and criminal justice professional. The designer claims that the robot can be the most effective system to record a crime investigation because it can capture a location in 360 degrees in high-definition video and high-resolution stills. The MABMAT has been touted to assist human investigators and members of the jury to reach proper decisions in and out of the courtroom. With the help of the MABMAT, jurors would be able to accurately observe crime scenes, and investigators can study footage without traveling to the scene.

Information about the MABMAT was revealed in August 2016. As of November 2016, the rover is still in development.

History

The MABMAT was developed by Mehzeb Chowdhury, a PhD researcher in forensic science and criminal investigations from Durham University.

Before development of the MABMAT, Chowdhury, a Barrister-at-Law by trade, had been observing how judges study crime scenes and how new technology was being implemented into crime investigations.

Chowdhury published an article on "The Conversation" noting how jurors are seldom allowed to visit crime scenes and the incredible difficulties that befall everyone (judges, lawyers, law enforcement and the jurors themselves) involved when they do. Chowdhury explained that by the time a juror visits and studies a crime scene, degradation would result in a marked difference in every aspect. Photography and sketching are crucial parts of gathering and using evidence but, they do not provide accurate representations of crime scenes due to the subjective nature of these methods.

Chowdhury believes that investigators can begin to rely on new technology that is specifically designed for crime investigation investigation, especially those capable of 3D imaging and virtual reality. Chowdhury discussed how researchers at Staffordshire University, led by Dr Caroline Sturdy Colls used virtual reality headsets and video game software to produce virtual crime scenes. He explained how virtual crime scenes can be used as a supplement to photographs and videos of crime scenes, allowing for jurors to decide on their own which articles of evidence should be prioritized and given weight. He has noticed the very high prices of the virtual reality headsets such as the HTC Vive, Oculus Rift, and the PlayStation VR. He believes that much cheaper and more competent pieces of technology are capable of transforming pictures and videos to 3D-rendered crime scene animations. The flaws of crime investigation and the improvements of technology led to the creation of the MABMAT.

According to Chowdhury, approximately fifty police departments in the United States and the United Kingdom have provided crime scene investigation data to support the MABMAT project. The system is expected to be tested in police departments in 2017.

Specifications

Since the development of the MABMAT is self-funded, Chowdhury and his team only spent 299 pounds (or 374 U.S. dollars) on all parts that were required to build the rover.

Chowdhury described all the parts that were used to create the MABMAT:

- off-the-shelf parts such as metal pieces and circuits
- a 360-degree camera that captures photographs and videos, which can be played on any computer. This camera can automatically capture pictures and record videos by itself.
- a Google Cardboard—a virtual reality headset that provides a virtual reality experience similar to that of the HTC Vive, Oculus Rift, and the Playstation VR. However, unlike those three headsets, the Google Cardboard does not render three-dimensional graphics and does not have a power central processing unit. This device only costs about ten dollars, while headsets like the Oculus Rift cost at least seven hundred dollars. This—along with the metal pieces and circuits—may have been the reason for the MABMAT's low budget.
- ultrasonic, motion, and infrared sensors which help the MABMAT navigate crime scene.

- Arduino—a microcontroller board that have built-in open-source software which allow user to program and create interactive objects such as the MABMAT
- Raspberry Pi—another microcontroller board with its own open-source software

The MABMAT is to be controlled with a tablet, smartphone, or a Bluetooth remote.

The team of researchers stated that the design of the MABMAT is inspired by NASA's "Curiosity"—a rover that is investigating Mars.

Trace Evidence

Trace evidence is created when objects contact. Material is often transferred by heat or induced by contact friction.

The importance of trace evidence in criminal investigations was shown by Dr. Edmond Locard in the early 20th Century. Since then, forensic scientists use trace evidence to reconstruct crimes, and to describe the people, places and things involved in them. Studies of homicides published in the forensic science literature show how trace evidence is used to solve crimes. Trace evidence is important in accident investigation, where movement of one part against another will often leave a tell-tale mark. Such analysis is of great use in forensic engineering.

Examples

Vehicular accident reconstruction relies on such marks to estimate vehicle speed before and during an accident, as well as braking and impact forces. Fabric prints of clothing worn by pedestrians in the paint and/or road grime of the striking vehicle can match a specific vehicle involved in a hit-and-run collision. Such traces are also known as "witness marks", especially in engineering and may be critical in understanding how a product failed. A typical witness mark could be an impact depression which broke a product, especially if that mark can be matched to the product which made the impact such as a hammer or nail. Such marks are also commonly encountered in criminal cases, and include bite marks, puncture marks, bullet holes etc.

Protection

The first preservation is to photograph *in situ*, and then remove the objects showing key traces, protect them, and analyse under controlled laboratory conditions.

Many techniques are used in the protection of trace evidence from criminal investigations, although all must be photographed as soon as possible, and while still in place. Samples may be collected by shaking, brushing, taping, vacuuming, swabbing and hand picking. Great care may be needed to prevent contamination with other substances (such as natural oil and sweat on the hand of the collector). In some cases, such as with oil or grease, a solvent extraction can be used to collect the evidence for analysis. The method used for collection is generally dependent on both the type of evidence and from where or what sort of object it is being collected.

Trace Evidence is also found in much smaller amounts at crime scenes.

Analysis

Analysis of trace materials most often begins with a visual examination of the evidence usually involving macrophotography. This is then usually followed by microscopic analysis, of which a number of different types are available depending on the type of material to be analysed, such as a stereomicroscope, scanning electron microscope (SEM) or comparison microscope. SEM is especially useful because X-ray analysis can be conducted on selected areas of the sample, so is a form of microanalysis. It is useful where chemical residues can show unusual elements present which may indicate chemical attack of the product. A car accident caused by a diesel fuel leak, for example, showed traces of sulfur on the cracked tube indicative of attack by sulfuric acid from the battery.

Gunshot residue may be identified by elemental analysis using atomic absorption or with a scanning electron microscope equipped with an energy dispersive spectroscope. Small amounts of explosives, volatile hydrocarbons, and other chemicals are identified with the use of analytical instruments, such as gas chromatography, mass spectrometry, and infrared spectroscopy, all of which separate out the components of the chemicals.

Similar comments apply to damaged items from an accident scene, but care is needed in ensuring that the sample is not damaged by the testing, or sampling for testing. Such nondestructive testing must always be used first before considering destructive methods which involve taking small samples from the item for more detailed tests, such as spectroscopic analysis. Use of all such methods must be done in consultation with other experts and the relevant authorities, such as lawyers on both sides of a case.

Problems

False positives and contamination by subsequent handling or nearby objects (e.g. mixing of blood from victim and attacker), for example, are problems owing to the presence of many common substances and the necessity of human involvement in the collection of trace evidence. Both can occur with DNA traces and fingerprints. Partial fingerprints are even more vulnerable to false positives. Samples from accidents or crimes should therefore be protected as much as possible by enclosure in a sealable container as soon as possible, after an incident is under investigation.

References

- Horace Cox, ed. (1905). The Law Times: The Journal and Record: The Law and The Lawyers. vol. CXIX. London: The Law Times. p. 563
- Ashbaugh, David (1999). Quantitative-Qualitative Friction Ridge Analysis: An Introduction to Basic and Advanced Ridgeology. Boca Raton, Florida: CRC Press. pp. 11–19. ISBN 0-8493-7007-8
- "Peer Reviewed Glossary of the Scientific Working Group on Friction Ridge Analysis, Study and Technology (SWGFAST)" (PDF). Retrieved 2012-09-14
- Wang, Yongchang; D. L. Lau; L. G. Hassebrook (2010). "Fit-sphere unwrapping and performance analysis of 3D Fingerprints" (PDF). Applied Optics. 49 (4): 592–600. doi:10.1364/ao.49.000592
- Dalrymple, BE; Duff, JM; Menzel, ER. (1977). "Inherent fingerprint luminescence – detection by laser". Journal of Forensic Sciences. 22 (1): 106–115

- Cole, Simon (2001). Suspect Identities: A history of fingerprinting and criminal identification. Cambridge, Massachusetts: Harvard University Press. pp. 60–61. ISBN 0-674-00455-8
- Fiebig, Tobias; Krissler, Jan; Hänsch, Ronny (August 2014). Security Impact of High Resolution Smartphone Cameras. Usenix Association. Retrieved 5 February 2015
- Herschel, William James (November 25, 1880). "Skin furrows of the hand" (PDF). Nature. 23 (578): 76. Bibcode:1880Natur..23...76H. doi:10.1038/023076b0
- Vokey, J.R., Tangen, J.M. and Cole, S.A, (2009), "On the preliminary psychophysics of fingerprint identification", The Quarterly Journal of Experimental Psychology, Vol 62, Iss 5, pp 1023–1040
- Robinson, James L. (2008). "Blood residue and bloodstains". In Ayn Embar-seddon, Allan D. Pass (eds.). Forensic Science. Salem Press. p. 152. ISBN 978-1-58765-423-7
- "O'Dougherty Urges All Be Fingerprinted: U.S. Attorney Describes Sciences of Crime Detection to Democrats". The Brooklyn Daily Eagle. March 8, 1938. Retrieved July 1, 2014
- Faulds, Henry (October 28, 1880). "On the skin-furrows of the hand" (PDF). Nature. 22 (574): 605. Bibcode:-1880Natur..22..605F. doi:10.1038/022605a0
- Hortolà, Policarp (2002). "Red blood cell haemotaphonomy of experimental human bloodstains on techno-prehistoric lithic raw materials". Journal of Archaeological Science. 29 (7): 733–739. doi:10.1006/jasc.2001.0782
- Herschel, William J (1916). The Origin of Finger-Printing (PDF). Oxford University Press. ISBN 978-1-104-66225-7
- Alberge, Dalya (9 December 2012). "Vital clue ignored for 50 years". London: Independent. Retrieved 28 December 2015
- Wong M, Choo SP, Tan EH (July 2009). "Travel warning with capecitabine". Annals of Oncology. 20 (7): 1281. PMID 19470576. doi:10.1093/annonc/mdp278
- Miller, K.W.P.; Dawson, J.L.; Hagelberg, E. (1996). "A concordance of nucleotide substitutions in the first and second hypervariable segments of the human mtDNA control region". International Journal of Legal Medicine. 109: 107–113. doi:10.1007/bf01369668
- Hueske, Edward. Firearms and Fingerprints. Facts on File/Infobase Publishing, New York. 2009. ISBN 978-0-8160-5512-8
- Stephen Musil (22 September 2013). "Hackers claim to have defeated Apple's Touch ID print sensor". Cnet. CBS Interactive Inc. Retrieved 23 September 2013
- Bieber Frederick; et al. (2006). "Finding Criminals Through DNA of Their Relatives". Science. 312 (5778): 1315–16. PMID 16690817. doi:10.1126/science.1122655

6

Forensic Science: Tools and Techniques

The tools and techniques used in forensic science are fingerprint powder, facial recognition system, bloodstain pattern analysis, autopsy, gait analysis, etc. The powder used by investigators in brushing for fingerprints is known as fingerprint powder whereas the application used in identifying a person's face is known as facial recognition system. The aspects elucidated in this chapter are of vital importance, and provide a better understanding of forensic science.

Fingerprint Powder

Fingerprint powders are fine powders used in dusting for fingerprints by crime scene investigators and others in law enforcement. The process of dusting for fingerprints involves various methods intended to get the particles of the powder to adhere to residue left by friction ridge skin on the fingers, palms, or feet.

Physical development of fingerprints using powders is just one of a selection of methods used to develop fingerprints. Fingerprints often leave residues of oils in the shape of the friction ridges, but the friction ridge skin itself does not secrete oils, and so some fingerprints will only leave a residue of amino acids and other compounds which the powder does not adhere to well. For this reason, 'dusting' is used as part of an array of techniques to develop fingerprints, but is often used on larger areas in a crime scene which cannot be removed for analysis, or cannot be subject to more rigorous analysis for other reasons.

Fingerprint powders have various formulations, and the appropriate powder must be used on the appropriate surface. For example, dark coloured powders will show up a fingerprint far better on a light surface.

Application

Powders may be applied with a fingerprint brush, a brush with extremely fine fibers designed to hold powder, and deposit it gently on the fingerprint to be revealed, without rubbing away the often delicate residue of the fingerprint itself. They may also be applied by blowing the powder across the fingerprint, or by pouring the powder onto the print, and then blowing away the excess.

Magnetic powders are also used, where a fine magnetic powder is held by a magnetic applicator, which may then be gently moved across the fingerprint. As no bristles touch the surface, this often damages the print less than other methods of developing the print.

Composition

Modern fingerprint powders have a variety of compositions, and are often a matter of personal choice by the expert using them or down to the standard procedure of the department or agency. Many agencies use proprietary powders produced by independent companies, and so the exact formulation of these powders is not revealed.

Some surfaces, such as organic ones, do not take to fingerprint powders at all and use of alternate methods is necessary. Other media, such as certain types of glue, can be "smoked" over these surfaces with fair results.

Historically, Lycopodium powder, the spores of Lycopodium and related plants, was used as a fingerprint powder.

Factor Influencing Fingerprint Powder Quality

There are several factors influencing the effectiveness of fingerprint powders.

Fineness

> The powder must be fine enough to show the detail of the fingerprint. Finer powders would be theoretically capable of displaying greater detail than coarser powders.

Adhesion

> The powder must display the right level of adhesion, so that it will adhere to the residue of the fingerprint (often oils) and not adhere to the rest of the surface where it would obscure the view of the print. When a powder coats a surface, this is known as 'painting'.

Sensitivity

> Sensitivity is related to adhesion, and is how well the powder adheres to a surface. For example, aluminum flake is more sensitive than aluminum powder, but greater sensitivity is not always desirable.

Color

> The fingerprint powder must be a suitable color for the surface in question.

Flow

> To a lesser extent, it is important that the powder can flow, and does not 'cake' into a solid block, which would render it useless.

As these various qualities are not normally all present in any one material, compositions of various materials are generally used. For example, lampblack is particularly black in color, absorbing around 98% of incident visible light, but other materials may have greater adhesion, or flow more effectively, producing a better overall powder than either alone.

Examples of Materials

- Metal powders

Of these, one of the more common powders in current use is aluminum powder, as it will show up on a variety of surfaces.

Facial Recognition System

Swiss European surveillance: face recognition and vehicle make, model, color and license plate reader

Close-up of the infrared illuminator. The light is invisible to the human eye, but creates a day-like environment for the surveillance cameras.

A face recognition system is a computer application capable of identifying or verifying a person from a digital image or a video frame from a video source. One of the ways to do this is by comparing selected facial features from the image and a face database.

It is typically used in security systems and can be compared to other biometrics such as fingerprint or eye iris recognition systems. Recently, it has also become popular as a commercial identification and marketing tool.

Techniques for Face Acquisition

Traditional

Some face recognition algorithms identify facial features by extracting landmarks, or features, from an image of the subject's face. For example, an algorithm may analyze the relative position, size, and/or shape of the eyes, nose, cheekbones, and jaw. These features are then used to search for other images with matching features. Other algorithms normalize a gallery of face images and then compress the face data, only saving the data in the image that is useful for face recognition. A probe image is then compared with the face data. One of the earliest successful systems is based on template matching techniques applied to a set of salient facial features, providing a sort of compressed face representation.

Recognition algorithms can be divided into two main approaches, geometric, which looks at distinguishing features, or photometric, which is a statistical approach that distills an image into values and compares the values with templates to eliminate variances.

Popular recognition algorithms include principal component analysis using eigenfaces, linear discriminant analysis, elastic bunch graph matching using the Fisherface algorithm, the hidden Markov model, the multilinear subspace learning using tensor representation, and the neuronal motivated dynamic link matching.

3-dimensional Recognition

A newly emerging trend, claimed to achieve improved accuracy, is three-dimensional face recognition. This technique uses 3D sensors to capture information about the shape of a face. This information is then used to identify distinctive features on the surface of a face, such as the contour of the eye sockets, nose, and chin.

One advantage of 3D face recognition is that it is not affected by changes in lighting like other techniques. It can also identify a face from a range of viewing angles, including a profile view. Three-dimensional data points from a face vastly improve the precision of face recognition. 3D research is enhanced by the development of sophisticated sensors that do a better job of capturing 3D face imagery. The sensors work by projecting structured light onto the face. Up to a dozen or more of these image sensors can be placed on the same CMOS chip—each sensor captures a different part of the spectrum.

Even a perfect 3D matching technique could be sensitive to expressions. For that goal a group at the Technion applied tools from metric geometry to treat expressions as isometries A company called Vision Access created a firm solution for 3D face recognition. The company was later acquired by the biometric access company Bioscrypt Inc. which developed a version known as 3D FastPass.

A new method is to introduce a way to capture a 3D picture by using three tracking cameras that point at different angles; one camera will be pointing at the front of the subject, second one to the side, and third one at an angle. All these cameras will work together so it can track a subject's face in real time and be able to face detect and recognize.

Skin Texture Analysis

Another emerging trend uses the visual details of the skin, as captured in standard digital or scanned images. This technique, called skin texture analysis, turns the unique lines, patterns, and spots apparent in a person's skin into a mathematical space.

Tests have shown that with the addition of skin texture analysis, performance in recognizing faces can increase 20 to 25 percent.

Thermal Cameras

A different form of taking input data for face recognition is by using thermal cameras, by this procedure the cameras will only detect the shape of the head and it will ignore the subject accessories such as glasses, hats, or make up. A problem with using thermal pictures for face recognition is that the databases for face recognition is limited. Diego Socolinsky, and Andrea Selinger (2004) research the use of thermal face recognition in real life, and operation sceneries, and at the same time build a new database of thermal face images. The research uses low-sensitive, low-resolution ferro-electric electrics sensors that are capable of acquire long wave thermal infrared (LWIR). The results show that a fusion of LWIR and regular visual cameras has the greater results in outdoor probes. Indoor results show that visual has a 97.05% accuracy, while LWIR has 93.93%, and the Fusion has 98.40%, however on the outdoor proves visual has 67.06%, LWIR 83.03%, and fusion has 89.02%. The study used 240 subjects over the period of 10 weeks to create the new database. The data was collected on sunny, rainy, and cloudy days.

Notable users and Deployments

The Australian and New Zealand Customs Services have an automated border processing system called SmartGate that uses face recognition. The system compares the face of the individual with the image in the e-passport microchip to verify that the holder of the passport is the rightful owner.

Law enforcement agencies in the United States, including the Los Angeles County Sheriff, use arrest mugshot databases in their forensic investigative work. Law enforcement has been rapidly building a database of photos in recent years.

The U.S. Department of State operates one of the largest face recognition systems in the world with 117 million American adults including mostly law abiding citizens in its database. The photos are typically drawn from driver's license photos. Although it is still far from completion, it is being put to use in certain cities to give clues as to who was in the photo. The FBI uses the photos as an investigative lead not for positive identification.

In recent years Maryland has used face recognition by comparing people's faces to their driver's license photos. The system drew controversy when it was used in Baltimore to arrest unruly protesters after the death of Freddie Gray in police custody. Many other states are using or developing a similar system however some states have laws prohibiting its use.

The FBI has also instituted its Next Generation Identification program to include face recognition, as well as more traditional biometrics like fingerprints and iris scans, which can pull from both criminal and civil databases.

The Tocumen International Airport in Panama operates an airport-wide surveillance system using hundreds of live face recognition cameras to identify wanted individuals passing through the airport.

Major Canadian airports will be using a new facial recognition program as part of the Primary Inspection Kiosk program that will compare people's faces to their passports. This program will first come to Ottawa International Airport in early 2017 and to other airports in 2018.

In 2017, Time & Attendance company ClockedIn released facial recognition as a form of attendance tracking for businesses and organisations looking to have a more automated system of keeping track of hours worked as well as for security and health & safety control.

Additional uses

In addition to being used for security systems, authorities have found a number of other applications for face recognition systems. While earlier post-9/11 deployments were well publicized trials, more recent deployments are rarely written about due to their covert nature.

At Super Bowl XXXV in January 2001, police in Tampa Bay, Florida used Viisage face recognition software to search for potential criminals and terrorists in attendance at the event. 19 people with minor criminal records were potentially identified.

In the 2000 presidential election, the Mexican government employed face recognition software to prevent voter fraud. Some individuals had been registering to vote under several different names, in an attempt to place multiple votes. By comparing new face images to those already in the voter database, authorities were able to reduce duplicate registrations. Similar technologies are being used in the United States to prevent people from obtaining fake identification cards and driver's licenses.

There are also a number of potential uses for face recognition that are currently being developed. For example, the technology could be used as a security measure at ATMs. Instead of using a bank card or personal identification number, the ATM would capture an image of the customer's face, and compare it to the account holder's photo in the bank database to confirm the customer's identity.

Face recognition systems are used to unlock software on mobile devices. An independently developed Android Marketplace app called Visidon Applock makes use of the phone's built-in camera to take a picture of the user. Face recognition is used to ensure only this person can use certain apps which they choose to secure.

Face detection and face recognition are integrated into the iPhoto application for Macintosh, to help users organize and caption their collections.

Also, in addition to biometric usages, modern digital cameras often incorporate a facial detection system that allows the camera to focus and measure exposure on the face of the subject, thus guaranteeing a focused portrait of the person being photographed. Some cameras, in addition, incorporate a smile shutter, or automatically take a second picture if someone blinks during exposure.

Because of certain limitations of fingerprint recognition systems, face recognition systems could be used as an alternative way to confirm employee attendance at work for the claimed hours.

Another use could be a portable device to assist people with prosopagnosia in recognizing their acquaintances.

Advantages and Disadvantages

Compared to other Technologies

Among the different biometric techniques, face recognition may not be most reliable and efficient. However, one key advantage is that it does not require the cooperation of the test subject to work. Properly designed systems installed in airports, multiplexes, and other public places can identify individuals among the crowd, without passers-by even being aware of the system. Other biometrics like fingerprints, iris scans, and speech recognition cannot perform this kind of mass identification. However, questions have been raised on the effectiveness of face recognition software in cases of railway and airport security.

Weaknesses

Face recognition is far from perfect and struggles to perform under certain conditions. Ralph Gross, a researcher at the Carnegie Mellon Robotics Institute, describes one obstacle related to the viewing angle of the face: "Face recognition has been getting pretty good at full frontal faces and 20 degrees off, but as soon as you go towards profile, there've been problems."

Current face recognition still often misidentifies people which can sometimes led to controversy. Google was criticized for racism in its system when a black couple were misidentified as gorillas. Face recognition software generally doesn't do as well in identifying minorities when most of the subjects used in testing the technology were from the majority group.

Other conditions where face recognition does not work well include poor lighting, sunglasses, hats, scarves, beards, long hair, makeup or other objects partially covering the subject's face, and low resolution images.

Another serious disadvantage is that many systems are less effective if facial expressions vary. Even a big smile can render the system less effective. For instance: Canada now allows only neutral facial expressions in passport photos.

There is also inconstancy in the datasets used by researchers. Researchers may use anywhere from several subjects to scores of subjects, and a few hundred images to thousands of images. It is important for researchers to make available the datasets they used to each other, or have at least a standard dataset.

Effectiveness

Critics of the technology complain that the London Borough of Newham scheme has, as of 2004, never recognized a single criminal, despite several criminals in the system's database living in the Borough and the system having been running for several years. "Not once, as far as the police know, has Newham's automatic face recognition system spotted a live target." This information seems to conflict with claims that the system was credited with a 34% reduction in crime (hence why it was rolled out to Birmingham also). However it can be explained by the notion that when the public is regularly told that they are under constant video surveillance with advanced face recognition technology, this fear alone can reduce the crime rate, whether the face recognition system technically works or does not. This has been the basis for several other face recognition based security systems, where the technology itself does not work particularly well but the user's perception of the technology does.

An experiment in 2002 by the local police department in Tampa, Florida, had similarly disappointing results.

A system at Boston's Logan Airport was shut down in 2003 after failing to make any matches during a two-year test period.

As of 2016, facial recognition is still not effective for most applications even though the accuracy has been substantially improved. Although systems are often advertised as having accuracy near 100%, this is misleading as the studies often uses much smaller sample sizes than would be necessary for large scale applications. Because facial recognition is not completely accurate, it creates a list of potential matches. A human operator must then look through these potential matches and studies show the operators pick the correct match out of the list only about half the time. This causes the issue of targeting the wrong suspect.

Privacy Issues

Civil rights right organizations and privacy campaigners such as the Electronic Frontier Foundation and the ACLU express concern that privacy is being compromised by the use of surveillance technologies. Some fear that it could lead to a "total surveillance society," with the government and other authorities having the ability to know the whereabouts and activities of all citizens around the clock. This knowledge has been, is being, and could continue to be deployed to prevent the lawful exercise of rights of citizens to criticize those in office, specific government policies or corporate practices. Many centralized power structures with such surveillance capabilities have abused their privileged access to maintain control of the political and economic apparatus, and to curtail populist reforms.

Face recognition can be used not just to identify an individual, but also to unearth other personal data associated with an individual – such as other photos featuring the individual, blog posts, social networking profiles, Internet behavior, travel patterns, etc. – all through facial features alone. Moreover, individuals have limited ability to avoid or thwart face recognition tracking unless they hide their faces. This fundamentally changes the dynamic of day-to-day privacy by enabling any marketer, government agency, or random stranger to secretly collect the identities and associated personal information of any individual captured by the face recognition system.

Social media web sites such as Facebook have very large numbers of photographs of people, annotated with names. This represents a database which may be abused by governments for face recognition purposes. Face recognition was used in Russia to harass women allegedly involved in online pornography. In Russia there is an app 'FindFace' which can identify faces with about 70% accuracy using the social media app called VK. This app would not be possible in other countries which do not use VK as their social media platform photos are not stored the same way as with VK.

In July 2012, a hearing was held before the Subcommittee on Privacy, Technology and the Law of the Committee on the Judiciary, United States Senate, to address issues surrounding what face recognition technology means for privacy and civil liberties.

In 2014, the National Telecommunications and Information Association (NTIA) began a multi-stakeholder process to engage privacy advocates and industry representatives to establish guidelines regarding the use of face recognition technology by private companies. In June 2015, privacy advocates left the bargaining table over what they felt was an impasse based on the industry representatives being unwilling to agree to consent requirements for the collection of face recognition data. The NTIA and industry representatives continued without the privacy representatives, and draft rules are expected to be presented in the spring of 2016.

States have begun enacted legislation to protect citizen's biometric data privacy. Illinois enacted the Biometric Information Privacy Act in 2008. Facebook's DeepFace has become the subject of several class action lawsuits under the Biometric Information Privacy Act, with claims alleging that Facebook is collecting and storing face recognition data of its users without obtaining informed consent, in direct violation of the Biometric Information Privacy Act. The most recent case was dismissed in January 2016 because the court lacked jurisdiction. Therefore, it is still unclear if the Biometric Information Privacy Act will be effective in protecting biometric data privacy rights.

History

Pioneers of automated face recognition include Woody Bledsoe, Helen Chan Wolf, and Charles Bisson.

During 1964 and 1965, Bledsoe, along with Helen Chan and Charles Bisson, worked on using the computer to recognize human faces (Bledsoe 1966a, 1966b; Bledsoe and Chan 1965). He was proud of this work, but because the funding was provided by an unnamed intelligence agency that did not allow much publicity, little of the work was published. Given a large database of images (in effect, a book of mug shots) and a photograph, the problem was to select from the database a small set of records such that one of the image records matched the photograph. The success of the method could be measured in terms of the ratio of the answer list to the number of records in the database. Bledsoe (1966a) described the following difficulties:

> "This recognition problem is made difficult by the great variability in head rotation and tilt, lighting intensity and angle, facial expression, aging, etc. Some other attempts at face recognition by machine have allowed for little or no variability in these quantities. Yet the method of correlation (or pattern matching) of unprocessed optical data, which is often used by some researchers, is certain to fail in cases where the variability is great. In particular, the correlation is very low between two pictures of the same person with two different head rotations"
>
> — *Woody Bledsoe, 1966*

This project was labeled man-machine because the human extracted the coordinates of a set of features from the photographs, which were then used by the computer for recognition. Using a graphics tablet (GRAFACON or RAND TABLET), the operator would extract the coordinates of features such as the center of pupils, the inside corner of eyes, the outside corner of eyes, point of widows peak, and so on. From these coordinates, a list of 20 distances, such as width of mouth and width of eyes, pupil to pupil, were computed. These operators could process about 40 pictures an hour. When building the database, the name of the person in the photograph was associated with the list of computed distances and stored in the computer. In the recognition phase, the set of distances was compared with the corresponding distance for each photograph, yielding a distance between the photograph and the database record. The closest records are returned.

Because it is unlikely that any two pictures would match in head rotation, lean, tilt, and scale (distance from the camera), each set of distances is normalized to represent the face in a frontal orientation. To accomplish this normalization, the program first tries to determine the tilt, the lean, and the rotation. Then, using these angles, the computer undoes the effect of these transformations on the computed distances. To compute these angles, the computer must know the three-dimensional geometry of the head. Because the actual heads were unavailable, Bledsoe (1964) used a standard head derived from measurements on seven heads.

After Bledsoe left PRI in 1966, this work was continued at the Stanford Research Institute, primarily by Peter Hart. In experiments performed on a database of over 2000 photographs, the computer consistently outperformed humans when presented with the same recognition tasks (Bledsoe 1968). Peter Hart (1996) enthusiastically recalled the project with the exclamation, "It really worked!"

By about 1997, the system developed by Christoph von der Malsburg and graduate students of the University of Bochum in Germany and the University of Southern California in the United States outperformed most systems with those of Massachusetts Institute of Technology and the University of Maryland rated next. The Bochum system was developed through funding by the United States Army Research Laboratory. The software was sold as ZN-Face and used by customers such as Deutsche Bank and operators of airports and other busy locations. The software was "robust enough to make identifications from less-than-perfect face views. It can also often see through such impediments to identification as mustaches, beards, changed hair styles and glasses—even sunglasses".

In about January 2007, image searches were "based on the text surrounding a photo," for example, if text nearby mentions the image content. Polar Rose technology can guess from a photograph, in about 1.5 seconds, what any individual may look like in three dimensions, and claimed they "will ask users to input the names of people they recognize in photos online" to help build a database. Identix, a company out of Minnesota, has developed the software, FaceIt. FaceIt can pick out someone's face in a crowd and compare it to databases worldwide to recognize and put a name to a face. The software is written to detect multiple features on the human face. It can detect the distance between the eyes, width of the nose, shape of cheekbones, length of jawlines and many more facial features. The software does this by putting the image of the face on a faceprint, a numerical code that represents the human face. Face recognition software used to have to rely on a 2D image with the person almost directly facing the camera. Now, with FaceIt, a 3D image can be compared to a 2D image by choosing 3 specific points off of the 3D image and converting it into a 2D image using a special algorithm that can be scanned through almost all databases. In 2006, the performance of the latest face recognition algorithms were evaluated in the Face Recognition Grand Challenge (FRGC). High-resolution face images, 3-D face scans, and iris images were used in the tests. The results indicated that the new algorithms are 10 times more accurate than the face recognition algorithms of 2002 and 100 times more accurate than those of 1995. Some of the algorithms were able to outperform human participants in recognizing faces and could uniquely identify identical twins.

U.S. Government-sponsored evaluations and challenge problems have helped spur over two orders-of-magnitude in face-recognition system performance. Since 1993, the error rate of automatic face-recognition systems has decreased by a factor of 272. The reduction applies to systems that match people with face images captured in studio or mugshot environments. In Moore's law terms, the error rate decreased by one-half every two years.

Low-resolution images of faces can be enhanced using face hallucination. Further improvements in high resolution, megapixel cameras in the last few years have helped to resolve the issue of insufficient resolution.

Emotion Detection

Facial recognition systems have been used for emotion recognition In 2016 Facebook acquired emotion detection startup FacioMetrics.

Anti Facial Recognition Systems

In January 2013 Japanese researchers from the National Institute of Informatics created 'privacy visor' glasses that uses nearly infrared light to make the face underneath it unrecognizable to face recognition software. The latest version uses a titanium frame, light-reflective material and a mask which uses angles and patterns to disrupt facial recognition technology through both absorbing and bouncing back light sources. In December 2016 a form of anti-CCTV and facial recognition sunglasses called 'reflectacles' were invented by a custom-spectacle-craftsmen based in Chicago named Scott Urban. They reflect infrared and, optionally, visible light which makes the users face a white blur to cameras. The project easily surpassed its crowdfunding goal of $28,000 and reflectacles will be commercially available by June 2017. It is conceivable that such technology might be fused with future head-mounted displays such as potential successors of HoloLens.

Bloodstain Pattern Analysis

Bloodstain pattern analysis (BPA), one of several specialties in the field of forensic science, involves the study and analysis of bloodstains at a known or suspected violent crime scene with the goal of helping investigators draw conclusions about the nature, timing and other details of the crime.

The use of bloodstains as evidence is not new; however, the application of modern science has brought it to a higher level since the 1970s and '80s. New technologies, especially advances in DNA analysis, are available for detectives and criminologists to use in solving crimes and apprehending offenders.

The science of bloodstain pattern analysis applies scientific knowledge from other fields to solve practical problems. Bloodstain pattern analysis draws on the scientific disciplines of biology, chemistry, mathematics and physics. If an analyst follows a scientific process, this applied science can produce strong, solid evidence, making it an effective tool for investigators, although care does need to be taken when relying on bloodstain pattern analysis in criminal cases. A report released by The National Academy of Sciences calls for more standardization within the field. The report highlights the ability of blood spatter analysts to overstate their qualifications and the reliability of their methods in the court room.

History

Bloodstain pattern analysis has been used informally for centuries, but the first modern study of blood stains was in 1895. Dr. Eduard Piotrowski of the University of Kraków published a paper titled "On the formation, form, direction, and spreading of blood stains after blunt trauma to the head." A number of publications describing various aspects of blood stains were published, but his publication did not lead to a systematic analysis. LeMoyne Snyder's widely used book *Homicide Investigation* (first published in 1941 and updated occasionally through at least the 1970s) also briefly mentioned details that later bloodstain experts would expand upon (e.g., that blood dries at a relatively predictable rate; that arterial blood is a brighter red color than other blood; that bloodstains tend to fall in certain patterns based on the motion of an attacker and victim).

The second modern origin of the study of bloodstain pattern analysis is the Sam Sheppard case in 1954, when the wife of an osteopathic physician was beaten to death in her home. Further growth of interest and use of the significance of bloodstain evidence is a direct result of the scientific research and practical applications of bloodstain theory by Herbert Leon MacDonell of Corning, New York. His research resulted in his publication of the first modern treatise on bloodstain analysis, entitled "Flight Characteristics and Stain Patterns of Human Blood" (1971).

The first formal bloodstain training course was given by MacDonnel in 1973 in Jackson, Mississippi. In 1983, the International Association of Bloodstain Pattern Analysts was founded by a group of blood stain analysts to help develop the emerging field of bloodstain pattern analysis.

Blood

Blood is a tissue that is circulated within the body to assist other parts of the body. This connective tissue has specialized cells that allow it to carry out its complex functions. For a healthy person, approximately 8% of their total weight is blood. For a 70 kg (154 lb.) individual, this equates to 5.6 L (12 US pints).

Biological Considerations

Blood contains three components or blood cells that are suspended within plasma. The three components are erythrocytes, leukocytes, and trombocytes.

- *Erythrocytes*, also known as red blood cells, are transporters. The role of erythrocytes is to transport oxygen. To do this, they contain great quantities of hemoglobin, which carry oxygen molecules and give blood its distinct red colour. Blood that has passed through the heart and been oxygenated (oxygenated blood travels through the arteries) tends to have a brighter shade of red as opposed to blood that is returning to the heart (in the veins). There are about 30 trillion erythrocytes circulating in the human blood at any given time.
- *Leukocytes*, also known as white blood cells, are the body's defenders. The role of leukocytes is to defend against harmful bacteria, viruses and microorganisms. There are five different types of leukocytes. They all have different sizes, shapes, structures, and functions. Leukocytes fight infection and disease. There are about 430 billion leukocytes circulating in the human blood at any given time (~1 per 700 erythrocytes). Pus is made up of leukocytes left in an affected area during and after fighting harmful substances or organisms that infect the body.
- *Platelets* are formed in the bone marrow. These particular blood cells contain cytoplasm

and are enclosed by a membrane, but do not have a nucleus. They play a major role in hemostasis (control of bleeding) by plugging up a breach in a vessel. They are important for forming blood clots. If a person has an abnormally low platelet count, a condition known as thrombocytopenia, blood clots more slowly.

Plasma is the yellowish fluid that carries the erythrocytes, leukocytes, and platelets. It is composed of water (92%), proteins (7%), and other materials such as salts, waste, and hormones, among others. Many of these proteins are clotting factors, which are important along with platelets for forming blood clots; clotting factor deficiencies can cause prolonged and excessive bleeding, a condition called hemophilia. Plasma makes up about 55% of blood. The remaining 45% is the blood cells. Because plasma is less dense than the blood cells, it can be easily separated. Plasma does not separate from blood cells whilst circulating in the bloodstream because it is in a constant state of agitation.

Chemical Considerations

Upon exiting the body, bloodstains transit from bright red to dark brown, which is attributed to oxidation of oxy-hemoglobin (HbO_2) to methemoglobin (met-Hb) and hemichrome (HC). The fractions of HbO_2, met-Hb and HC in a bloodstain can be used for age determination of bloodstains and can be measured by Reflectance Spectroscopy 1.

- *In vivo* hemoglobin molecules are mainly present in two forms: one without oxygen, de-oxy-hemoglobin (Hb) and one saturated with oxygen, oxy-hemoglobin (HbO_2), both have iron in the Fe^{2+} state. HbO_2 can auto-oxidize into met-Hb, which contains iron in the Fe^{3+} state. Met-Hb is incapable of binding oxygen. When met-Hb is formed in vivo it will be reduced back to Hb by reductase protein cytochrome b5, resulting in a small part (<1%) of met-Hb in a healthy in vivo situation.
- *Outside the body* hemoglobin saturates completely with oxygen in the ambient environment to HbO_2. Due to a decreasing availability of cytochrome b5, necessary for reduction of met-Hb, the transition of HbO_2 into met-Hb will, in contrast to inside the body, no longer be reversed. Once hemoglobin is autooxidized to met-Hb it will denature to hemichrome (HC), which is formed by an internal conformation change to the heme group.

Physical Considerations

In physics there are two continuous physical states of matter, solid and fluid. Once blood has left the body it behaves as a fluid and all physical laws apply.

- *Gravity* acts on blood (without the body's influence) as soon as it exits the body. Given the right circumstances blood can act according to ballistic theory.
- *Viscosity* is the amount of internal friction in the fluid. It describes the resistance of a liquid to flow.
- *Surface tension* is the force that maintains the shape of a drop of liquid, such as blood. When two fluids are in contact with each other (blood and air) there are forces attracting all molecules to each other.

Blood Spatter Flight Characteristics

Experiments with blood have shown that a drop of blood tends to form into a sphere in flight rather than the artistic teardrop shape. This is what one would expect of a fluid in freefall. The formation of the sphere is a result of surface tension that binds the molecules together.

This spherical shape of blood in flight is important for the calculation of the angle of impact (incidence) of blood spatter when it hits a surface. That angle will be used to determine the point from which the blood originated which is called the Point of Origin or more appropriately the Area of Origin.

A single spatter of blood is not enough to determine the Area of Origin at a crime scene. The determination of the angles of impact and placement of the Area of Origin should be based on the consideration of a number of stains and preferably stains from opposite sides of the pattern to create the means to triangulate.

Determining Angles of Impact

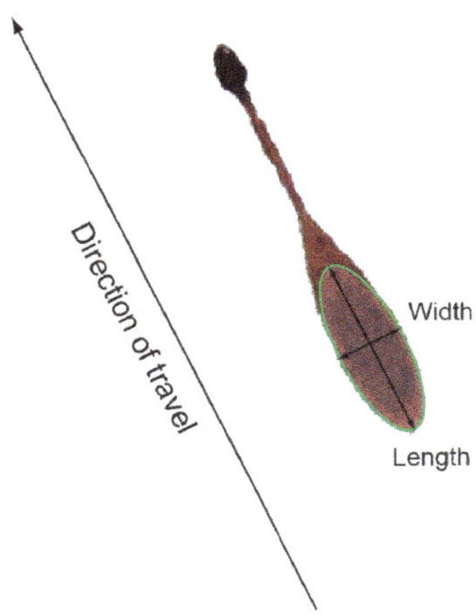

Fig. (a) Upward moving bloodstain showing proper ellipse placement.

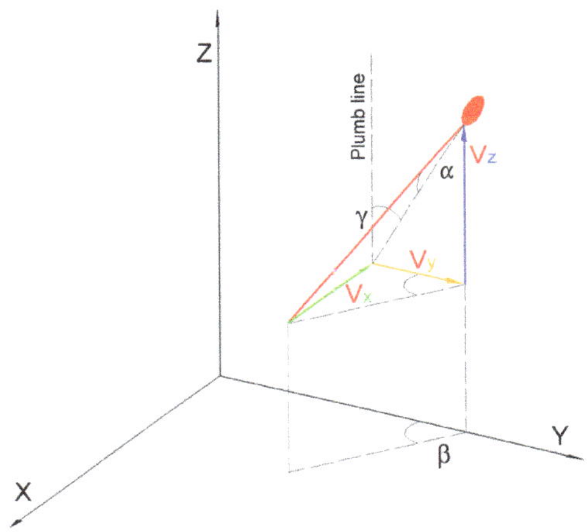

Fig.(b) Angles of Impact

As mentioned earlier, a blood droplet in freefall has the shape of an oscillating sphere. Should the droplet strike a surface and a well-formed stain is produced, an analyst can determine the angle at which this droplet struck the surface. This is based on the relationship between the length of the major axis, minor axis, and the angle of impact.

A well-formed stain is in the shape of an ellipse (see figure a). Dr. Victor Balthazard, and later Dr. Herbert Leon MacDonell, realized that the width-length ratio of the ellipse is the sine of the impact angle. Accurate measurement of the stain thus allows easy calculation of the impact angle.

Angles of Impact

Because of the three-dimensional aspect of trajectories there are three angles of impact:

- alpha (α), the impact angle of the bloodstain path moving out from the surface.

- beta (β), the angle of the bloodstain path pivoting about the vertical (z) axis (see figure b with beta extended to the floor).
- gamma (γ), the angle of the bloodstain path measured from the true vertical (plumb) of the surface (see figure b showing plumb line and extended angle from stain).

All three angles are related through the following trigonometric equations:

$$\sin\alpha = \left(\frac{w}{l}\right)$$

$$\tan\beta = \frac{\tan\alpha}{\sin\gamma}$$

where

l = length of ellipse (major axis)

w = width of ellipse (minor axis)

Accurately measuring the stain and calculating the angle of impact requires due diligence of the analyst. In the past analysts have used a variety of instruments. Methods currently used include:

- Viewing loupe with an embedded scale in 0.2 mm increments or better that is placed over the stain. The analyst then uses a scientific calculator or spreadsheet to complete the angle calculations.
- Bloodstain Pattern Analysis (BPA) software that superimposes an ellipse over a scaled close-up image of an individual bloodstain, then automatically calculates the angles of impact.

Using BPA software such as HemoSpat produces a very accurate result that is measurable and reproducible.

Point and Area of Convergence

To determine the point/area of convergence an analyst has to determine the path the blood droplets travelled. The tangential flight path of individual droplets can be determined by using the angle of impact and the offset angle of the resulting bloodstain. "Stringing" stains is a method of visualizing this. For the purpose of the point of convergence, only the top view of the flight paths is required. Note that this is a two-dimensional (2D) and not a three-dimensional (3D) intersection.

- The *point of convergence* is the intersection of two bloodstain paths, where the stains come from opposite sides of the impact pattern. (see figure c)
- The *area of convergence* is the box formed by the intersection of several stains from opposite sides of the impact pattern. (see figure d)

In the past, some analysts have drawn lines along the major axes of the stains and brought them to an area of convergence on the wall. Instead of using a top-down view, they used a front view. This provides a false point/area of convergence.

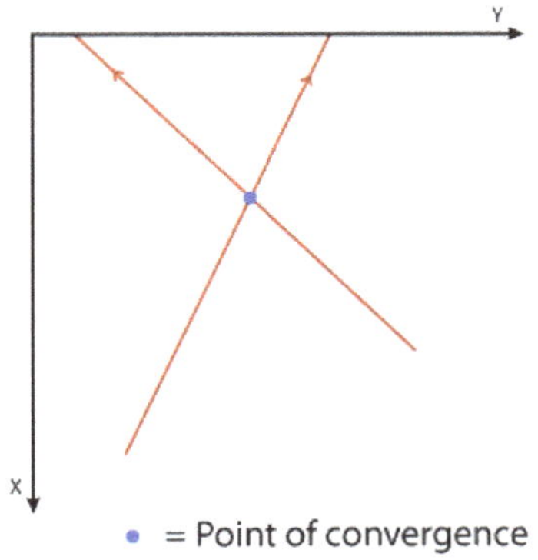

Fig. (c) Point of convergence

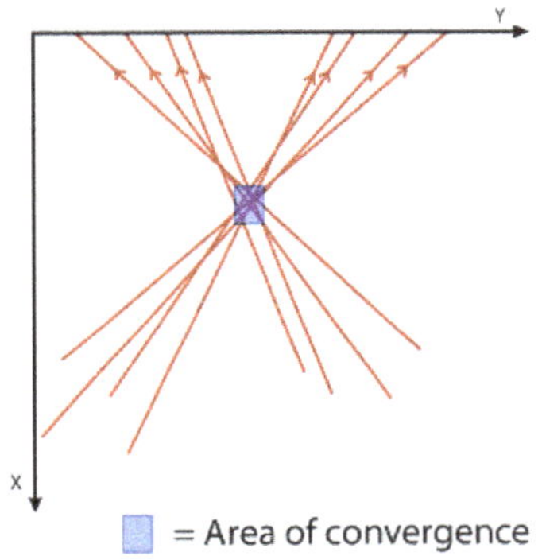

Fig. (d) Area of convergence

Area of Origin

The area of origin is the area in three-dimensional space where the blood source was located at the time of the bloodletting incident. The area of origin includes the area of convergence with a third dimension in the z direction. Since the z-axis is perpendicular to the floor, the area of origin has three dimensions and is a volume.

The term *point of origin* has also been accepted to mean the same thing. However, it has been argued, there are problems associated to this term. First, a blood source is not a point source. To produce a point source the mechanism would have to be fixed in three-dimensional space and have an aperture where only a single blood droplet is released at a time, with enough energy to create a pattern. This does not seem likely. Second, bodies are dynamic. Aside from the victim physically moving, skin is elastic and bones break. Once a force is applied to the body there will be an equal and opposite reaction to the force applied by the aggressor (Newton's third law of motion). Part of the force will move the blood source, even a millimetre, and change the origin while it is still producing blood. So the source becomes *contained* in a three-dimensional volume, or region.

As with the area of convergence, the area of origin is easily calculated by using BPA software. There are other longer, mathematical methods of determining the area or origin, one of which is the tangential method.

IABPA definition:

- Point (Area) of Origin - The common point (area) in three-dimensional space to which the trajectories of several blood drops can be retraced. (see figure e)

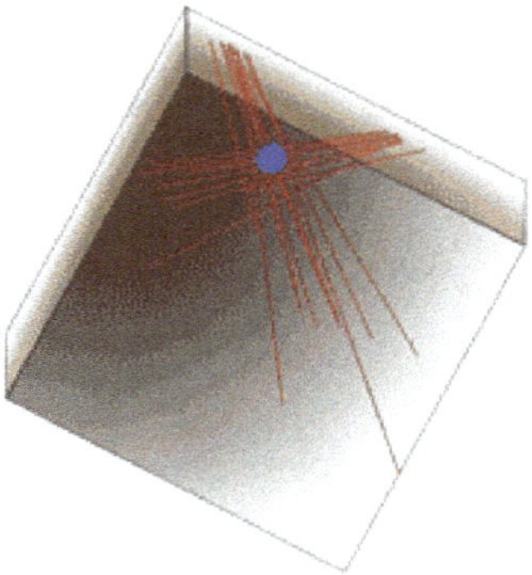

Fig. (e) Area of origin (blue area representing a volume in 3D space)

Once the angle of impact and the point and or area of convergence are identified, there are techniques that can be used to find where the bloodshed most likely occurred. The most basic and longest applied technique is the string method. A blood spatter analyst positions their protractor at the location of the blood stain and projects a string at the angle of impact in the direction of the point or area of convergence. This will predict a general origin of the blood loss. Another technique applicable is the trigonometric method, which is fairly similar to the string method. Since we know the point of convergence, we can measure the distance from the blood stain to that point. With this measurement along with the angle of impact, we can use basic trigonometric rules to solve for where in space the origin of blood shed is. By taking the tangent of the angle of impact and multiplying by the distance from the point of convergence, we can find the approximate height of the origin.

Photography

Crime scene photography has some unique requirements. When there is a bloodletting scene, the basics are still required but special attention must be given to the bloodstains. The current means of documenting the scene include 35 mm (B&W, colour, and specialty film), digital cameras, and video (Hi-8, DV, and other formats). Each method has its pros and cons. Often the scene is documented using multiple methods. (Videography has been included here because it follows the same principles and provides crime scene images.)

There are three types of crime scene photos:

- Overall – wide-angle images (28–35 mm range) that capture the scene as it is. This type of image provides anyone who has not been in the scene a good overall layout.
- Mid-range – images taken with a normal lens (45–55 mm range) give greater detail than the overall shots. In the case of a bloodletting scene, the mid-range image could capture a single bloodstain pattern.
- Close-up – images taken with a macro lens giving the greatest amount of detail. For example, a medium velocity impact pattern can contain thousands of individual stains where

there is a preponderance of small stains (1–3 mm in diameter) some of which require individual images.

Many times an analyst cannot attend a bloodletting scene, and must work from the crime scene images and notes of the person who attended. An appropriate sized scale should be in overall, mid-range, and close-up images. For overall images the scales should be parallel and perpendicular to the floor. This provides the analyst, and anyone else who looks at the images, a proper perspective on what they are observing. (Note: in some cases overall and mid-range images are taken with and *without* a scale.)

Reliability

While bloodstain pattern analysis has a solid foundation in science and can be a useful tool for investigators, the reliability of courtroom testimony by bloodstain pattern analysts has come under fire in recent years. Care needs to be taken to ensure that the bloodstain pattern analyst has appropriate credentials and training as well as uses appropriate methods. Even with proper training and methods, there are still many times where reputable analysts disagree on their findings, which calls into question the reliability of their conclusions and its value as evidence in court.

In the criminal case against David Camm, who was tried three times for the murder of his family largely on the basis of blood spatter evidence, both prosecution and the defense used expert bloodstain pattern analysts to interpret the source of the approximately 8 drops of blood on his shirt. The prosecution's experts included Tom Bevel and Rod Englert, who testified that the stains were high velocity impact spatter. Paul Kish, Barton Epstein, Paulette Sutton, Barrie Goetz and Stuart H. James testified for the defense that the stains were transferred from his shirt brushing against his daughter's hair. Dr. Robert Shaler, Founding Director of the Penn State Forensic Science Program, decried blood spatter analysis as unreliable in the Camm case. "The problem in this case is the number of stains are minimal," he said. "I think you're really on the edge of reliability." All of the blood spatter analysts involved in the case are "experts" in the traditional sense. The problem is "We have two opinions in this case. That, in essence, is a 50 percent error rate." An unacceptable level of reliability in a court case when the perception of guilt beyond a reasonable doubt is what is required.

Further complicating matters was the testimony of Rob Stites. Stites testified for the prosecution that he was an expert blood spatter analyst. It was later uncovered that he had no training and his credentials were fabrications by the prosecutor. His testimony that the blood on Camm's shirt was high velocity impact spatter aided in the conviction of David Camm. Dr. Shaler pointed out that one limitation of blood spatter analysis testimony is that "you do not have the supporting underlying science" to back up your conclusions. When Stites testified, the jury had no way of knowing that he was not the expert that he purported to be. Even among the expert witnesses, it is unknown which set of experts interpreted the stains accurately as there is no objective way of determining which bloodstain pattern analyst has applied the science correctly.

Other times, bloodstain patterns from different causes can mimic each other. In the 2008 trial of Travis Stay for the murder of Joel Lovelien, prosecution witness Terry Laber testified that the blood spatter on Stay's clothing came from blows to Lovelien during a fist fight. After a review of the evidence by Paul Kish, another bloodstain pattern analyst, Laber reviewed the report submitted by Kish and revised his findings to include the possibility that the blood came from expiration by Lovelien.

In Popular Culture

- Sam Tyler, the time-travelling detective in episode 3 of the Emmy Award-winning BBC TV series *Life on Mars*, asks his colleague Chris Skelton to make a blood pattern analysis, quickly realizing by his puzzled expression that in 1973 such techniques are not known.
- Serial killer Dexter Morgan of the *Dexter* novels and Showtime series is a blood spatter analyst for the fictitious Miami Metro Police Department.
- Julie Finlay is a blood spatter analyst on the CBS series *CSI: Crime Scene Investigation*.

Forensic Firearm Examination

Forensic firearm examination is the forensic process of examining the characteristics of firearms as well as any cartridges or bullets left behind at a crime scene. Specialists in this field are tasked with linking bullets and cartridges to weapons and weapons to individuals. Obliterated serial numbers can be raised and recorded in an attempt to find the registered owner of the weapon. Examiners can also look for fingerprints on the weapon and cartridges, and then viable prints can be processed through fingerprint databases for a potential match.

By examining unique striations, or markings, left behind on the bullet as it passes through the barrel and on the cartridge as it is hit by the firing pin, individual spent rounds can be linked back to a specific weapon. Known exemplars taken from a seized weapon can be directly compared to samples recovered from the scene using a comparison microscope. Striation images can also be uploaded to any existing national databases. Furthermore, these markings can be compared to other images in an attempt to link one weapon to multiple crime scenes. Like all forensic specialties, forensic firearm examiners are subject to being called to testify in court as expert witnesses.

History

The ability to compare ammunition is a direct result of the invention of rifling around the turn of the 16th century. By forcing the bullet to spin as it travels down the barrel of the weapon the bullet's accuracy greatly increases. At the same time, the rifling leaves marks on the bullet that are indicative of that particular barrel. Prior to mass production of firearms, each barrel and bullet mold was hand made by gunsmiths making them unique. The first successful documented case of forensic firearm examination occurred in 1835 when a member of the Bow Street Runners in London matched a recovered bullet from a murder victim to a specific mold in a suspect's home confirming that he made the bullet. Further evidence that the bullet maker was the perpetrator was found in his home and he was convicted. As manufacturing and automation replaced hand tools, the ability to compare bullets became impossible due to the standardization of molds within a specific company. However, experts in the field postulated that there were microscopic differences on each barrel left during the manufacturing process. These differences were a result of wear on the machines and since each new weapon caused a tiny amount of wear, each barrel would be slightly different from every other barrel produced by that company. Also, each bullet fired from a specific barrel would be printed with the same marks, allowing investigators to identify the weapon that fired a specific bullet.

One of the first uses of this knowledge was in 1915 to exonerate Charles Stielow of the murder of his neighbors. Stielow was sentenced to death and appealed to Charles S. Whitman, the Governor of New York, who was not convinced by the evidence used to convict Stielow. Whitman halted the execution until an inquiry could be conducted and after further examination it was shown that Stielow's firearm could not have fired the bullets recovered from the victims. The invention of the comparison microscope by Calvin Goddard and Phillip O. Gravelle in 1925 modernized the forensic examination of firearms. Simultaneous comparison of two different objects at the same time allowed to closely examine striations for matches and therefore make a more definitive statement as to whether or not they matched.

One of the first true tests of this new technology was in the aftermath of the Saint Valentine's Day Massacre in 1929. During the Prohibition Era, competing gang members were fighting over bootlegging operations within the city of Chicago. Members of the Chicago Outfit and the Egan's Rats led by Al Capone attempted to remove all competition from Chicago by eliminating the North Side Gang leader Bugs Moran. The massacre missed Moran, who was not present, but killed seven members of the North Side Gang. The murderers attempted to cover up their crime by posing as police officers, even dressing in police uniforms. Witnesses saw two "officers" leaving the scene, which implicated the Chicago police department as the perpetrators of the massacre. High levels of police corruption during that time period made it seem likely that the police department committed the killings. The investigation stalled until December 1929 when Fred Burke, a member of the Egan's Rats, shot and killed a police officer in St. Joseph, Michigan. Officers searching for Burke were led to a home in nearby Stevensville. While Burke was not there, inside officers found an arsenal of weapons including two Thompson submachine guns. The Chicago police department was contacted and the weapons were brought back to Chicago for testing. Goddard was asked to compare the weapons to collected evidence found at the massacre using his new "ballistic-forensics" technique. After test firing the guns, Goddard proved that the weapons were those used to kill the members of the North Side Gang, absolving the Chicago police department of all involvement. The successful use of Goddard's technique resulted in the solidification of his place as the father of forensic firearm examination.

Examination of the Firearm

Any firearm collected during the course of an investigation could yield viable evidence if examined. For forensic firearm examination specific evidence that can be recovered include weapon serial numbers and potentially fingerprints left on the weapon's surface.

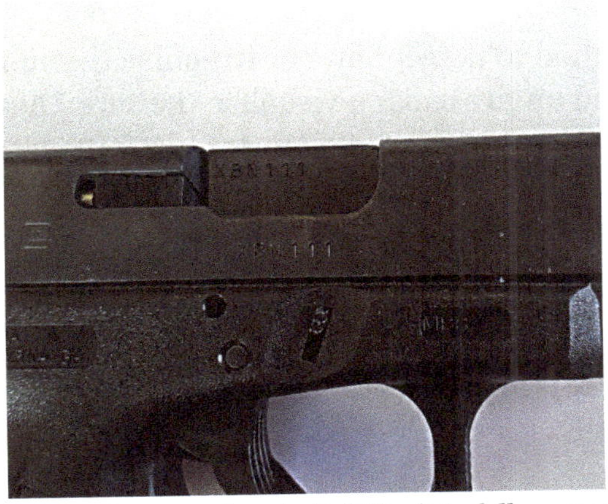

Multiple serial numbers provide redundancy and make it difficult to fully remove the numbers from a weapon.

Fingerprint Recovery

Fingerprint recovery from the surface of firearms is done with cyanoacrylate (more commonly known as superglue) fuming. Firearms are placed in a specially designed fume hood designed to evenly distribute fumes instead of removing them. Liquid superglue is placed in a container and heated until it is in a gaseous state. The circulating fumes adhere to the oils left behind by the fingerprint, turning the print white. The resulting white print can be enhanced with fingerprint powder to increase the contrast of the white print against the weapon's finish. While using the fuming technique on recovered guns is commonplace, the recovery of fingerprints from the surfaces of a firearm is challenging due to the textured grip and the general condition of recovered weapons. If fingerprints are recovered, they can be processed through fingerprint databases such as the Integrated Automated Fingerprint Identification System (IAFIS). Various parts of the recovered weapon can also be tested for touch DNA left by whomever handled it. However, the low levels of DNA that can be recovered presents numerous issues such as contamination and analysis anomalies such as allele drop-out and drop-in.

Serial Number Recovery

Serial numbers became commonplace after the United States passed the Gun Control Act of 1968. This law mandated that all guns manufactured or imported into the country have a serial number. Prior to 1968, many firearms either did not have a serial number or the serial numbers were not unique and were reused by a manufacturer on multiple firearms. If a recovered weapon has had the serial numbers altered or destroyed, examiners can attempt to recover the original numbers. The two main methods for the restoration of serial numbers are magnetic particle inspection and chemical restoration. It is recommended that magnetic particle inspection be performed first due to the nondestructive nature of the method. If magnetic particle inspection fails, chemical restoration is the next step in the forensic analysis.

If the serial number is successfully restored it can be used to help investigators track the weapon's history, as well as potentially determine who owns the weapon. Firearm databases such as the National Crime Information Center of the United States and INTERPOL's Firearm Reference Table can be used by investigators to track weapons that have been lost, stolen, or used previously in other crimes.

Magnetic Particle Inspection

Originally developed as a method to detect flaws or irregularities in magnetic materials, magnetic particle inspection can be used on firearms to visualize the serial number underneath the obliterated area. When performing this technique, examiners place the weapon in a magnetic field. The irregularities in the metal, in this case the serial number, cause the field to deform. When a solution of ferrous particles is added to the weapon's magnetized surface they will be attracted to the area where the magnetic field has deformed and will build up in the area. If fluorescent particles are added to the ferrous solution, ultraviolet light can be used to make it easier to visualize any recovered serial number.

Chemical Restoration

Chemical restoration is a type of chemical milling. Typically, chemical milling is used to slowly remove material to create a desired shape. In serial number restoration, small amounts of metal are removed until the serial number is brought back to the surface. This can be performed due to the depth that serial numbers are engraved into the weapon. However, chemical restoration is limited by that depth and is only successful when the obliteration of the serial number is superficial. Examiners performing a restoration first sand the area where the serial number used to be. This removes any debris from the area left when the serial number was obliterated. The examiner then chooses a chemical, usually an acid, that will be used to slowly bring the number back to the surface. The type of chemical that is used depends on the material the weapon is made of. These acids can range from Fry's Reagent for a magnetic metal, which is a mixture of hydrochloric acid, cupric chloride, and distilled water, to an acidic ferric chloride solution for a non-magnetic, non-aluminum material.

Examination of Cartridges

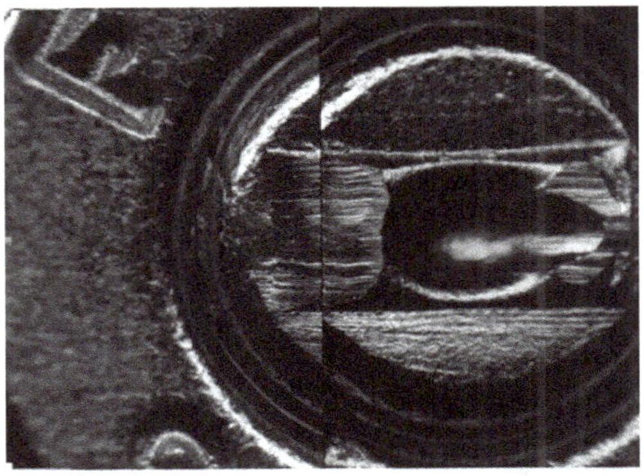

Two test-fired cartridges under magnification. Matching striations can be seen.

Spent cartridges found at a scene can be examined for physical evidence such as fingerprints or compared to samples that match them to a weapon. The examination of the cartridge relies on the unique tool marks left by the various parts of the weapon including the firing pin and the ejector in semi and fully automatic firearms. These markings can be compared and matched to known exemplars fired from the same weapon using the same parts. The examination of the marks left on the cartridge is done using a comparison microscope. Examiners view the questioned cartridge and the known exemplar simultaneously, looking for similar microscopic marks left during the firing process.

Example of microstamping. Insert shows a close up of the serial number imprinted into the cartridge.

Cartridges are also routinely examined for fingerprints as the act of loading the ammunition into the magazine, or chamber, leaves recoverable impressions. These fingerprints can survive the firing processes and, while a rare occurrence, fingerprints have been obtained from cartridges recovered from the scene. Cartridges are subjected to cyanoacrylate fuming and examined for any usable prints. Usable prints are photographed and can be uploaded to fingerprint databases such as IAFIS for comparison with known exemplars. Cartridges can also be swabbed for trace DNA left by the individual who loaded the magazine. The extremely low levels of recoverable DNA present the same issues as swabbing a firearm for DNA.

Advancements in microscopic stamping have led to a push for the inclusion of firing pin microstamping. The microstamp is etched onto the firing pin and is transferred to the cartridge during the firing process. Each firing pin would have a unique serial number allowing investigators to trace casings found at a crime scene to a known firearm. The practice is not in use as of 2017, although California has enacted legislation that requires microstamping on all newly sold firearms. The law, and microstamping in general, has received significant opposition from gun manufacturers due to increased costs associated with introducing the microstamps into the manufacturing lines.

Examination of Bullets

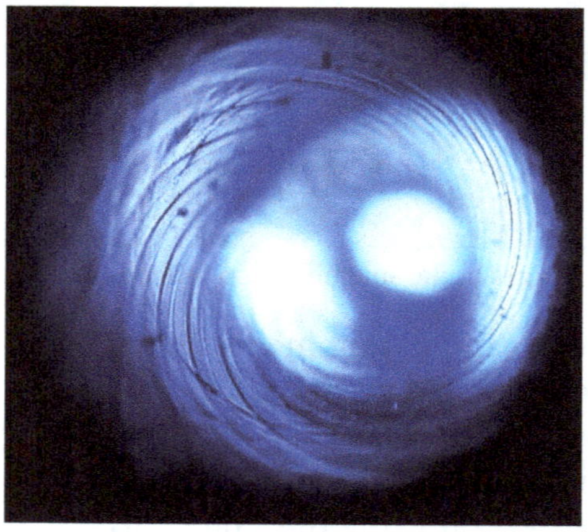

Rifing pattern for a Remington rifle showing a clockwise (right-handed) twist.

Class Characteristics

Preliminary examination of the bullet can exclude a large number of weapons by examining the general characteristics of a recovered bullet. By determining general aspects of the fired ammunition, a number of weapons can be immediately excluded as being incapable of firing that type of bullet. The make and model of the weapon can also be inferred from the combination of different class characteristics that are common to specific manufactures. The three main class characteristics of all bullets are the lands and grooves, the caliber of the bullet, and the rifling twist. All three can be tied directly to the type of barrel that was used to fire the bullet. The lands and grooves of barrel are the bumps and valleys created when the rifling is created. The caliber is the diameter of the barrel. The twist is the direction of the striations left by the barrel's rifling, clockwise (right-handed) or counterclockwise (left-handed). Most barrels will have a right-handed twist with the exception of weapons created by the Colt's Manufacturing Company which uses left-handed twists. Weapon barrels that match the class characteristics of recovered bullets can be examined further for individual characteristics to determine if the bullet came from that particular weapon.

Individual Characteristics

In order to compare individual striations, examiners must obtain a known sample using the seized weapon. For slower-traveling bullets, such as pistols or revolvers, known bullet exemplars are created by firing the weapon into a water tank. The spent bullet can be recovered, intact, as the water slows down the bullet before it can reach the tank walls, allowing for it to be recovered. For faster traveling bullets, such as those fired from high-powered rifles and military style weapons, water tanks cannot be used as the tank will not provide enough stopping power for the projectiles. To examine these weapons, investigators must fire them at a target at a controlled range with enough backing to stop the bullet and collect the spent round after it has been fired.

Once a known exemplar is produced, the evidence sample can be compared to the known by examining both at the same time with a comparison microscope. Striations that line up are examined more closely, looking for multiple consecutive matches. There is no set number of consecutive matches that equates to a match declaration, and examiners are trained to use the phrase "sufficient agreement" when testifying. The degree to which an examiner can make that determination is based on their training and expertise. All findings by examiners are subject to questioning by both sides, prosecution and defense, during testimony in court.

Striation Databasing

Bullets and casings found at a scene require a known example to compare to in order to match them to a weapon. Without a weapon, the striation pattern can be uploaded to a database such as the National Integrated Ballistic Identification Network (NIBIN) maintained by the ATF or the United Kingdom's National Ballistics Intelligence Service (NABIS). Information uploaded to these databases can be used to track gun crimes and to link crimes together. Maintainers of these databases recommend that every recovered firearm be test fired and the resulting known exemplar be uploaded into the database.

Criticisms

Firearm examiners have attempted to determine the shooter's position by the location of spent bullet casings. The use of ejection pattern studies were originally part of incident reconstruction and methods for determining shooter location continue to be explained in major crime scene examination books. However, the validity of ejection pattern analysis has been brought into question by multiple studies that look at the reproducibility and end determination of shooter position by qualified examiners. Studies have shown that over 25% of spent casings land somewhere other than to the right and rear of the shooter. This is the most commonly accepted location for where spent cartridge casings should fall, and the large percentage of casings that end up somewhere else raises concerns for the validity of the examination technique. Investigators should only present a location gained from an ejection pattern study as a tentative estimate when using the information in a courtroom setting.

Prior to September 2005, comparative bullet-lead analysis was performed on bullets found at a scene that were too destroyed for striation comparison. The technique would attempt to determine the unique elemental breakdown of the bullet and compare it to seized bullets possessed by a suspect. Review of the method found that the breakdown of elements found in bullets could be significantly different enough to potentially allow for two bullets from separate sources to be correlated to each other. However, there is not enough differences to definitely match a bullet from a crime scene to one taken from a suspect's possession. An additional report in 2004 from the National Academy of Sciences (NAS) found that the testimony given regarding comparative bullet-lead analysis was overstated and potentially "misleading under the federal rules of evidence". In 2005, the Federal Bureau of Investigation indicated that they would no longer be performing this type of analysis.

Further criticism came from the 2009 NAS report on the current state of various forensic fields in the United States. The report's section on firearm examination focused on the lack of defined requirements that are necessary in order to determine "matches" between known and unknown striations. The NAS stated that, "sufficient studies have not been done to understand the reliability and repeatability of the methods." Without defined procedures on what is and what isn't considered "sufficient agreement" the report states that forensic firearm examination contains fundamental problems that need to be addressed by the forensic community through a set of repeatable scientific studies that outline standard operating procedures that should be adopted by all firearm examiners. Another report issued in 2016 by the United States President's Council of Advisors on Science and Technology confirmed the NAS's findings, finding only one appropriately designed study that examined the rate of false positives and reliability amongst firearm examiners.

Autopsy

An autopsy (also known as a post-mortem examination, obduction, necropsy, or autopsia cadaverum) is a highly specialized surgical procedure that consists of a thorough examination of a corpse by dissection to determine the cause and manner of death and to evaluate any disease or injury that may be present. It is usually performed by a specialized medical doctor called a pathologist. Usually only a small portion of deaths require an autopsy; in most cases, a medical examiner or coroner can determine cause of death without one.

Autopsies are performed for either legal or medical purposes. For example, a forensic autopsy is carried out when the cause of death may be a criminal matter, while a clinical or academic autopsy is performed to find the medical cause of death and is used in cases of unknown or uncertain death, or for research purposes. Autopsies can be further classified into cases where external examination suffices, and those where the body is dissected and internal examination is conducted. Permission from next of kin may be required for internal autopsy in some cases. Once an internal autopsy is complete the body is reconstituted by sewing it back together.

Purpose

The principal aim of an autopsy is to determine the cause of death, the state of health of the person before he or she died, and whether any medical diagnosis and treatment before death was appropriate.

In most Western countries the number of autopsies performed in hospitals has been decreasing every year since 1955. Critics, including pathologist and former *JAMA* editor George Lundberg, have charged that the reduction in autopsies is negatively affecting the care delivered in hospitals, because when mistakes result in death, they are often not investigated and lessons therefore remain unlearned.

When a person has given permission in advance of their death, autopsies may also be carried out for the purposes of teaching or medical research.

An autopsy is frequently performed in cases of sudden death, where a doctor is not able to write a death certificate, or when death is believed to result from an unnatural cause. These examinations are performed under a legal authority (Medical Examiner or Coroner or Procurator Fiscal) and do not require the consent of relatives of the deceased. The most extreme example is the examination of murder victims, especially when medical examiners are looking for signs of death or the murder method, such as bullet wounds and exit points, signs of strangulation, or traces of poison. Some religions including Judaism and Islam usually discourage the performing of autopsies on their adherents. Organizations such as Zaka in Israel and Misaskim in the United States generally guide families how to ensure that an unnecessary autopsy is not made.

Autopsies are used in clinical medicine to identify medical error.

A study that focused on myocardial infarction (heart attack) as a cause of death found significant errors of omission and commission, i.e. a sizable number cases ascribed to myocardial infarctions (MIs) were not MIs and a significant number of non-MIs were actually MIs.

A systematic review of studies of the autopsy calculated that in about 25% of autopsies a major diagnostic error will be revealed. However, this rate has decreased over time and the study projects that in a contemporary US institution, 8.4% to 24.4% of autopsies will detect major diagnostic errors.

A large meta-analysis suggested that approximately one-third of death certificates are incorrect and that half of the autopsies performed produced findings that were not suspected before the person died. Also, it is thought that over one fifth of unexpected findings can only be diagnosed histologically, i.e. by biopsy or autopsy, and that approximately one quarter of unexpected findings, or 5% of all findings, are major and can similarly only be diagnosed from tissue.

One study found that (out of 694 diagnoses) "Autopsies revealed 171 missed diagnoses, including 21 cancers, 12 strokes, 11 myocardial infarctions, 10 pulmonary emboli, and 9 endocarditis, among others".

Focusing on intubated patients, one study found "abdominal pathologic conditions--abscesses, bowel perforations, or infarction--were as frequent as pulmonary emboli as a cause of class I errors. While patients with abdominal pathologic conditions generally complained of abdominal pain, results of examination of the abdomen were considered unremarkable in most patients, and the symptom was not pursued".

Types

There are four main types of autopsies:

- *Medico-Legal Autopsy or Forensic* or *coroner's autopsies* seek to find the cause and manner of death and to identify the decedent. They are generally performed, as prescribed by applicable law, in cases of violent, suspicious or sudden deaths, deaths without medical assistance or during surgical procedures.

- *Clinical* or *Pathological autopsies* are performed to diagnose a particular disease or for research purposes. They aim to determine, clarify, or confirm medical diagnoses that remained unknown or unclear prior to the patient's death.
- *Anatomical* or *academic autopsies* are performed by students of anatomy for study purpose only.
- *Virtual* or *medical imaging autopsies* are performed utilizing imaging technology only, primarily magnetic resonance imaging (MRI) and computed tomography (CT).

Forensic Autopsy

Autopsy room of the Charité Berlin

A forensic autopsy is used to determine the cause and manner of death. Forensic science involves the application of the sciences to answer questions of interest to the legal system.

Medical examiners attempt to determine the time of death, the exact cause of death, and what, if anything, preceded the death, such as a struggle. A forensic autopsy may include obtaining biological specimens from the deceased for toxicological testing, including stomach contents. Toxicology tests may reveal the presence of one or more chemical "poisons" (all chemicals, in sufficient quantities, can be classified as a poison) and their quantity. Because post-mortem deterioration of the body, together with the gravitational pooling of bodily fluids, will necessarily alter the bodily environment, toxicology tests may overestimate, rather than underestimate, the quantity of the suspected chemical.

Following an in-depth examination of all the evidence, a medical examiner or coroner will assign one of the manners of death provided for in the fact-finder's jurisdiction and will detail the evidence on the mechanism of the death.

United States of America

In most United States of America jurisdictions, each death is categorized as taking place in one of five "manners of death":

- Natural

- Accident, including both *a*) deaths resulting from a risk that is either reasonable or neither deliberately assumed nor intentionally created by another person and *b*) deaths resulting from deliberate assumption of unreasonable risk (contrast the definition of "accident" used in England and Wales)
- Homicide
- Suicide
- Undetermined

Most states require the state medical examiner to complete an autopsy report, and many mandate that the autopsy be videotaped.

England and Wales

Although England and Wales use the "accident" designation, in those jurisdictions the term applies to deaths resulting from a risk that is either *a*) reasonable (whether assumed deliberately or not) or *b*) neither *i*) voluntarily assumed nor *ii*) intentionally created by another party; for deaths resulting from deliberate assumption of unreasonable risk, England and Wales use the category "misadventure."

Other Jurisdictions

Some jurisdictions place deaths in absentia, such as deaths at sea and missing persons declared dead in a court of law, in the "Undetermined" category on the grounds that due to the fact-finder's lack of ability to examine the body, the examiner has no personal knowledge of the manner of (assumed) death; others classify such deaths in an additional category "Other," reserving "Undetermined" for deaths in which the fact-finder has access to the body but the information provided by the body and examination of it is insufficient to provide sufficient grounds for a determination.

Clinical Autopsy

Clinical autopsies serve two major purposes. They are performed to gain more insight into pathological processes and determine what factors contributed to a patient's death. Autopsies are also performed to ensure the standard of care at hospitals. Autopsies can yield insight into how patient deaths can be prevented in the future.

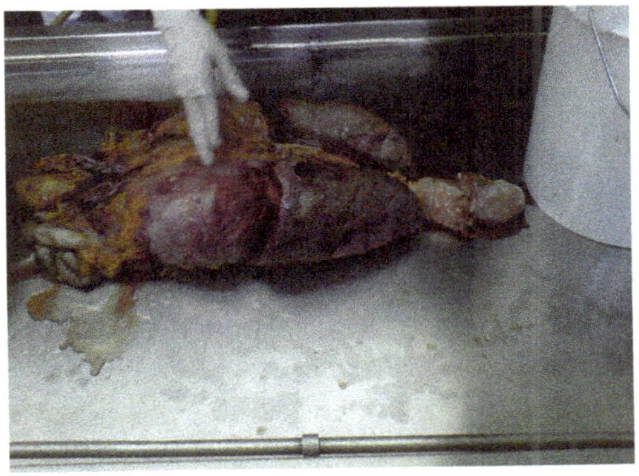

Pathologist performing a human dissection of the abdominal and thoracic organs in an autopsy room.

Within the United Kingdom, clinical autopsies can be carried out only with the consent of the family of the deceased person as opposed to a medico-legal autopsy instructed by a Coroner (England & Wales) or Procurator Fiscal (Scotland) to which the family cannot object.

Overtime, autopsies have not only been able to determine the cause of death, but also lead to discoveries of various diseases such as fetal alcohol syndrome, Legionnaire's disease, and even viral hepatitis.

Prevalence

In 2004 in England and Wales, there were 514,000 deaths of which 225,500 were referred to the coroner. Of those, 115,800 (22.5% of all deaths) resulted in post-mortem examinations and there were 28,300 inquests, 570 with a jury.

The rate of consented (hospital) autopsy in the UK (and worldwide) has declined rapidly over the past 50 years. Turnbull and colleagues from Imperial College London showed that in the UK in 2013 only 0.7% of inpatient adult deaths were followed by consented autopsy.

In the United States, autopsy rates fell from 17% in 1980 to 14% in 1985 and 11.5% in 1989, although the figures vary notably from country to country.

Process

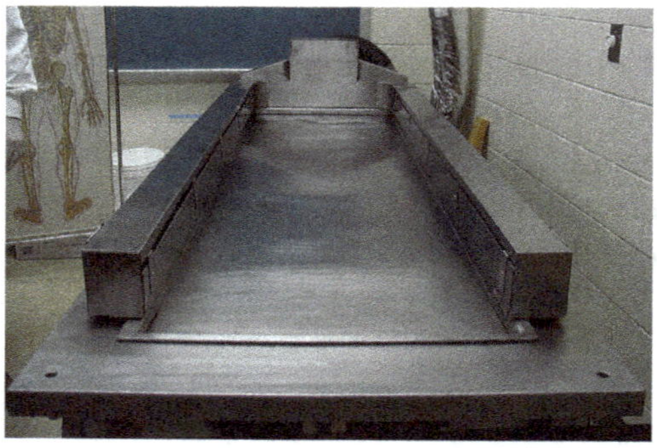

Cadaver dissection table. Similar to those used in medical or forensic autopsies.

The body is received at a medical examiner's office or hospital in a body bag or evidence sheet. A new body bag is used for each body to ensure that only evidence from that body is contained within the bag. Evidence sheets are an alternative way to transport the body. An evidence sheet is a sterile sheet that the body is covered in when it is moved. If it is believed there may be any significant evidence on the hands, for example, gunshot residue or skin under the fingernails, a separate paper sack is put around each hand and taped shut around the wrist.

There are two parts to the physical examination of the body: the external and internal examination. Toxicology, biochemical tests and/or genetic testing/molecular autopsy often supplement these and frequently assist the pathologist in assigning the cause or causes of death.

External Examination

At many institutions the person responsible for handling, cleaning, and moving the body is often called a diener, the German word for *servant*. In the UK this role is performed by an Anatomical Pathology Technologist who will also assist the pathologist in eviscerating the body and reconstruction after the autopsy. After the body is received, it is first photographed. The examiner then notes the kind of clothes and their position on the body before they are removed. Next, any evidence such as residue, flakes of paint or other material is collected from the external surfaces of the body. Ultraviolet light may also be used to search body surfaces for any evidence not easily visible to the naked eye. Samples of hair, nails and the like are taken, and the body may also be radiographically imaged. Once the external evidence is collected, the body is removed from the bag, undressed, and any wounds present are examined. The body is then cleaned, weighed, and measured in preparation for the internal examination. The scale used to weigh the body is often designed to accommodate the cart that the body is transported on; its weight is then deducted from the total weight shown to give the weight of the body.

If not already within an autopsy room at the city, county or state morgue, the body is transported to one and placed on a table. A general description of the body as regards ethnicity, sex, age, hair color and length, eye color and other distinguishing features (birthmarks, old scar tissue, moles, tattoos, etc.) is then made. A handheld voice recorder or a standard examination form is normally used to record this information. In some countries e.g. France, Germany, and Canada, an autopsy may comprise an external examination only. This concept is sometimes termed a "view and grant". The principles behind this being that the medical records, history of the deceased and circumstances of death have all indicated as to the cause and manner of death without the need for an internal examination.

Internal Examination

If not already in place, a plastic or rubber brick called a "body block" is placed under the back of the body, causing the arms and neck to fall backward while stretching and pushing the chest upward to make it easier to cut open. This gives the prosector, a pathologist or assistant, maximum exposure to the trunk. After this is done, the internal examination begins. The internal examination consists of inspecting the internal organs of the body by dissection for evidence of trauma or other indications of the cause of death. For the internal examination there are a number of different approaches available:

- a large and deep Y-shaped incision can be made starting at the top of each shoulder and running down the front of the chest, meeting at the lower point of the sternum. This is the approach most often used.
- a T-shaped incision made from the tips of both shoulder, in a horizontal line across the region of the collar bones to meet at the sternum (breastbone) in the middle.
- a single vertical cut is made from the middle of the neck (in the region of the 'adam's apple' on a male body)
- a U-shaped incision is made at the tip of both shoulders, down along the side of the chest to the bottom of the rib cage, following along it. This is typically used on women and during chest only autopsies.

In all of the above cases the cut then extends all the way down to the pubic bone (making a deviation to either side of the navel).

Bleeding from the cuts is minimal, or non-existent, because the pull of gravity is producing the only blood pressure at this point, related directly to the complete lack of cardiac functionality. However, in certain cases there is anecdotal evidence that bleeding can be quite profuse, especially in cases of drowning.

At this point, shears are used to open the chest cavity. It is also possible to utilise a simple scalpel blade. The prosector uses the tool to saw through the ribs on the lateral sides of the chest cavity to allow the sternum and attached ribs to be lifted as one chest plate; this is done so that the heart and lungs can be seen in situ and that the heart, in particular the pericardial sac is not damaged or disturbed from opening. A scalpel is used to remove any soft tissue that is still attached to the posterior side of the chest plate. Now the lungs and the heart are exposed. The chest plate is set aside and will be eventually replaced at the end of the autopsy.

At this stage the organs are exposed. Usually, the organs are removed in a systematic fashion. Making a decision as to what order the organs are to be removed will depend highly on the case in question. Organs can be removed in several ways: The first is the en masse technique of Letulle whereby all the organs are removed as one large mass. The second is the en bloc method of Ghon. The most popular in the UK is a modified version of this method which is divided into four groups of organs. Although these are the two predominant evisceration techniques in the UK variations on these are widespread.

One method is described here: The pericardial sac is opened to view the heart. Blood for chemical analysis may be removed from the inferior vena cava or the pulmonary veins. Before removing the heart, the pulmonary artery is opened in order to search for a blood clot. The heart can then be removed by cutting the inferior vena cava, the pulmonary veins, the aorta and pulmonary artery, and the superior vena cava. This method leaves the aortic arch intact, which will make things easier for the embalmer. The left lung is then easily accessible and can be removed by cutting the bronchus, artery, and vein at the hilum. The right lung can then be similarly removed. The abdominal organs can be removed one by one after first examining their relationships and vessels.

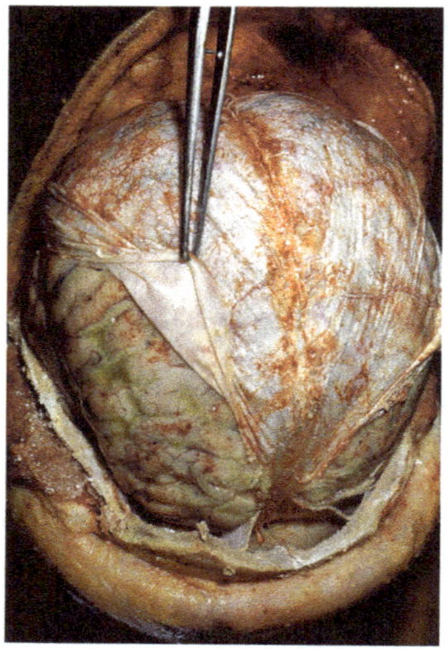

A brain autopsy demonstrating signs of meningitis. The forceps (center) are retracting the dura mater (white). Underneath the dura mater are the leptomeninges, which appear to be edematous and have multiple small hemorrhagic foci.

Some pathologists, however, prefer to remove the organs all in one "block". Then a series of cuts, along the vertebral column, are made so that the organs can be detached and pulled out in one piece for further inspection and sampling. During autopsies of infants, this method is used almost all of the time. The various organs are examined, weighed and tissue samples in the form of slices are taken. Even major blood vessels are cut open and inspected at this stage. Next the stomach and intestinal contents are examined and weighed. This could be useful to find the cause and time of death, due to the natural passage of food through the bowel during digestion. The more area empty, the longer the deceased had gone without a meal before death.

The body block that was used earlier to elevate the chest cavity is now used to elevate the head. To examine the brain, an incision is made from behind one ear, over the crown of the head, to a point behind the other ear. When the autopsy is completed, the incision can be neatly sewn up and is not noticed when the head is resting on a pillow in an open casket funeral. The scalp is pulled away from the skull in two flaps with the front flap going over the face and the rear flap over the back of the neck. The skull is then cut with a circular (or semicircular) bladed reciprocating saw to create a "cap" that can be pulled off, exposing the brain. The brain is then observed in situ. Then the brain's connection to the cranial nerves and spinal cord are severed, and the brain is lifted out of the skull for further examination. If the brain needs to be preserved before being inspected, it is contained in a large container of formalin (15 percent solution of formaldehyde gas in buffered water) for at least two but preferably four weeks. This not only preserves the brain, but also makes it firmer allowing easier handling without corrupting the tissue.

Reconstitution of the Body

An important component of the autopsy is the reconstitution of the body such that it can be viewed, if desired, by relatives of the deceased following the procedure. After the examination, the body has an open and empty chest cavity with chest flaps open on both sides, the top of the skull is missing, and the skull flaps are pulled over the face and neck. It is unusual to examine the face, arms, hands or legs internally.

In the UK, following the Human Tissue Act 2004 all organs and tissue must be returned to the body unless permission is given by the family to retain any tissue for further investigation. Normally the internal body cavity is lined with cotton wool or an appropriate material, the organs are then placed into a plastic bag to prevent leakage and returned to the body cavity. The chest flaps are then closed and sewn back together and the skull cap is sewed back in place. Then the body may be wrapped in a shroud and it is common for relatives to not be able to tell the procedure has been done when the body is viewed in a funeral parlor after embalming.

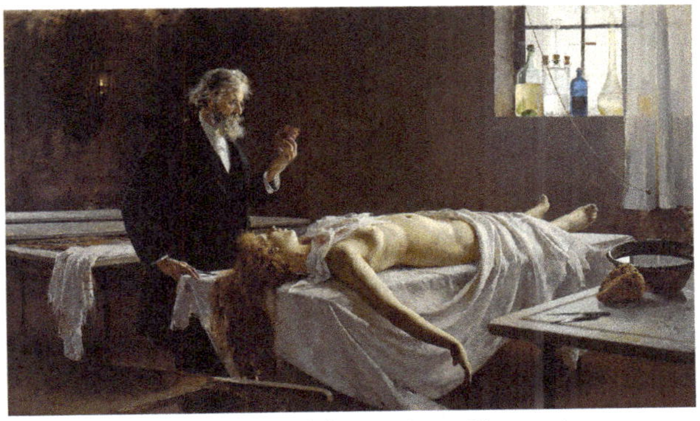

Autopsy (1890) by Enrique Simonet.

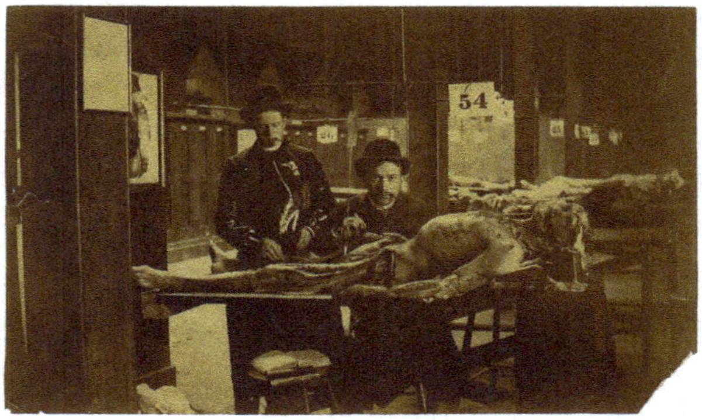

Dissection, 19th century US.

The word "autopsy" has been used since around the 17th century, it refers to the examination of inside the dead human body to discover diseases and cause of death. Around 3000 BC ancient Egyptians were one of the first civilizations to practice the removal and examination of the internal organs of humans in the religious practice of mummification.

Autopsies that opened the body to determine the cause of death were attested at least in the early third millennium BC, although they were opposed in many ancient societies where it was believed that the outward disfigurement of dead persons prevented them from entering the afterlife (as with the Egyptians, who removed the organs through tiny slits in the body). Notable Greek autopsists were Galen (AD 129- c. 200/ 216), Erasistratus and Herophilus of Chalcedon, who lived in 3rd century BC Alexandria, but in general, autopsies were rare in ancient Greece. In 44 BC, Julius Caesar was the subject of an official autopsy after his murder by rival senators, the physician's report noting that the second stab wound Caesar received was the fatal one. Julius Caesar had been stabbed a total of 23 times. By around 150 BC, ancient Roman legal practice had established clear parameters for autopsies.

The dissection of human remains for medical or scientific reasons continued to be practiced irregularly after the Romans, for instance by the Arab physicians Avenzoar and Ibn al-Nafis. In Europe they were done with enough regularity to become skilled, as early as 1200, and successful efforts to preserve the body, by filling the veins with wax and metals. Until recently, it was thought that the modern autopsy process derived from the anatomists of the Renaissance. Giovanni Morgagni (1682–1771), celebrated as the father of anatomical pathology, wrote the first exhaustive work on pathology, *De Sedibus et Causis Morborum per Anatomen Indagatis* (The Seats and Causes of Diseases Investigated by Anatomy, 1769).

Carl von Rokitansky and colleagues at the Second Vienna Medical School began to undertake dissections as a means to improve diagnostic medicine, for the first time applying scientific techniques.

In 1543 Andreas Vesalius conducted a public dissection of the body of a former criminal. He asserted and articulated the bones, this became the worlds oldest surviving anatomical preparation. It is still displayed at the Anatomical museum at the University of Basel.

The great 19th-century medical researcher Rudolf Virchow, in response to a lack of standardization of autopsy procedures, established and published specific autopsy protocols (one such protocol still bears his name). He also developed the concept of pathological processes.

Other Animals

A field post-mortem exam of an ewe.

Post-mortem examination, or necropsy, is far more common in veterinary medicine than in human medicine. For many species that exhibit few external symptoms (sheep), or that are not suited to detailed clinical examination (poultry, cage birds, zoo animals), it is a common method used by veterinarians to come to a diagnosis. A necropsy is mostly used like an autopsy to determine cause of death. The entire body is examined at the gross visual level, and samples are collected for additional analyses.

Microstamping

Microstamping is a ballistics identification technology. Microscopic markings are engraved onto the tip of the firing pin and onto the breech face of a firearm with a laser. When the gun is fired, these etchings are transferred to the primer by the firing pin and to the cartridge case head by the breech face, using the pressure created when a round is fired. After being fired, if the cases are recovered by police, the microscopic markings imprinted on the cartridges can then be examined by forensic ballistics experts to help trace the firearm to the last registered owner. A California law requiring the use of microstamping technology in all new semiautomatic firearms sold in the state has attracted controversy.

Legal Jurisdictions in the United States

California

Microstamping legislation was passed in California AB 1471 and signed into law on October 14, 2007, but specifically exempts law enforcement. The law has generated controversy.

This technology was to be required in California starting in 2010, however, it is on hold and law enforcement is specifically exempt. One group, the Calguns Foundation, paid a $555 fee to keep the patent active in order to delay implementation. On May 17, 2013, California Attorney General Kamala Harris announced that micro-stamping had cleared all technological and patenting hurdles and would be required on newly sold semiautomatics, effective immediately. However, handguns already approved for sale but lacking this technology may still be sold as long as they remain on the Roster of Not Unsafe Handguns.

In January 2014, the two largest handgun manufacturers in the U.S., Smith & Wesson and Sturm, Ruger & Co., announced their intent to stop selling new semi-automatic handguns in California. They cited the microstamping law as their reason.

Two trade groups, the National Shooting Sports Foundation (NSSF) and the Sporting Arms and Ammunition Manufacturers Institute (SAAMI), have filed a lawsuit seeking both declaratory and injunctive relief against what the groups perceive as an attempt to ban semi-automatic handguns in the state. In February 2015 a federal judge upheld the microstamping requirement, ruling that it does not violate the Second Amendment.

On December 1, 2016, a California Appellate Court reversed the Fresno Superior Court's dismissal of the NSSF and the SAAMI lawsuit seeking an injunction to block enforcement of the state's ammunition microstamping law and remanded the case back to the lower court to hear arguments.

Other Jurisdictions

Similar legislation is under consideration in New York, Connecticut, Rhode Island, Massachusetts, Maryland, Wisconsin, and Illinois.

Federal bill H.R.5266, the National Crime Gun Identification Act of 2008, was written by House Rep. Xavier Becerra (D-CA). Senator Edward Kennedy (MA) introduced an identical companion bill in the Senate.

US National Research Council Study

The United States National Research Council released a report in 2008 that endorsed the investigation of microstamping as an alternative to ballistic markings. It had concluded that a national database of ballistic markings is unworkable and that there is not enough scientific evidence that, "every gun leaves microscopic marks on bullets and cartridge cases that are unique to that weapon and remain the same over repeated firings". It described microstamping as a "promising method" that could "attain the same basic goal as the proposed database".

Objections

The SAAMI trade group raises these objections:

- Unscrupulous individuals could collect discarded brass from a firing range and salt crime scenes with microstamped cases, thereby providing false evidence against innocent people and increasing the workload for investigators.
- Firing a large number of rounds will wear down the microstamp.
- Microstamping is an immature, sole source technology, and has not been subjected to suf-

ficient independent testing. Transfer of microstamped marks to the cases is less reliable than proponents claim.

- High costs for testing the efficacy of the technique must be passed on to customers, increasing the cost of firearms for those who obtain them legally.
- Guns manufactured before an effective date are exempt and the bill does not extend to guns outside of California. There's no possibility that this bill would ever cover enough guns to provide the investigative advantage claimed for it by the proponents.

Specific to California, the chief of the Oakland Police Department says:

- Firearms sold to law-enforcement are exempt. Problems could arise if a police officer's firearm is used in a crime or stolen, and the fact that a firearm is "unsafe" if not provided with stamping technology exposes the police to liability.

Most firearms used in crime are stolen or purchased in the secondary market.

Manufacturer

The proprietary technology was invented and patented by Todd Lizotte and is presently owned by a company he founded called NanoMark, a division of ID Dynamics of Seattle, Washington. They are the only company from which this technology can be purchased.

Gait Analysis

Gait analysis is the systematic study of animal locomotion, more specifically the study of human motion, using the eye and the brain of observers, augmented by instrumentation for measuring body movements, body mechanics, and the activity of the muscles. Gait analysis is used to assess and treat individuals with conditions affecting their ability to walk. It is also commonly used in sports biomechanics to help athletes run more efficiently and to identify posture-related or movement-related problems in people with injuries.

Gait analysis laboratory equipped with infrared cameras and floor mounted force platforms

The study encompasses quantification (i.e. introduction and analysis of measurable parameters of gaits), as well as interpretation, i.e. drawing various conclusions about the animal (health, age, size, weight, speed etc.) from its gait pattern.

History

The pioneers of scientific gait analysis were Aristotle in *De Motu Animalium* (On the Gait of Animals) and much later in 1680, Giovanni Alfonso Borelli also called *De Motu Animalium (I et II)*. In the 1890s, the German anatomist Christian Wilhelm Braune and Otto Fischer published a series of papers on the biomechanics of human gait under loaded and unloaded conditions.

With the development of photography and cinematography, it became possible to capture image sequences that reveal details of human and animal locomotion that were not noticeable by watching the movement with the naked eye. Eadweard Muybridge and Étienne-Jules Marey were pioneers of these developments in the early 1900s. For example, serial photography first revealed the detailed sequence of the horse "gallop", which was usually misrepresented in paintings made prior to this discovery.

Although much early research was done using film cameras, the widespread application of gait analysis to humans with pathological conditions such as cerebral palsy, Parkinson's disease, and neuromuscular disorders, began in the 1970s with the availability of video camera systems that could produce detailed studies of individual patients within realistic cost and time constraints. The development of treatment regimes, often involving orthopaedic surgery, based on gait analysis results, advanced significantly in the 1980s. Many leading orthopaedic hospitals worldwide now have gait labs that are routinely used to design treatment plans and for follow-up monitoring.

Development of modern computer based systems occurred independently during the late 1970s and early 1980s in several hospital based research labs, some through collaborations with the aerospace industry. Commercial development soon followed with the emergence of commercial television and later infrared camera systems in the mid-1980s.

Process and Equipment

A typical gait analysis laboratory has several cameras (video and / or infrared) placed around a walkway or a treadmill, which are linked to a computer. The patient has markers located at various points of reference of the body (e.g., iliac spines of the pelvis, ankle malleolus, and the condyles of the knee), or groups of markers applied to half of the body segments. The patient walks down the catwalk or the treadmill and the computer calculates the trajectory of each marker in three dimensions. A model is applied to calculate the movement of the underlying bones. This gives a complete breakdown of the movement of each joint. One common method is to use Helen Hayes Hospital marker set, in which a total of 15 markers are attached on the lower body. The 15 marker motions are analyzed analytically, and it provides angular motion of each joint.

To calculate the kinetics of gait patterns, most labs have floor-mounted load transducers, also known as force platforms, which measure the ground reaction forces and moments, including the magnitude, direction and location (called the center of pressure). The spatial distribution of forces can be measured with pedobarography equipment. Adding this to the known dynamics of each body segment enables the solution of equations based on the Newton–Euler equations of motion permitting computations of the net forces and the net moments of force about each joint at every stage of the gait cycle. The computational method for this is known as inverse dynamics.

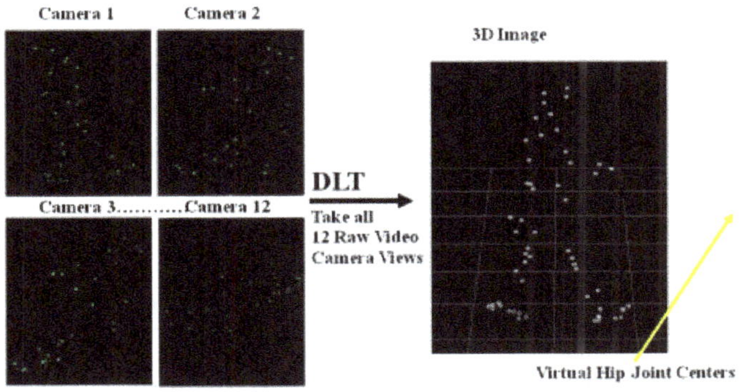

Acquisition of information on the position of the markers in 2D through the chambers of the left and right, this combination of information gives rise to a 3D image on the position of the markers

This use of kinetics, however, does not result in information for individual muscles but muscle groups, such as the extensor or flexors of the limb. To detect the activity and contribution of individual muscles to movement, it is necessary to investigate the electrical activity of muscles. Many labs also use surface electrodes attached to the skin to detect the electrical activity or electromyogram (EMG) of muscles. In this way it is possible to investigate the activation times of muscles and, to some degree, the magnitude of their activation—thereby assessing their contribution to gait. Deviations from normal kinematic, kinetic or EMG patterns are used to diagnose specific pathologies, predict the outcome of treatments, or determine the effectiveness of training programs.

Factors and Parameters

The gait analysis is modulated or modified by many factors, and changes in the normal gait pattern can be transient or permanent. The factors can be of various types:

- *Extrinsic: such as terrain, footwear, clothing, cargo*
- *Intrinsic: sex (male or female), weight, height, age, etc.*
- *Physical: such as weight, height, physique*
- *Psychological: personality type, emotions*
- *Physiological: anthropometric characteristics, i.e., measurements and proportions of body*
- *Pathological: for example trauma, neurological diseases, musculoskeletal anomalies, psychiatric disorders*

The parameters taken into account for the gait analysis are as follows:

- *Step length*
- *Stride length*
- *Cadence*

- *Speed*
- *Dynamic Base*
- *Progression Line*
- *Foot Angle*
- *Hip Angle*
- *Squat Performance*

Techniques

Gait analysis involves measurement, where measurable parameters are introduced and analyzed, and interpretation, where conclusions about the subject (health, age, size, weight, speed, etc.) are drawn. The analysis is the measurement of the following:

Temporal / Spatial

It consists in the calculation of "speed, the length of the rhythm, pitch, and so on. These measurements are carried out through:

- Stopwatch and marks on the ground.
- Walking on a pressure mat.
- Range laser sensors scanning a plane a few centimeters above the floor.
- Inertial sensors and software to interpret 3D gyroscopes and 3D accelerometric data.

Kinematics

1. Chronophotography is the most basic method for recording of movement. Strobe lighting at known frequency has been used in the past to aid in the analysis of gait on single photographic images.
2. Cine film or video recordings using footage from single or multiple cameras can be used to measure joint angles and velocities. This method has been aided by the development of analysis software that greatly simplifies the analysis process and allows for analysis in three dimensions rather than two dimensions only.
3. Passive marker systems, using reflective markers (typically reflective balls), allows for accurate measurement of movements using multiple cameras (typically five to twelve cameras), simultaneously. The cameras utilize high-powered strobes (typically red, near infrared or infrared) with matching filters to record the reflection from the markers placed on the body. Markers are located at palpable anatomical landmarks. Based on the angle and time delay between the original and reflected signal, triangulation of the marker in space is possible. Software is used to create three dimensional trajectories from these markers that are subsequently given identification labels. A computer model is then used to compute joint

angles from the relative marker positions of the labeled trajectories. These are also used for motion capture in the motion picture industry.

4. Active marker systems are similar to the passive marker system but use "active" markers. These markers are triggered by the incoming infra red signal and respond by sending out a corresponding signal of their own. This signal is then used to triangulate the location of the marker. The advantage of this system over the passive one is that individual markers work at predefined frequencies and therefore, have their own "identity". This means that no post-processing of marker locations is required, however, the systems tend to be less forgiving for out-of-view markers than the passive systems.

5. Inertial (cameraless) systems based on MEMS inertial sensors, biomechanical models, and sensor fusion algorithms. These full-body or partial body systems can be used indoors and outdoors regardless of lighting conditions.

Markerless Gait Capture

Markerless gait capture systems utilize one or more color cameras or 2.5D depth sensors (i.e. Kinect) to directly calculate the body joint positions from a sequence of images. The markerless system allows non-invasive human gait analysis in a natural environment without any marker attachment. Eliminating markers can expand the applicability of human gait measurement and analysis techniques, considerably reduce the preparation time, and enable efficient and accurate motion assessment in all kinds of applications. Currently, the main markerless system is the video-based motion capture with monocular camera or multiple camera studio. Nowadays, the depth sensor-based gait analysis for clinical applications becomes more and more popular. Since depth sensors can measure the depth information and provide a 2.5D depth image, they have effectively simplified the task of foreground/background subtraction and significantly reduced pose ambiguities in monocular human pose estimation.

Kinetics

Is the study of the forces involved in the production of movements.

Dynamic Electromyography

Is the study of patterns of muscle activity during gait.

Applications

Gait analysis is used to analyze the walking ability of humans and animals, so this technology can be used for the following applications:

Medical Diagnostics

Pathological gait may reflect compensations for underlying pathologies, or be responsible for causation of symptoms in itself. Cerebral palsy and stroke patients are commonly seen in gait labs. The study of gait allows diagnoses and intervention strategies to be made, as well as permitting future developments in rehabilitation engineering. Aside from clinical applications, gait analysis is used in professional sports training to optimize and improve athletic performance.

Gait analysis techniques allow for the assessment of gait disorders and the effects of corrective orthopedic surgery. Options for treatment of cerebral palsy include the artificial paralysis of spastic muscles using Botox or the lengthening, re-attachment or detachment of particular tendons. Corrections of distorted bony anatomy are also undertaken (osteotomy).

Chiropractic and Osteopathic Utilizations

Observation of gait is also beneficial for diagnoses in chiropractic and osteopathic professions as hindrances in gait may be indicative of a misaligned pelvis or sacrum. As the sacrum and ilium biomechanically move in opposition to each other, adhesions between the two of them via the sacrospinous or sacrotuberous ligaments (among others) may suggest a rotated pelvis. Both doctors of chiropractic and osteopathic medicine use gait to discern the listing of a pelvis and can employ various techniques in order to restore a full range of motion to areas involved in ambulatory movement. Chiropractic adjustment of the pelvis has shown a trend in helping restore gait patterns as has osteopathic manipulative therapy (OMT).

Biometric Identification and Forensics

Minor variations in gait style can be used as a biometric identifier to identify individual people. The parameters are grouped to spatial-temporal (step length, step width, walking speed, cycle time) and kinematic (joint rotation of the hip, knee and ankle, mean joint angles of the hip/knee/ankle, and thigh/trunk/foot angles) classes. There is a high correlation between step length and height of a person.

The approach above belongs to the model-based approach. Another appearance-based approach recognizes individuals through binary gait silhouette sequences. For example, silhouette sequences of full gait cycles can be treated as 3D tensor samples, and multilinear subspace learning, such as the multilinear principal component analysis, can be employed to learning features for classification.

Comparative Biomechanics

By studying the gait of non-human animals, more insight can be gained about the mechanics of locomotion, which has diverse implications for understanding the biology of the species in question as well as locomotion more broadly.

Popular Media

- G. K. Chesterton premised one of his Father Brown mysteries, “The Queer Feet”, on gait recognition.
- Cory Doctorow makes much of gait recognition as a security technique used in a high school in his book *Little Brother*.
- Arthur Conan Doyle has Sherlock Holmes use gait analysis to identify the height of the *Rache* killer in A Study in Scarlet

Hair Analysis

Hair analysis may refer to the chemical analysis of a hair sample, but can also refer to microscopic analysis or comparison. Chemical hair analysis may be considered for retrospective purposes when blood and urine are no longer expected to contain a particular contaminant, typically three months or less. Its most widely accepted use is in the fields of forensic toxicology and, increasingly, environmental toxicology. Several alternative medicine fields also use various hair analyses for environmental toxicology but these uses are controversial, evolving and not standardized.

Microscopic hair analysis has traditionally been used in forensics as well. Analysts examine a number of different characteristics of hairs under a microscope, usually comparing hair taken from a crime scene and hair taken from a suspect. It is still acknowledged as a useful technique for confirming hairs do not match, but the ability of the field to identify a specific person has fallen into disrepute after DNA analysis showed that many claimed matches from this technique were false.

In Forensic Toxicology

Hair analysis is used for the detection of many therapeutic drugs and recreational drugs, including cocaine, heroin, benzodiazepines and amphetamines. Hair analysis is less invasive than a blood test, if not quite as universally applicable. In this context, it has been reliably used to determine compliance with therapeutic drug regimes or to check the accuracy of a witness statement that an illicit drug has not been taken. Hair testing is an increasingly common method of assessment in substance misuse, particularly in legal proceedings, or in any situation where a subject may have decided not to tell the entire truth about his or her substance-using history. It is also used by private employers who test their employees. Hair analysis has the virtue of showing a 'history' of drug use due to hair's slow growth. Urine analysis might detect drugs taken in the past three days; hair analysis can sometimes stretch back as far as a month, although certain cosmetic treatments (e.g. dyeing hair) can interfere with this. Hair analysis has the ability to measure a large number of potentially interacting elements, although that trait is shared with many other drug tests.

The judicial admissibility of the test in the United States is guided by the Daubert standard. A notable court case was *United States v. Medina, 749 F.Supp. 59 (E.D.N.Y.1990).*

Microscopic Hair Analysis in Forensics

Microscopic hair analysis is the science of comparing several strands of hair under a microscope and attempting to deduce if the strands 'match'. It became established as a forensic science by the 1950s. Researchers often monitored more than a dozen attributes, including pigment distribution and scale patterns. This technique has been used in criminal investigations to try to tie hair found at a crime scene, or other location of note, and confirm if the hair matches that of a suspect. While a simple hair color match might be *consistent* with a certain suspect having been at the scene – black hair at the scene when the suspect has black hair – microscopic hair analysis began to claim a stronger standard by the 1970s. Rather than merely "narrow the field" of possibilities, hair analysts claimed to actually match a specific person, such that the hair could be 'proof' of a specific suspect's presence. While the typed reports often hedged the certainty of microscopic hair analysis, witnesses in court would not always be as modest; the manager of the Montana state crime lab testified there was a "1 in 10,000 chance" that hairs found at a crime scene did not come from the suspect in one case, for example. Microscopic hair analysis has a long tradition of being used in fiction as well; it was originally popularized by Sherlock Holmes before it was even used by the police. Fictional works involving detectives have continued to use it since, including *Columbo, Quincy, ME, Dexter*, and *CSI*.

Skepticism about the stronger claims used by witnesses in the 1970s and 80s existed then; researchers said in 1974 that the whole process was inherently subjective, and the FBI wrote in 1984 that hair analysis cannot positively match one single person. In the 1990s, DNA profiling was introduced as a key new technique into forensics investigations and introduced a new level of certainty into them. DNA analysis of old cases in the 1970s and 80s, however, contradicted a number of earlier matches on the basis of hair analysis. In 1994, the Justice Department created a task force which would eventually review 6,000 cases by 2004, focusing on the work of one particularly zealous examiner, Michael Malone. These reviews came after reports that sloppy work by examiners at the FBI lab was producing unreliable forensic evidence in court trials. At first, these investigations were largely kept quiet; *The Washington Post* reported that "Instead of releasing those findings, they made them available only to the prosecutors in the affected cases." A study of FBI Laboratory hair analysis cases between 1996 and 2000 was released in 2002 by Max M. Houck and Bruce Budowle. The study showed that 11% of hair analysis "matches" were contradicted by DNA analysis. As the set of cases analyzed was one which would be expected to favor matches strongly in any case – only hair of individuals the police already believed were potential suspects was sent in – this error rate was seen as extremely high.

Kirk Odom was convicted of rape in 1982 by no physical evidence except microscopic hair analysis performed by the FBI Crime Laboratory. Combined with a witness's identification in a line-up (another technique which modern research has shown to be less reliable than previously thought), Odom was sentenced to twenty or more years in jail. DNA analysis, however, proved that Odom was entirely innocent. While Odom had been released from prison in 2003, he was officially exonerated in 2012. In a similar case, Santae Tribble was convicted of murder in 1979 due to a hair analysis match of hair found at the scene, despite having three witnesses who gave him an alibi when the crime was committed. The prosecutor went even further than the expert witness, saying in his closing statement that "There is one chance, perhaps for all we know, in 10 million that it could [be] someone else's hair." DNA testing in January 2012 showed that the prosecution's key piece of evidence, the hair, did not in fact match the defendant. Tribble was exonerated in December 2012, despite having already served 28 years in prison.

The outcry from defense attorneys has forced the FBI to open up on disputed hair analysis matches since 2012. The Justice department began an "unprecedented" review of old cases involving hair analysis in July 2013, examining more than 21,000 cases referred to the FBI Lab's hair unit from 1982 through 1999, and including as many as 27 death penalty convictions in which FBI experts may have exaggerated the reliability of hair analysis in their testimony. The review is still in progress, but in 2015, it released findings on 268 trials examined so far in which hair analysis was used. The review concluded that in 257 of these 268 trials, the analysts gave flawed testimony that overstated the accuracy of the findings in favor of the prosecution. About 1200 cases remain to be examined. In 2017, new Attorney General Jeff Sessions announced that this investigation would be suspended.

In Environmental Toxicology

Analysis of hair samples has many advantages as a preliminary screening method for the presence of toxic substances deleterious to health after exposures in air, dust, sediment, soil and water, food and toxins in the environment. The advantages of hair analysis include the non-invasiveness, low cost and the ability to measure a large number of, potentially interacting, toxic and biologically essential elements. Hence, head hair analysis is now increasingly being used as a preliminary test to see whether individuals have absorbed poisons linked to behavioral or health problems.

Detection of Long Term Elemental Effects

There appears to be genuine validity to the use of hair analysis in the measurement of lifelong, or long-term heavy metal burden, if not the measurement of general elemental analysis. Several interesting studies including the analysis of Ludwig van Beethoven's hair have been conducted in conjunction with the National Institutes of Health, and Centers for Disease Control and Prevention to name a few.

A 1999 study on hair concentrations of calcium, iron, and zinc in pregnant women and effects of supplementation, it was concluded that "From the analyses, it was clear that hair concentrations of Ca, Fe, and Zn could reflect the effects of supplementation... Finally, it could be concluded that mineral element deficiencies might be convalesced by adequate compensations of mineral element nutrients."

Occupational, Environmental and Alternative Medicine

Hair analysis has been used in occupational, environmental and some branches of alternative medicine as a method of investigation to assist screening and/or diagnosis. The hair is sampled, processed and analyzed, studying the levels of mineral and metals in the hair sample. Using the results, as part of a proper examination or test protocol, practitioners screen for toxic exposure and heavy metal poisoning. Some advocates claim that they can also diagnose mineral deficiencies and that people with autism have unusual hair mineral contents. These uses are often controversial, and the American Medical Association states, "The AMA opposes chemical analysis of the hair as a determinant of the need for medical therapy and supports informing the American public and appropriate governmental agencies of this unproven practice and its potential for health care fraud." A recent review of scientific literature by Dr Kempson highlighted analysis of metals/minerals in hair can be applied in large population studies for researching epidemiology and groups of chronically exposed populations, however any attempt to provide a diagnosis based on hair for an individual is not possible. An exception to this can be in advanced analyses for acute poisoning.

Forensic Seismology

Forensic seismology is the forensic use of the techniques of seismology to detect and study distant phenomena, particularly explosions, including those of nuclear weapons.

Because of the efficiency with which seismic waves propagate through the Earth and the technical difficulties of decoupling explosions to diminish their seismic radiation, forensic seismology is a critical technique in the enforcement of bans on underground nuclear testing.

In addition to nuclear explosions, the signatures of many other kinds of explosions can also be detected and analyzed by forensic seismology, and even other phenomena such as ocean waves (the global microseism), the movement of icebergs across the sea floor or in collision with other icebergs, or explosions within submarines.

Organizations with expertise in forensic seismology include AWE Blacknest, Los Alamos National Laboratory, Sandia National Laboratory, and Lawrence Livermore National Laboratory.

Seismic Nuclear Detonation Detection

Forensic Seismology is one of several other methods used by the global community to determine compliance with the Comprehensive Nuclear Test-Ban Treaty (CTBT). A network of approximately 170 seismic stations, along with data generated from sources such as Infrasound, Hydroacoustics, and Radionucleotide detection, is used to identify and locate nuclear detonations. Forensic seismology is specifically used to locate nuclear detonations that may have occurred underneath the ground.

Seismic stations record underground pressure waves and transmit this data for processing via secure communication links. There are many challenges involved with trying to differentiate a nuclear explosion from other natural and man-made phenomena, such as earthquakes, mining explosions, and construction. Nuclear explosions exceeding 150 kilotons generate pressure waves that primarily travel through the Earth's core and mantle. These types of explosions are straightforward to identify because the mixture of rock the signals pass through is fairly homogeneous and the signals generated are free from noise. Smaller nuclear explosions are more difficult to identify because pressure waves primarily travel through the Earth's upper mantle and crust, leading to signal distortion due to the heterogeneity of rocks at this depth.

Nations may also conduct clandestine underground tests that are not easily identifiable. One method of hiding an underground nuclear detonation is called decoupling. This involves detonating a nuclear warhead in an underground cavity in order to significantly muffle the amplitude of the subsequent underground pressure waves. Another proposed method of hiding nuclear detonations is called mine masking. This technique uses a larger explosion to mask a smaller nuclear explosion. The feasibility of mine masking has been called into question because seismic events large enough to mask a nuclear explosion are exceedingly rare and would draw suspicion. Smaller nuclear detonation yields may also be hard to detect because they produce readings similar to small earthquakes or other natural events.

When seismic data is gathered, it has to be processed to produce meaningful information. Algorithms are used to isolate patterns, remove noise, and generate estimates. The development of efficient algorithms for nuclear detonation detection has led to many advancements in other fields such as kriging, an advanced method of interpolation used primarily in geostatistics. Algorithms are used to identify key characteristics of wave forms, such as peak-to-peak distance, amplitude, phase, P-wave amplitude, and S-wave amplitude. P-waves, or primary waves, are compression waves that propagate quickly through rock, and are generally the first waves to reach seismic stations. S-waves, or shear waves, arrive after P-waves. The ratio of P to S waves is one of several important values used to characterize seismic events. When a nuclear detonation has been identified, algorithms are used to estimate the detonation time and explosive yield

References

- Vo-Dinh, T.; Cullum, B. (2000). "Biosensors and biochips: Advances in biological and medical diagnostics". Fresenius' Journal of Analytical Chemistry. 366 (6–7): 540–551. doi:10.1007/s002160051549
- R. Brunelli, Template Matching Techniques in Computer Vision: Theory and Practice, Wiley, ISBN 978-0-470-51706-2, 2009 ([1] TM book)
- Krause, Mike (2002-01-14). "Is face recognition just high-tech snake oil?". Enter Stage Right. ISSN 1488-1756. Archived from the original on 2002-01-24. Retrieved 2011-06-30
- Cavalcanti A, Shirinzadeh B, Zhang M, Kretly LC (2008). "Nanorobot Hardware Architecture for Medical Defense" (PDF). Sensors. 8 (5): 2932–2958. doi:10.3390/s8052932
- Hongo, Jun. "Eyeglasses with Face Un-Recognition Function to Debut in Japan". Wall Street Journal. Retrieved 9 February 2017
- National Research Council (2009). Strengthening Forensic Science in the United States: A Path Forward (PDF). National Academies Press. ISBN 0-309-13131-6. Retrieved June 12, 2016
- Willing, Richard (2003-09-02). "Airport anti-terror systems flub tests; Face-recognition technology fails to flag 'suspects'" (Abstract). USA Today. Retrieved 2007-09-17
- Donzella, V; Crea, F (June 2011). "Optical biosensors to analyze novel biomarkers in oncology". J Biophotonics. 4 (6): 442–52. doi:10.1002/jbio.201000123
- Brodbeck, Silke (2012). "Introduction to bloodstain pattern analysis" (PDF). Journal for Police Science and Practice. 2: 51–57. doi:10.7396/IE_2012_E
- Strasser, Russell S. (2008). "Autopsies". In Ayn Embar-seddon, Allan D. Pass (eds.). Forensic Science. Salem Press. p. 95. ISBN 978-1-58765-423-7
- Cornell BA; BraachMaksvytis VLB; King LG; et al. (1997). "A biosensor that uses ion-channel switches". Nature. 387 (6633): 580–583. Bibcode:1997Natur.387..580C. PMID 9177344. doi:10.1038/42432
- Hamby, James (Summer 1999). "The History of Firearm and Toolmark Identification". Association of Firearm and Tool Mark Examiners Journal. 31 (3). Retrieved January 16, 2016
- Rothenberg, Kelly (2008). "The Autopsy Through History". In Ayn Embar-seddon, Allan D. Pass (eds.). Forensic Science. Salem Press. p. 100. ISBN 978-1-58765-423-7
- "740 ILCS 14/ Biometric Information Privacy Act.". www.ilga.gov. Archived from the original on 2016-04-16. Retrieved 2016-04-05
- Krupin, O.; Wang, C.; Berini, P. "Optical plasmonic biosensor for leukemia detection". SPIE Newsroom (22 January 2016). doi:10.1117/2.1201512.006268
- Thomas, Dylan (February 25, 2016). "A high-tech approach to tracking gun crimes". Southwest Journal. Retrieved June 20, 2016
- Schafer, Elizabeth D. (2008). "Ancient science and forensics". In Ayn Embar-seddon, Allan D. Pass (eds.). Forensic Science. Salem Press. p. 43. ISBN 978-1-58765-423-7
- "In the Public Eye: Finding Fingerprints on Firearms is Actually Very Rare". Forensic Magazine. September 2, 2015. Retrieved May 31, 2016
- Hanahan, Douglas; Weinberg, Robert A. (2011). "Hallmarks of Cancer: The Next Generation". Cell. 144: 646–74. PMID 21376230. doi:10.1016/j.cell.2011.02.013

- Williams, M.; & Sigman, M. (2007). "Performance Testing of Commercial Containers for Collection and Storage of Fire Debris Evidence". Journal of Forensic Sciences. 52: 579–585. doi:10.1111/j.1556-4029.2007.00435
- Best, Russell; Begg, Rezaul (2006). "Overview of Movement Analysis and Gait Features". In Begg, Rezaul; Palaniswami, Marimuthu. Computational Intelligence for Movement Sciences: Neural Networks and Other Emerging Techniques. Idea Group (published 2006-03-30). pp. 11–18. ISBN 978-1-59140-836-9
- "FBI Laboratory Announces Discontinuation of Bullet Lead Examinations" (Press release). FBI National Press Office. September 1, 2005. Retrieved December 28, 2016

Permissions

All chapters in this book are published with permission under the Creative Commons Attribution Share Alike License or equivalent. Every chapter published in this book has been scrutinized by our experts. Their significance has been extensively debated. The topics covered herein carry significant information for a comprehensive understanding. They may even be implemented as practical applications or may be referred to as a beginning point for further studies.

We would like to thank the editorial team for lending their expertise to make the book truly unique. They have played a crucial role in the development of this book. Without their invaluable contributions this book wouldn't have been possible. They have made vital efforts to compile up to date information on the varied aspects of this subject to make this book a valuable addition to the collection of many professionals and students.

This book was conceptualized with the vision of imparting up-to-date and integrated information in this field. To ensure the same, a matchless editorial board was set up. Every individual on the board went through rigorous rounds of assessment to prove their worth. After which they invested a large part of their time researching and compiling the most relevant data for our readers.

The editorial board has been involved in producing this book since its inception. They have spent rigorous hours researching and exploring the diverse topics which have resulted in the successful publishing of this book. They have passed on their knowledge of decades through this book. To expedite this challenging task, the publisher supported the team at every step. A small team of assistant editors was also appointed to further simplify the editing procedure and attain best results for the readers.

Apart from the editorial board, the designing team has also invested a significant amount of their time in understanding the subject and creating the most relevant covers. They scrutinized every image to scout for the most suitable representation of the subject and create an appropriate cover for the book.

The publishing team has been an ardent support to the editorial, designing and production team. Their endless efforts to recruit the best for this project, has resulted in the accomplishment of this book. They are a veteran in the field of academics and their pool of knowledge is as vast as their experience in printing. Their expertise and guidance has proved useful at every step. Their uncompromising quality standards have made this book an exceptional effort. Their encouragement from time to time has been an inspiration for everyone.

The publisher and the editorial board hope that this book will prove to be a valuable piece of knowledge for students, practitioners and scholars across the globe.

Index

www.ingramcontent.com/pod-product-compliance
Lightning Source LLC
LaVergne TN
LVHW080653210926
848485LV00003B/371
* 9 7 8 1 6 3 5 4 9 7 1 5 1 *